COMING TO
ARIZONA

The Complete Guide
for Future Arizonans:
Job-Seekers, Retirees and Snowbirds

By Don W. Martin & Betty Woo Martin

Pine Cone Press • Columbia, California

BOOKS BY DON AND BETTY MARTIN

NORTHERN CALIFORNIA DISCOVERY GUIDE ● 1993
OREGON DISCOVERY GUIDE ● 1993
THE ULTIMATE WINE BOOK ● 1993
THE BEST OF NEVADA ● 1992
THE BEST OF THE WINE COUNTRY ● 1991
INSIDE SAN FRANCISCO ● 1991
COMING TO ARIZONA ● First printing, 1991; second printing, 1993
THE BEST OF ARIZONA ● 1990; revised 1993
THE BEST OF THE GOLD COUNTRY ● First printing, 1987; second printing, 1990; revised 1992
SAN FRANCISCO'S ULTIMATE DINING GUIDE ● 1988
THE BEST OF SAN FRANCISCO ● 1986; revised 1990, 1994

Library of Congress Catalog-in-Publication Data
Martin, Don, 1934; Martin, Betty, 1941—
Coming to Arizona
Includes index
1. Arizona—Description and travel—Guidebooks
2. Moving, job-seeking, retiring—Arizona
979.1'053; 646.7'9—dc19

ISBN 0-942053-09-5
Library of Congress catalog card number: 91-60180

Book design & production ● **Charles L. Beucher, Jr.**, and **Don W. Martin**
Charts & graphs ● **Jil Weil**
Photography ● **Don** or **Betty Martin**, unless otherwise credited

THE COVER ● *The "Coffee Pot" is one of the many striking red rock formations around Sedona, a popular art colony and retirement community in beautiful Oak Creek Canyon.*

CONTENTS

4

ARIZONA: A STATE FOR EVERYONE

Most relocation guides focus on a particular group—usually job-hunters, moving families or retirees. Why not, we wondered, produce a re-lo guide for everyone? Whatever your reasons for contemplating a move to Arizona, you all share common interests and curiosities. You'll want to know the nature, character, physical appearance and amenities of your future home town. You'll be concerned about climate, cultural lures and nearby attractions.

If you're coming to Arizona, for whatever reason, this is your book.

It's not only full of information; it's straightforward and honest. Our reviews of communities are based on facts, not chamber of commerce puffery. If an area is depressed, if a community is scalding hot in summer, if a town is just hound dog homely, we say so.

Like all of our guides, **Coming to Arizona** contains no paid listings or advertising, so it's free of outside bias. No agency, organization or community listed herein have asked to be included. All of the information, and opinions, comes from our own research and observations.

Of course, most of what we say about Arizona is positive, because it's a positive, growing, vibrant and attractive place.

We spent months prowling about the state recently, in researching an earlier book, **The Best of Arizona**. We soon discovered why Arizona has been, and will continue to be, one of America's fastest growing states. It's amazingly diverse, with pine forests as well as cactus deserts. It offers two major metropolitan centers with their cultural variety, fine dining and—yes—commute-hour traffic. Or, one can settle in a tiny hamlet where nothing changes but the stoplight—if there is one.

Phoenix is America's ninth largest city, with a population topping a million, and Tucson has nearly half a million. Yet overall, the state ranks 40th in population density, with just over 30 folks per square mile.

Many people think of Arizona primarily as a Sunbelt state. Indeed, eighty-five percent of its population resides in its warmer climes. Yet, you can live under the pines of Flagstaff and ski the slopes of the next-door San Francisco Peaks. You can play cowboy, or be a real one, on the high prairies of the state's southeastern corner.

You can run rivers, hike the high country, fish in crystalline streams and explore prehistoric ruins of the very first Americans. On the flip side of the activity coin, you can attend opening night at Tucson's opera, dine in style in a Phoenix skyroom, prowl through excellent museums, putter around fine golf courses and—obviously—laze at pool side. It's one of the few places on earth where you can soak up both culture and toasty sunshine in January. Other than the absence of an ocean, Arizona offers a bit of everything, and most of it is bathed in warm sunshine.

One of the state's biggest attractions is its home prices, which are considerably less than in most of America's other good-weather growth areas.

We were so charmed by this attractive and affordable state that we came within an inch of buying a piece of cactus-studded land in the Santa Catalina foothills above Tucson. Although we didn't make the move, we've formally adopted Arizona as our second home after California.

We intend to continue exploring and enjoying the Grand Canyon State's grand diversity. And who knows? We may yet buy that cactus patch with a view.

Care to join us?

THANK YOU —

Guides and reference books are authored by individuals but written by committee. The thousands of facts must come from many sources and they're checked by many more.

Our single most useful source was the Arizona Department of Commerce. Its statewide and community profiles are virtual treasure-troves of Arizona facts and figures. Also valuable was input from various chambers of commerce, along with information from officials of the state's assorted national parks and monuments.

These individuals were particularly helpful in providing and/or checking many of the thousands of facts in this book: **Mobin Qaheri**, senior economic specialist of the Arizona Department of Commerce; **Dan Anderson** and **Fernando M. Vender** of the Arizona Department of Economic Security; **Linda Tudan** of the Arizona Department of Insurance; **Holly Penix**, Division of Economic and Business Research, College of Business and Public Administration, University of Arizona; **Sue Scholz**, Arizona Association of Realtors; **Zale Delp** of Century 21 All Properties realty in Phoenix; **Judi E. Ross**, division director and **Alberto Gutier**, deputy administrator, Motor Vehicle Division.

CLOSING INTRODUCTORY THOUGHTS
Keeping up with the changes

Nobody's perfect, but we try. This book contains thousands of facts, and a few are probably wrong. If you catch an error, let us know. Also, drop us a note if you find that a phone number, office location or other bit of information has changed in this ever-changing state.

All who provide useful data will earn a free copy of any other publication on our list. (See the back of this book.)

Address your comments to:

Pine Cone Press
P.O. Box 1494
Columbia, CA 95310
(209) 532-2699

A BIT ABOUT THE AUTHORS

The husband and wife team of Don and Betty Martin has written more than ten guidebooks. Don, who provides most of the adjectives, has been a journalist since he was 17. He was a Marine correspondent in the Orient, then he worked on the editorial side of several West Coast newspapers. Later, he served as associate editor of the California State Automobile Association's travel magazine. A member of the Society of American Travel Writers, he now devotes his time to writing, photography, travel and—for some curious reason—collecting squirrel and chipmunk artifacts.

Betty, who does much of the research, photography and editing, offers the curious credentials of a doctorate in pharmacy and a California real estate broker's license. She's also a freelance travel writer and photographer who has sold material to assorted newspapers and magazines. The Martins live in Columbia State Historic Park in the California Gold Country.

A third and most essential member of the team is *Ickybod*, a green 1979 Volkswagen camper, the Martins' home on the road. Without *Ick*, they might have been tempted to solicit free lodging and meals, and their guidebooks wouldn't be quite so honest.

The impossibly slender pinnacle of Spider Rock pierces skyward from Canyon de Chelly, a little-known national monument in Arizona's Navajo Nation.

PART ONE

THE STATE

Like a sunny magnet, Arizona lures millions of people across its borders each year. About eighteen million tourists annually sample the state's seductive climate and its rich variety of scenic attractions, historic and cultural offerings.

But while some come to play, many come to stay. Hundreds of thousands of families, soured by January blizzards and stagnating economies back home, snip their roots and head for Arizona. Additional legions of retirees choose to spend their golden years under the state's smiling sun. Another million "Snowbirds" fly south to winter here.

In this section, you'll meet the state itself. You'll learn about its history, its alluring desert climate (and how to handle it) and its various departments and services. Later chapters discuss schooling, job prospects and the best places for retirees and winter visitors.

Chapter One

WHY ARIZONA?

MAKING THE DECISION

During the past decade, more than a million people have come to Arizona—to stay. They made a profound decision—to pack their families, their worldly goods and possibly their pets. They chose to relinquish the comfort of familiar terrain, friends and relatives.

Uprooting and relocating a family is not a task taken lightly. What prompted so many to undertake such a move? Why Arizona?

We'll sum it up in two sentences, then spend the rest of this book on elaboration.

1. Arizona offers that rare combination of pleasant climate, natural attractions, cultural and recreational offerings and essential services.

2. It's all wrapped in an alluring package of affordability.

If you and your family are planning to join this statistical surge to Arizona, this is your book. It's packed with information for job-seekers, retirees and long-term temporary residents—the winter Snowbirds. On the pages that follow, we'll tell you everything you need to know about the Grand Canyon State—how to find a job, which communities offer the best climate, cultural opportunities, schools, retirement facilities and housing prices.

Arizona was the third fastest growing state in the nation during the decade of the Eighties. (Nevada and Alaska were first and second.) According to census figures, its population leaped 35 percent, from 2,716,546 in 1980 to 3,665,228 in 1990. It has become western America's third most populous state, after California and Washington. A survey taken a few years ago revealed that nearly 70 percent of the greater Phoenix area residents had been in the state less than 20 years. Indeed, when we traveled about the state to research *The Best of Arizona* recently, we were hard-pressed to find a native.

Growth slowed a bit toward the end of the decade as the economy flattened. The slow-down is attributed to a temporary glut in housing and commercial office space—a typical consequence of construction booms. Flow charts never really flow; they're comprised of peaks and valleys.

But even as we write this, the state is showing signs of a resurgence. A recent U.S. Supreme Court decision awarding Arizona a larger share of precious Colorado River water should accelerate growth even further. Since the great majority of Arizona's residents live in the desert, water obviously is the key to its future.

During the Nineties, Arizona will resume its role as America's fastest growing state, predicts the U.S. Census Bureau. Nevada will outperform it percentage-wise, but with a larger population base, Arizona will gain more people. At century's end, its population will nudge five million, say the experts.

Much of Arizona's growth is rooted in tourism. This is no accident, since the state operates one of America's most aggressive tourist promotion campaigns. Officials realize that visitors and conventioneers require few services and leave behind lots of money.

"Arizona: If you knew it, you'd do it," proclaims the state government's multi-million dollar publicity campaign.

The state-sponsored **Arizona Highways** magazine has wooed visitors for decades. Its pages brim with color pictures of pristine canyons, handsome Native Americans and cactus wrens looking quite at home in giant saguaros. The slick magazine has projected Arizona's vast sweeps of sunny terrain into millions of American households.

Tourists, having seen the other side of the fence, often are tempted to close the gate behind them. Most Arizona communities work to lure and accommodate newcomers. Phoenix, for instance, is unabashedly pro-growth. The Phoenix metropolitan area, which local promoters like to call the "Valley of the Sun," cradles 60 percent of the state's population. Its bedroom communities of Mesa, Scottsdale, Gilbert, Glendale, Chandler and Tempe are among the swiftest growing cities in America.

According to the 1990 census, Mesa ranked second in growth among the country's 195 cities with populations over 100,000. It skyrocketed from 152,404 in 1980 to 288,091 in 1990, an increase of nearly 80 percent. Scottsdale ranked 20th in growth rate, going from 88,622 to 130,069.

Little of this happened by accident. Phoenix promoters have placed ads in **Fortune** magazine, the **Wall Street Journal** and other publications, touting the Valley of the Sun as a sunny place for business.

Tucson, while not quite as growth-obsessed, isn't exactly locking its gates to newcomers. Its population swelled by 20 percent from 330,537 in 1980 to 403,575 at decade's end. Recent estimates approach half a million.

Both population hubs have broadened their employment bases by attracting high tech industries and promoting white-collar and service jobs. Several major corporations have moved their headquarters to the state. Service industries, including tourism, account for 25 percent of

PERCENTAGE OF SUNNY DAYS
(Source : National Oceanic and Atmospheric Administration)

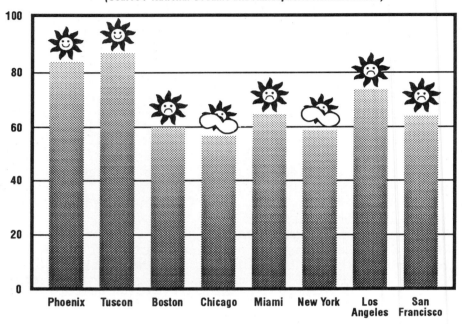

Arizona's payroll. Another 20 percent comes from retail trades and 12 percent stems from manufacturing.

Other factors that motivate migration to the Grand Canyon State are home prices and a rather conservative state government that tries to keep the lid on taxes. Although housing prices and taxes are rising, they're still far below those of some other Sunbelt states, notably neighboring California. A couple of examples: Home prices in the San Francisco Bay Area and Los Angeles Basin are double those in Phoenix and Tucson. And the maximum rate for Arizona's state income tax is eight percent, compared with nearly 10 percent in the Golden State.

Arizona's Department of Commerce and Department of Economic Security collect and eagerly disseminate statistics that track, and thus promote, Arizona's economic boom. The commerce department issues in-depth community profiles of 117 cities and towns and 23 Indian communities. They cover employment, population, climate, history, transportation, communications, utilities, educational facilities, churches, recreational and cultural lures, nearby attractions and lodgings—all crowded onto a single two-sided sheet. For a loose-leaf binder of these profiles, send $18 (or $15 without the binder) to:

Economic Research Division
Arizona Department of Commerce
3800 N. Central Ave., Phoenix, AZ 85012

If you just can't wait to start your Arizona planning, call **(602) 280-1321**; the accommodating folks will send out your packet and bill you. Incidentally, individual profiles are available for 15 cents each. You also can receive a list of the department's other publications by calling the above number.

WEATHER OR NOT

Many families or retirees contemplating a move to Arizona are concerned about summer temperatures. Certainly, it's a great place for a winter retreat, but can one handle the August heat? Bear in mind that Phoenix set an all-time record of 124 degrees during the summer of 1990.

Sizzling summers don't seem to bother the state's residents. Eighty-five percent of them live in desert climes, well below the cooling heights of northern Arizona. With air conditioning and a little common sense, they do just fine.

Heat is not a problem if you keep a cool head. For one thing, Arizona's desert heat is dry. Humidity, not heat alone, causes the greatest discomfort. It inhibits perspiration, which is the body's natural cooling mechanism. For instance, at zero humidity, 115 degrees has a "discomfort rating" of only 103. (Only?) It's like a wind-chill factor in reverse. However, if the mercury hits 115 and the humidity is 40 percent, the discomfort factor spirals to 151, which would make survival impossible. Fortunately, that combination never occurs in the Arizona desert.

We often travel about the Southwest in summer and we function quite comfortably. On the other hand, during trips to the soggy tropics, we've wilted at 85 degrees. That temperature, coupled with 80 percent humidity, feels like 100.

Beating the heat

Follow these steps to keep your cool when the weather's not:

⁕ Don't be a mad dog or an Englishman. Plan your outdoor activities in the early morning and evening.

⁕ Avoid dehydration by drinking plenty of water. And we mean plenty. A gallon a day will keep heatstroke away.

⁕ Avoid sweet drinks or alcohol (which speeds up dehydration). Besides, you chubby little rascal, the average soft drink contains twelve teaspoons of sugar.

⁕ Don't take a lot of salt, despite what they told you in boot camp. Salt causes your body to retain water, and you want to perspire. That's what keeps you cool. The key is to keep plenty of fluid circulating through your system.

⁕ Don't exert yourself on a hot day. Your body will lose more fluid than you can replace.

⁕ Wear light-colored, reflective clothing—preferably cotton or linen. Avoid nylon and polyester, since these fabrics don't "breathe" and this traps body heat against your skin.

* If you must work outdoors in the heat, dip your shirt or blouse in water frequently. Its evaporation—along with that from your body—will help keep you cool.

Shielding the sun

Arizona suffers the distinction of having America's highest skin cancer rate. Because of the state's southern latitude, clear air and relatively high altitude (for a desert climate), more of the sun's damaging ultraviolet rays reach the earth.

Skin cancer can develop late in life, even years after you've stopped getting your annual tan. And one form—melanoma— can be deadly. Even if you don't get skin cancer, which is nearly 100 percent preventable, constant sun exposure will lead to premature wrinkling.

Some drugs increase your skin's sensitivity to the sun, so check with your pharmacist. Among the suspect items are hormone- based drugs including birth control pills, some tranquilizers, diuretics, sulfa drugs and antibiotics such as vibramycin. Even some sweeteners and perfumes are suspect.

Take these precautions to keep your hide from being fried:

* Use sunscreen with a high PABA concentration; it ranges from five to 33 percent (which is a virtual sun-block). Even if you're working on a tan, use sunblock on sensitive areas, such as your lips, nose and—yes—the tops of your ears. (In case you're curious, PABA stands for para-aminobenzoic acid. No wonder people use the acronym!) A few individuals are allergic to PABA; if a rash appears, try something else.

* Bear in mind that suntan lotion tends to rinse off in water, so re-lather yourself after you've taken a dip.

* If you spend a lot of time outdoors, some specialists recommend getting a careful, light tan. Moderately tanned skin will resist sunburn—up to a point. You can still get singed from prolonged exposure. Get your tan very slowly. After all, you've moved to Arizona, so what's the rush? Limit your initial exposure to a few minutes a day. Do your tanning in the morning or late afternoon. Take Rudyard Kipling's advice; avoid the noonday sun.

* Always wear a broad-brimmed hat or visor outdoors. It'll protect your eyes from sun glare and shield your face from sunburn. The *vaqueros* knew what they were doing when they created the sombrero.

I prefer to keep moving as I work on my tan—walking, swimming, bike-riding and such. If you baste yourself in the sun, you may doze off and get too much exposure. Besides, it's boring.

Incidentally, clouds don't block all ultraviolet rays, and reflections from sand, pool decks or water can intensify burning. Also, wet Tshirts may look rather fetching on the right bodies, but they offer almost no sun protection.

If you do get burned, ease the pain with a dip in the pool or a cool shower, then use one of those over-the-counter anesthetic sprays. (However, repeated use of anesthetics can create allergic reactions in some people.) Antihistamine will relieve the itch. That's right; the same stuff that you take for the sniffles. And keep your skin out of the sun until it's fully healed.

Surviving the desert

The Arizona desert occupies thousands of square miles of open spaces. These can become intimidating places if you're stranded. If you're tempted—as we often are—to explore this remote and beautiful world, save the urge for fall, winter or spring. Arizona summers are for pool-side lounging, not desert prowling.

When you venture into the wilds, let someone know where you're going, and when you intend to return. Keep these pointers in mind if you wander off the well-traveled asphalt:

✳ First, foremost and always, take plenty of water. Water to drink, to soak your clothes, to top off a leaky radiator. It's cheap, it's easily portable and it can save your life.

✳ Give your car, Jeep or RV a physical before going into the boonies, to ensure that it'll get you back.

Take extra engine oil, coolant and an emergency radiator sealant. Include spare parts such as fan belts, a water pump, radiator hoses— and tools to install these things. Toss an extra spare tire into the trunk, along with a tire pump, patching and sealant.

Take food with you—stuff that won't spoil. If you break down, you may be out there for a while. Also pack matches, a small shovel, aluminum foil (for signaling), a can opener, a powerful flashlight and a space blanket so you can snooze in the shade of your car.

✳ A CB radio or cellular phone can be a life-saver. Remember that channel 9 is the emergency CB band, monitored by rescue agencies.

✳ Never drive off-road, particularly in an on-road vehicle. Loose, sandy desert soil can trap your car in an instant, even if the ground looks solid. We don't leave established roadways as a matter of principle, because tires are hell on the fragile desert environment. And no, we don't approve of "off-road" areas.

✳ Even if you keep to the roads, you might get stuck in a sand-blown area or a soft shoulder. Carry a tow chain and tire supports for soft sand, like strips of carpeting. An inexpensive device called a "come-along"—sort of a hand-winch—can get you out of a hole, if you can find something for an anchor.

✳ If you become stranded in the desert, stay in the shade of your car—not in the vehicle itself. Don't try to walk out, particularly during the heat of the day. Besides, a vehicle is easier to spot than a lonely hiker. Use a mirror or aluminum foil as a signal device, and build a signal fire. A spare tire will burn, and a douse of oil will make the fire nice and smoky. Start your blaze in a cleared area away from your vehicle. You don't want to start a wildfire that might compound your predicament.

❋ If you're on a road and you know that you can reach civilization on foot, do your walking at night. Take all the water you can carry.

Incidentally, heat isn't your only problem in the desert. Flash floods can roar down dry washes and across roadway dips, particularly during the late spring and summer "monsoon season." If you're driving or hiking in the desert and a sudden rainstorm hits, keep to the high ground until it passes.

Avoiding "heat sickness"

One more sobering item, then we'll get back to the good stuff about Arizona. Heat exhaustion and its lethal cousin heatstroke are real dangers on hot summer days. Both are brought on by a combination of dehydration and sun.

Signs of heat exhaustion are weariness, muscle cramps and clammy skin. The pulse may slow and you may become unusually irritable. If left untreated, heat exhaustion can lead to deadly heatstroke. The skin becomes dry and hot, the pulse may quicken and you'll experience nausea and possibly a headache. Convulsions, unconsciousness, even death can follow.

At the first sign of heat sickness, get out of the sun and into the shade. Stay quiet and drink water—plenty of water. If you're near a pool, faucet or stream, douse your face and body with water, and soak your clothes. You **must** lower your body temperature quickly!

That's enough of the serious stuff. Let's begin getting acquainted with Arizona.

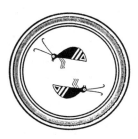

Chapter Two

GETTING TO KNOW YOU ⩗⩗⩗⩗⩗⩗

JUST THE FACTS

Size • 113,909 square miles; sixth largest state; about 340 miles wide by just under 400 miles deep.

Population • About 3,600,000; largest city is Phoenix with just under a million residents. State population density is 27.1 per square mile; ranks 40th among the states.

Elevations • Highest point, Humphreys Peak, 12,633 feet; lowest point, Colorado River as it enters Mexico, 100 feet.

Admitted to the Union • February 14, 1912, as the forty-eighth state; capital—Phoenix.

Time zone • Mountain; one hour later than the West Coast, two hours earlier than the East; only the Navajo Reservation observes summer Daylight Saving Time.

Telephone area code • (602) for the entire state.

Official things • State motto—**Didat Deus** (God enriches); **State seal** depicts the five "Cs" of copper, cotton, climate, citrus and cattle; state bird—**cactus wren** (medium-brown with speckled breast, likes to hang around saguaro cactus); **state flower**—saguaro cactus blossom (white with yellow center); **state tree**—paloverde (desert tree identified by green limbs, which is what *palo verde* means in Spanish); **state gem**—turquoise; **official neck-wear**—bola tie, which (perhaps unfortunately) originated here.

State nicknames • The Grand Canyon State and the Copper State (appropriate, since it produces more than half of America's copper supply).

Motorists' laws • A 1990 law requires front-seat occupants to wear safety belts. Also, children four or under, or weighing less than 40 pounds, must be secured by child restraints. Speed limit is 55 mph unless posted (65 on most freeways).

Drinking laws • See Chapter 3.

Indian reservations • They're regarded as sovereign territories, with their own laws—which may differ from those elsewhere in the state. (See Chapter 17.)

Getting there • Three interstate highways cross Arizona from east to west—I-40, I-10 and I-8. Several major airlines serve Phoenix and Tucson, and feeder lines fly to Bullhead City, Flagstaff, Kingman, Lake Havasu City, Page, Prescott, Sedona, Winslow and Yuma. Amtrak has two routes across Arizona, originating in Los Angeles and connecting to the East. One run stops in Yuma, Phoenix and Tucson; the other hits Kingman, Flagstaff and Winslow.

Road conditions • Call (602) 279-2000 and punch R-O-A-D to learn about driving conditions.

General information sources
(For more specific references, see Chapter 3)

Arizona Department of Commerce, 3800 N. Central Ave., Suite 1400, Phoenix, AZ 85017; phone 280-1321.

Arizona Office of Tourism, 1100 W. Washington St., Phoenix, AZ 85007; 542-TOUR.

Arizona State Parks, 800 W. Washington St., #415, Phoenix, AZ 85007; 542-4174.

Arizona Game & Fish Department, 2221 W. Greenway Rd., Phoenix, AZ 85023; 942-3000.

National Park Service, 202 E. Earll Dr., Phoenix, AZ 85012; 640-5250.

Native American Tourism Center, 4130 N. Goldwater Blvd., Suite 114, Scottsdale, AZ 85281; 945-0771.

U.S. Bureau of Land Management, 3707 N. Seventh St., Phoenix, AZ 85014; 241-5547.

Additional sources of information are listed in Chapter 3.

THE WAY IT IS • Asking someone to describe Arizona is like asking blind men to describe an elephant. It depends on what part they're feeling.

The state fits its desert stereotype. Indeed, two thirds of it is arid. It's the only state in the Union with two national monuments named for varieties of cactus—Organ Pipe and Saguaro.

At the same time, it defies this stereotype. Humphreys Peak north of Flagstaff is one of America's highest. A fourth of the state is covered by forest, and it shelters the largest stand of virgin ponderosa pines in the country. And of course, it contains the world's deepest gorge—the Grand Canyon of the Colorado River, which is Arizona's grandest stereotype of all.

The state's physical appearance is summed up rather well by Reg Manning, Pulitzer Prize-winning cartoonist for Phoenix's Arizona Republic. In his whimsical book, **What Is Arizona Really Like?**, he says the topography can be taken in three bites, starting from the Four Corners area in the northeast.

The first bite is a remote, often hauntingly beautiful semi-arid plateau containing the large Navajo and Hopi Indian reservations, Monument Valley and the Painted Desert. The second semi-circle, curving from the north central to the southeastern corner, is a green belt of ponderosa pines, including the forest-rimmed Grand Canyon. The Mogollon Rim, a great fault extending in a 200-mile arc, marks the edge of this high country.

The final bite—consuming nearly two-thirds of the state—is a great sweep of desert and high prairie, reaching from the northwest to the southeast corner. This is the Sunbelt. That term originated in Arizona and now is used to describe just about anyplace south of a Pennsylvania blizzard.

Although most of Arizona is desert, it isn't necessarily scalding hot. Much of this arid land, particularly in the central and northeastern areas, is high desert that's often quite cold in winter. Southeastern Arizona is more of a prairie than a desert. Naturally, the northwestern mountain regions get regular snowfall. Even in the southern Sunbelt, evenings can get quite cool, so don't put all your winter clothing in the Salvation Army collection box.

Nearly eighty-five percent of Arizona's population is focused in this warm belt—mostly in and around Phoenix and Tucson. These two metropolitan centers offer every imaginable service and convenience, and an abundance of cultural and recreational lures.

However, Arizona's greatest charms lie in its open spaces and scenic wonders; in its small towns with their affable wanna-be-cowboy attitudes. We found our Arizona in the high, silent reaches of the San Francisco Peaks and the hidden depths of the Grand Canyon. We discovered it in the dignity of the Indian nations and the scruffy charm of the Mexican border towns; in the solitude of a wilderness cactus garden reached only by a dusty road.

THE WAY IT WAS • Arizona is one of the youngest states in the union, admitted as the last of the Lower Forty-eight in 1912. Yet, river-runners and hikers in the Grand Canyon will see two-billion-year-old Precambrian schist, some of the oldest exposed rock on Planet Earth. Native Americans have occupied Arizona's deserts and high plateaus for about 20,000 years.

Its first residents were nomadic hunters who drifted down from the Great Plains. When droughts drove the mammoths and antelope away, they swapped their spears for plowshares and became—about eleven centuries ago—North America's first farmers. Freed from the constant search for food, they settled down to build substantial communities whose ruins survive today. The state is a treasure-trove of archaeological sites, ranging from mesa cities to tucked-away cliff dwellings.

Anthropologists call these early people Hohokam, Anasazi, Sinagua and Mogollon. We don't know what they called themselves, for they left no written language. Like most ancient tribes, they probably just referred to their kind as " The People."

Through the centuries, they evolved into highly-developed societies. They dug irrigation canals and thrived on a complete protein diet of squash, beans and corn, supplemented by hunting. Their pottery, weaving and other crafts were among the most advanced of the time. Ruins resembling amphitheaters and ball courts suggested that they had their own versions of major league sports.

Around eight hundred years ago, this highly developed civilization began coming apart at the seams. The great pueblos were abandoned and left to weather away in the hot Arizona sun. Scientists speculate that a persistent drought may have driven them from their fields. Some experts blame their downfall on disease, soil depletion or the arrival of more aggressive tribes.

People identify Navajos and Apaches with Arizona, yet these were latter-day arrivals, coming from the cold north about six hundred years ago. They were Athabaskans who drifted down from Canada. Warlike hunters, they may have driven off many of the native tribes. Ironically, they adopted some of the original residents' farming and weaving techniques.

Scientists have been unable to pinpoint the ultimate fate of the Hohokam, Sinagua or Mogollon. Similarities in culture and crafts suggest that today's Hopi may be descendants of the Anasazi.

What's in a name?

Historians have fun feuding over the origin of Arizona's name. There are four Indian versions: Arizuma, an Aztec word for "silver bearing;" Ali shonak or Ari-son, meaning "small spring" or "young spring," which were names of Pima settlements; and a Tohono O'odham term, Aleh-zone, also meaning young spring. Basque settlers insist that Arizona comes from Aritz ona, their term for "good oak." This was the name given to the site of a silver strike in 1736. Some unimaginative scholars suggest that state's name is merely a derivation of "arid zone."

"Arizona" first appeared in print in a 1750s document by one Padre Ortega, a Spanish missionary.

The years of the Spanish

Spaniards were the area's first outside visitors, and they got here by accident. In 1528, a group led by Alvar Cabeza de Vaca set out to explore Florida's west coast. Part of the group became lost after an Indian attack. They spent more than eight years wandering through what is now Texas, New Mexico, Arizona and northern Mexico. Some

ARIZONA DEPARTMENT OF ARCHIVES PHOTO

Spain was the first outside nation to explore Arizona. Francisco Vasquez de Coronado arrived in 1540 to check out rumors of golden cities.

accounts say they were befriended and protected by other Indians after De Vaca convinced them that he was a powerful medicine man.

Finally, four surviving members of the group stumbled across a party of other Spaniards in western Mexico. They told their rescuers of Indian legends about fabulously wealthy cities to the north.

Antonio de Mendoza, viceroy of New Spain, knew of an eighth century Moorish legend about seven golden cities, hidden somewhere in the unexplored world. Could these be the same? In 1539, with golden greed glittering in his eyes, he dispatched a party of explorers from Mexico City to find these treasure-laden towns. It was led by Franciscan Father Marcos de Niza. Accompanying the group—probably reluctantly—was a Moorish slave named Estevan, one of the survivors of the De Vaca trek.

As the Spaniards entered present-day Arizona, local Indians said the area through which they traveled was called "Cibola." Thus, the legend of the Seven Cities of Cibola was born. Learning that a Zuni pueblo lay ahead of them, Father de Niza sent an advance party to investigate, led by Estevan. The Zunis weren't very gracious hosts; they killed the visitors.

The intimidated de Niza kept his distance. But he drew near enough to see that the pueblos glittered in the sun. He returned home and advised the Viceroy of Mexico that he may have found one of the golden cities. Historians say the good padre was fooled by the glitter of mica, embedded in the adobe.

A year later, that great and brutal explorer, 30-year-old Francisco Vasquez de Coronado, traveled north to continue the search. Finding no gold, he pillaged a few pueblos and explored as far north as Kansas. After two years, he returned to Mexico City empty-handed. More than a century passed before the curious Spanish again began pestering natives of the Southwest. Then in the late 1600s, Father Eusebio Francisco Kino and other padres came to establish missions. Thousands of Indians were converted to Christianity. They were most likely encouraged by accompanying soldiers who set up military presidios to protect the missions.

Most of the Indians did not yield their land or their free spirits easily. Angered by abusive treatment from the Spanish intruders, they staged several violent revolts. The Hopi emptied their villages of Spaniards in a savage rebellion in 1680. Spanish occupation, punctuated by Indian uprisings, continued into the early 1800s.

When Mexico won its independence from Spain in the 1820s, most of the soldiers were withdrawn from what is now Arizona. Indians— primarily Apaches—again went on the warpath, driving frightened settlers to the safety of the walled cities of Tucson and Tubac.

The Americans arrive

Much of what is now Arizona and New Mexico was ceded to the United States in the 1848 Treaty of Guadalupe Hidalgo, at the end of the Mexican War. Sandwiched between California and Texas, they were lumped together as the New Mexico Territory. But as far as the Native Americans were concerned, this was still their land and warfare with the intruders continued. In the late 1800s, more than a dozen U.S. Army forts were built to protect American settlers. Not until Geronimo surrendered in 1886 was the territory safe for the intruders.

Arizona's early American settlement was spurred, indirectly, by an event next door. The California gold discovery in 1848 prompted the greatest human migration in history. Many gold-seekers traveled south through the New Mexico Territory, to avoid the precipitous Sierra Nevada range on California's eastern edge. Part of this southern route dipped into Mexico, so the government decided to make it all-American by negotiating the Gadsden Purchase. In 1854, cash-poor Mexico sold 30,000 square miles of its northern desert for $10 million. This would become a large chunk of southern Arizona.

Four years later, the government awarded the Butterfield Overland Stage Company a contract to forge a mail route through this area, from St. Louis to San Francisco, to link fast growing California with the rest of the U.S., which then ended at the Missouri border.

The New Mexico Territory, settled primarily by Southerners, was rather sympathetic with the South during the Civil War. A Texas militia seized Mesilla, New Mexico, in 1861, and claimed all the land from the Rio Grande to the Pacific as Confederate territory. But a column of Union-sympathizing Californians soon put an end to that. In 1862, the Confederates were routed in the Battle of Picacho Pass, south of Phoenix. Little more than a skirmish with only eight casualties, it was the Civil War's westernmost fracas.

The following year, President Lincoln signed a bill creating separate Arizona and New Mexico territories.

For the next two decades, the Arizona Territory epitomized the Wild West. Cattle barons battled over water and grazing rights and knocked down sod-busters' pesky fences. Tombstone and its O.K. Corral shoot-out and Yuma's infamous Territorial Prison became the stuff of which movie legends were made. In the 1880s, several minor gold strikes, major copper discoveries and Mormon migrations from Utah brought a more settled brand of citizens to the territory.

The railroad arrived late in the century to complete the taming of this last outpost of the Wild West. Then on St. Valentine's Day in 1912, portly President William Howard Taft signed the proclamation making Arizona the last of the contiguous 48 states.

Hampered by lack of water, the new state grew slowly in the first half of this century. Several military air bases were built in its wide open spaces during World War II, and many GIs stayed on. Then in the Fifties, Arizona's population began to swell. It was boosted by air conditioning, the creation of the Snowbird cult, and a court ruling granting it a larger share of Colorado River water.

To bring us up to date, Arizona paused to catch its breath in the closing years of the Eighties. It's now gathering momentum for another spate of rapid growth. Expect the Grand Canyon State to hit the ground running as it races toward the next century.

ARIZONA POPULATION GROWTH DURING THE PAST TEN YEARS

Source: Division of Economic and Business Research, University of Arizona

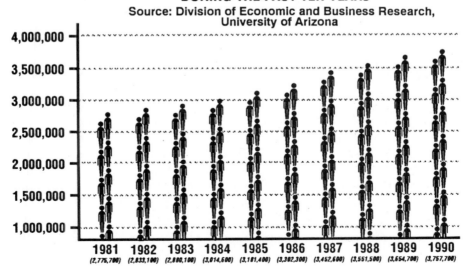

Chapter Three

ESSENTIAL ARIZONA

TAXES

As you contemplate coming to Arizona, it's a good guess that one of your first concerns will be taxes. By law and habit, Arizonans try to keep them down. Property tax has a cap of one percent of full value, similar to California's Proposition 13. With their basic pro-growth attitude, officials try to rein in business taxes down as well.

If you have any taxing questions, contact the **Arizona Department of Revenue**, 1600 W. Monroe St., Phoenix, AZ 85007; telephone 542-3572.

Individual income tax

Income received while you live in Arizona is subject to state income tax, whether or not you're a permanent resident. Tax credits are available for seniors, renters (including mobile home occupants) and low income people. Renters must occupy property in the state for more than six months to qualify for this credit. Other credits are given for installing solar energy equipment or groundwater measuring devices.

Tax rates are as follows, based on the adjusted gross income on your federal return (assuming it all was earned while you resided in Arizona):

Single taxpayers	Married couples	Tax rate
Up to $1,290	Up to $2,580	2 percent
$1,290 to $2,580	$2,580 to $5,160	3 percent
$2,580 to $3,870	$5,160 to $7,740	4 percent
$3,870 to $5,160	$7,740 to $10,320	5 percent
$5,160 to $6,450	$10,320 to $12,900	6 percent
$6,450 to $7,740	$12,900 to $15,480	7 percent
More than $7,740	More than $15,480	8 percent

Estate (inheritance) tax

Arizona is rather generous, allowing a $500,000 exemption on estate taxes. For estates valued higher, a return must be filed with the

Department of Revenue, Estate Tax Division, within nine months of the person's demise.

Property taxes

To help keep property taxes down, counties, cities and schools can increase their levies only by two per cent each year. Reevaluation of property for taxing purposes is limited to ten percent a year, even if the appraised value goes higher.

Owner-occupied property is assessed at 10 percent of its real value, with a tax-rate cap of one percent of the full cash value. Other rates are 15 percent for rental property, 16 percent for farm land and vacant property and 25 percent for commercial property.

The state takes a property tax bite of 47 cents per $100 assessed valuation. Above that, tax rates vary widely from one community to the next. They're listed in our community profiles in Part Two.

Like most states, Arizona offers property tax breaks for certain people, including surviving spouses and the disabled.

Sales tax

Arizona collects a five percent sales tax on most items purchased, except for food and pharmaceuticals. In addition, most cities levy another one or two percent, and they have the option of taxing food and drugs. The state also levies tax from three-eights percent to five percent on business sales.

THINGS AUTOMOTIVE

Since you'll likely be driving in Arizona, you'll need to know these things about vehicle taxes, insurance requirements, registration and such. For details, check with the nearest office of the **Motor Vehicle Division** or the main office at 1801 W. Jefferson (P.O. Box 2100), Phoenix, AZ 85001; or the nearest MVD office.

MOTOR VEHICLE AND FUEL TAXES ● Motorists pay a $8.25 per vehicle registration fee each year (and an extra $4 for new first-time registration), plus a Vehicle License Tax (VLT) in lieu of personal property tax. It's based on $4 per $100 of assessed value. New cars are assessed at 60 percent of the manufacturer's base retail price, and the assessment drops 15 percent a year. Vehicle taxes are paid annually, in the month the vehicle was first registered. And yes, you can get personalized license plates in Arizona for a one-time fee of $25.

State gasoline and diesel tax is 17 cents per gallon, plus whatever federal fuel tax is currently in vogue.

AUTO INSURANCE ● Arizona drivers are required to carry liability insurance in the amounts of $15,000 medical per person or $30,000 per accident plus $10,000 property damage. As an alternative to insurance, one can deposit a $40,000 surety bond or certificate of deposit with the state treasurer. Evidence of financial responsibility must be carried in the vehicle. This can be the policy itself or an insurance company's ID card.

If you can't prove financial responsibility, you face penalties of $250 for a first offense and possible suspension of your driving license and vehicle registration for 90 days. Penalties go up to $750 and a year's suspension for three violations within three years. Also, you must notify the Motor Vehicle Division within ten days of any change in liability coverage—such as switching vehicles or insurance companies.

AUTO REGISTRATION • See "Vehicle registration" below.

AUTO REPAIR • The Arizona Automobile Association **(AAA)** provides a list of approved auto repair establishments. Call 274-1116 in **Phoenix**, 949-7993 in **Scottsdale**, 979-3700 in **Peoria** (for the west side of the Valley of the Sun), 834-8296 in **Mesa** (east side), 296-7461 in **Tucson** and 783-3339 in **Yuma**.

AUTOMOTIVE LEMON LAW • The state has a "lemon law" that protects a new car buyer. It requires the dealer to offer a full refund or replacement vehicle if a defect can't be fixed after four tries within a year; or if the car is in the shop for repair more than 30 days during that year.

DRIVER'S LICENSE • If you become a resident, you must immediately obtain an Arizona driver's license. Seasonal visitors are not considered permanent residents and may use their back-home license. Arizona defines a resident as anyone who remains in the state for seven or more consecutive months in one year. Also, you become a resident if you enroll a child in school, set up a business or accept employment other than seasonal agricultural work.

For teen drivers, a restricted learner's permit can be obtained at 15 years and seven months, and a regular license at 16.

Fees are $2 for a learner's permit and $7 for a new or renewed vehicle or motorcycle license. State ID cards are $5. For a $3 charge, you can get a copy of your motor vehicle record (or $5 for a certified five-year record).

When applying for a license, you must surrender your license from the previous state, and show evidence that you have a clear driving record in that state. For details on fees and requirements, contact the nearest Driver's License Examining Station

DRUNK DRIVING LAWS • Arizona is tough on drunk drivers. You are presumed to be under the influence if you have a blood alcohol level of .10 percent. A law enforcement officer can require that you submit to a blood, breath or urine test if he has "reasonable grounds" to believe you were driving under the influence of alcohol or drugs. You can lose your license for a year if you refuse to submit to a test, even if you're cleared of the drunk-driving charge.

DWI conviction results in a mandatory jail sentence of at least 24 hours, a fine of $250 or more and a 90-day license suspension. A second offense within five years results in a year's license suspension, a heavy fine and a mandatory jail term.

The moral to this: get high on Arizona sunshine, not alcohol.

DRUNK DRIVING REPORTS • If you see someone driving erratically, call the police hot line at (800) 535-5555.

HANDICAPPED LICENSE PLATES • People with physical disabilities can obtain vehicle license plates that permit parking in blue spaces designated for the handicapped. They must first obtain a statement from a physician confirming their disability. To qualify, they must meet two of these requirements:

- Be physically unable to use public transit.
- Be extremely deformed or disfigured.
- Have a severe loss of dexterity and/or coordination.
- Be physically unable to perform manual activity for more than six hours.
- Be unable to climb a flight of stairs without a pause.
- Be unable to walk 50 yards without stopping to rest.

Plates may be obtained from any office of the **Motor Vehicle Division**. You also can get a temporary permit while recuperating from an illness or injury that has impaired your mobility. Again, a statement from a physician is required.

Able-bodied people who use handicapped parking spaces face a stiff fine.

MOTORCYCLE HELMET LAW • Anyone under age 18 must wear a safety helmet when riding on a motorcycle. Also, all motorcyclists must wear protective eyewear if their cycle is not equipped with a protective windshield.

SAFETY BELT LAW • A law that went into effect in 1990 requires front-seat vehicle occupants to wear safety belts. An earlier law stipulates that all children weighing up to 40 pounds, or age four and under, must be secured in an approved child restraint.

SMOG CHECKS • If you register a vehicle in Maricopa or Pima County (Phoenix or Tucson area), it must be checked to ensure that federally-required emissions equipment hasn't been tampered with, removed or bypassed. The fee is $5.40. To learn the location of the nearest vehicle testing station, call (800) 2-VIP-SITE. Electric and diesel powered vehicles and those with engines under 90cc are exempt.

VEHICLE REGISTRATION • If you become a resident, you must immediately register your car at a state Title and Registration office. Anyone who remains in Arizona for seven consecutive months in a year, enrolls a child in school or accepts employment is considered a resident. (See "Driver's license" above.) A vehicle must be checked at a testing station before it can be registered. To learn the location of the nearest testing station, call (800) 2-VIP-SITE.

Fees are $4 for a new title plus $8.25 annual registration and $1.50 Air Quality Fee. In addition, you must pay an annual Vehicle License Tax (VLT); see "Motor vehicle and fuel taxes" above.

Once your vehicle is registered, if you move or change your name, you must notify the Motor Vehicle Division within ten days.

EVERYTHING ELSE YOU NEED TO KNOW
and now you know where to ask

ACCOUNTANTS • To find an accountant, contact the **Arizona Society of CPAs**, 426 N. 44th St., Phoenix, AZ 85008; phone 273-0100.

ALCOHOL • Alcoholic beverage sales hours are 7 a.m. to 1 a.m. Monday through Saturday and noon to 1 a.m. Sunday. Legal age for buying, consuming or drinking alcohol is 21. It may not be drunk in a vehicle or in public areas in its original container.

ARCHITECTS • For a list of AIA members, contact the **American Institute of Architects**, 802 N. Fifth Ave., Phoenix, AZ 85003; phone 257-1924.

ATTORNEYS • To find a lawyer, contact the **Maricopa County Bar Association Lawyer Referral Service**, 333 W. Roosevelt St., Phoenix, AZ 85003; phone 257-4434 or the **Pima County Lawyer Referral Service**, 177 N. Church Ave., Tucson, AZ 85701; phone 623-4625.

BAD CHECKS • Writing a bad check in Arizona isn't just bad manners; it's a misdemeanor. Rubber check writers who don't make good within 12 days may be fined and/or jailed, in addition to having to cover the check.

BICYCLING • Bicycles are considered vehicles and are subject to the same basic traffic regulations as motor vehicles. In addition, they're required by law to have brakes (which seems logical). A front light and rear reflector are required for night riding.

BOAT REGISTRATION • Pleasure boats moored or used on public waterways must be registered with the Game and Fish Department, which will issue numbers that must be displayed prominently. For other specifics and tips on boating safety, get the Arizona Boating Guide from the **Arizona Game and Fish Department**, 2221 W. Greenway Rd., Phoenix, AZ 85023; phone 942-3000.

CAMPGROUNDS • For a directory of more than 250 campgrounds in the state, contact the **Arizona Office of Tourism**, 1100 W. Washington St., Phoenix, AZ 85007; 542-TOUR. Also see "Joining the RV clan?" in Chapter 7.

COMMUNITY PROFILES • Sketches of more than a hundred Arizona towns are available from the Arizona Department of Commerce,

3800 N. Central Ave., Suite 1400, Phoenix, AZ 85017; phone 280-1321. The price is $15 for the entire package, $18 for the packet with a binder, or 15 cents for profiles of individual communities.

CONSUMER PROTECTION • These agencies offer consumer protection services:

Arizona Board of Osteopathic Examiners, 1830 W. Colter St., Suite 4, Phoenix, AZ 85015; phone 255-1747.

Arizona Department of Real Estate, Office of the Commissioner, Consumer Representative, 202 E. Earll Dr., Suite 460, Phoenix, AZ 85012; phone 255-3232.

Better Business Bureau, 264-1721 or check your local phone directory.

Board of Medical Examiners, 2001 W. Camelback Rd., Phoenix, AZ 85015; phone 255-3751.

Consumer Products Safety (U.S.), 241-2397.

Registrar of Contractors, 800 W. Washington St., Phoenix, AZ 85007; 542-1525 or 416 W. Congress, Tucson, AZ 85701; 628-6345.

Securities Division, Arizona Corporation Commission, 1200 W. Washington St., Suite 201, Phoenix, AZ 85007; phone 542-4242.

State Department of Insurance, 3030 N. Third St., Suite 1100, Phoenix, AZ 85040, phone 255-5400.

Superintendent of Banks, 3225 N. Central Ave., Suite 815, Phoenix, AZ; phone 255-4421.

CONTRACTORS • They're listed with the **Registrar of Contractors** in Phoenix and Tucson (addresses above).

COUNTY GOVERNMENT • Arizona has 15 counties, each run by a three-member board of supervisors. Elected county officials—all serving four-year terms—are supervisors, county attorney, treasurer, superintendent of schools, recorder, assessor, sheriff and clerk of the superior court.

CROSS-COUNTRY SKIING • See "Winter sports" below.

DAY CARE • Anyone who cares for more than four children (not related to them) must be licensed by the Department of Health Services. For the publication Guidelines for Choosing a Day Care Center, contact: **Arizona Department of Health Services,** Division of Health Care Facilities, 701 E. Jefferson St., Phoenix, AZ 85034-2249; phone 542-1000. The office can also tell you if complaints have been lodged against a particular day care center.

These agencies also provide assistance in finding child care: **Association for Supportive Child Care**, 2510 S. Rural Rd., Tempe, AZ 85282, phone 829-0500; and **Tucson Association for Child Care**, 1030 N. Alvernon Way, Tucson, AZ 85711, phone 881-8940.

The Family Service Agency offers assistance in finding child care facilities as well as providing counseling for family problems, unplanned pregnancies and adoption services. The main office is at 1530

E. Flower St., Phoenix, AZ 85014; phone 264-9891. Other offices are in Tempe (966-0739), Scottsdale (994-0187), Mesa/Chandler (834-9290) and Phoenix Metrocenter (863-1862).

DENTISTS • Got a toothache? To find a dentist, contact the **Arizona Dental Association**, 4131 N. 36th St., Phoenix, AZ 85018; phone 957-4864.

DIVORCE LAWS • Arizona is a no-fault divorce state and a community property state. In ruling on alimony, courts will consider contributions made by one spouse to the other's earning ability, loss of potential earning power by spending years as a homemaker and other factors. The community property law simply means that property acquired by either marital partner during the marriage is considered the equal property of both.

DOCTORS • To find a medical doctor, contact the **Arizona Medical Association**, 810 W. Bethany Home Rd., Phoenix, AZ 85013; phone 246-8901 or the **Arizona Osteopathic Medical Association**, 5057 E. Thomas Rd., Phoenix, AZ 85018; phone 840-0460. Two county medical societies also provide names of local doctors: **Maricopa County Medical Society**, 326 E. Coronado Rd., Phoenix, AZ 85004; phone 252-2015 and the **Pima County Medical Society**, 5199 E. Farness St., Tucson, AZ 85712; phone 795-7985.

DRUG USE • Arizona gets mean about substance abuse. Possession of a "usable" amount of marijuana will earn you a $750 mandatory fine plus jail time or community service. If you're found with more of the stuff, or if you're arrested near a school grounds, the penalties get worse. You can imagine what they are for heroine and cocaine possession.

ELECTIONS • The state primary is held in September of even-numbered years, followed by the general election in November. You must pick a major party to vote in a primary, but not in a general election. The state doesn't conduct a Presidential primary. Precinct committeemen, who are elected to two-year terms, pick the state's party candidates.

Arizona's elected officials are the governor, secretary of state, attorney general and superintendent of public instruction, who all serve four-year terms; and the state mine inspector, who serves two years. Office holders are subject to recall elections if enough voters sign petitions. Voters also can place statewide initiatives and referendums on the ballot. (Also see "Legislature" and "Political parties" below.)

EMERGENCY PHONE NUMBERS • The 911 emergency phone number is active in virtually all areas. Other emergency numbers are: **Arizona Highway Patrol**—(800) 525-5555; **Poison control**—(800) 362-0101 or 253-3334 in Phoenix and 626-6016 in Tucson.

GOLFING • For a list of more than 150 golf courses in the state, contact the **Arizona Golf Association**, P.O. Box 13236, Phoenix, AZ 85002.

GUN CONTROL • With its Old West attitude, Arizona allows someone to buy a handgun or rifle without a waiting period and pack it in view. However, you can't own an automatic weapon or sawed-off shotgun. Also, you can't possess any weapon if you have a felony record or history of mental illness. A legally-owned weapon can't be concealed. You can, however, carry your Swiss army knife in your pocket.

HEALTH CARE • Arizona doesn't have a state-sponsored medical program or supplemental Medicare plan, although such plans are available through private insurance companies.

Persons interested in extended health care can get a directory of state-licensed facilities by contacting the **Office of Long Term Care** of the Arizona Department of Health Services, either at 701 E. Jefferson St., Phoenix, AZ 85034-2249; phone 255-1272, or at 402 W. Congress St., Tucson, AZ 85701; 628-5870. For information on nursing homes, contact the **Arizona Nursing Home Association**, 1817 N. Third St., Suite 200, Phoenix, AZ 85004; 258-8996.

HIGHWAY MAPS • See "Maps" below.

HOUSING • The best source for housing information is chambers of commerce and estate offices, since no one agency compiles data on prices and availability. (We provide pricing information in many of our community listings in Part Two.) If you want to build your own and need a contractor, contact the **Registrar of Contractors**, 800 W. Washington St., Phoenix, AZ 85007; 542-1525 or 416 W. Congress St., Tucson, AZ 85701; 628-6345. (Also see "Renting," below.)

HUNTING AND FISHING • Hunting and fishing licenses are required for anyone 14 and older, and are available at most sporting goods stores. Fishing license fees are $6.50 for residents and $25.50 for non-residents, or $18.50 for a nine-day and $12.50 for a five-day non-resident permit. Trout stamps are $6.50 for residents and $21.50 for out-of-staters. Combined hunting-fishing license is $18.50 for residents and $90.50 for non-residents. For specifics on limits and such, stop in at a sporting goods store or contact the **Arizona Game & Fish Department**, 2221 W. Greenway Rd., Phoenix, AZ 85023; 942-3000. State licenses aren't required for hunting and fishing on Indian reservations, but most have their own regulations and fees. (See "Other Indian nations" in Chapter 17.)

IDENTIFICATION CARDS • ID cards for non-drivers, handy for use in proving your age and identification, can be obtained for a fee from any office of the **Motor Vehicle Division**.

IMMIGRATION • For matters concerning immigration and naturalization, contact the **Immigration and Naturalization Service,** which has two offices in Arizona: 2035 N. Central Ave., Phoenix,

AZ 85004; phone 379-3122 and 301 W. Congress St., Tucson, AZ 85017; 629-6228.

INCORPORATING A BUSINESS • See "Starting a business" in Chapter 5.

INSURANCE • As in other states, insurance rates vary from city to city. Auto insurance rates are highest in busy Phoenix, somewhat lower in Tucson and lower still in smaller towns. The Department of Insurance will send you a survey of companies selling automobile and homeowners insurance in the state. It also maintains records of complaints against insurance carriers. To get a copy of the survey, send a self-addressed, stamped business-size envelope to: **State Department of Insurance**, 3030 N. Third St., Suite 1100, Phoenix, AZ 85040. The phone number is 255-5400. (Also see "Auto insurance" above.)

LEGISLATURE • Arizona is sliced into 30 legislative districts, and each sends one representative and one senator to the capital in Phoenix. Members of both houses serve two-year terms. The legislature convenes in early January and usually stays in session about four months. The **Senate information desk** (255-3559) and the **House of Representatives information desk** (255-4221) can tell you the status of a bill.

LIQUOR • See "Alcohol" above.

LOTTERY • The Arizona Lottery sells chances at $1 each and conducts computer drawings on Wednesdays and Saturdays. The jackpot often tops a million dollars; grand prize winners are paid over a period of twenty years. About two thirds of the money goes to prizes, and the other third is used for such programs as public transportation, street maintenance and senior vans.

You can pick your favorite numbers or let the computer do the choosing. Instant-winner scratch-off tickets also are sold. Hundreds of retailers displaying the Arizona Lottery logo sell tickets.

MAJOR LEAGUE SPORTS • Tickets for the **Phoenix Suns** of the National Basketball Association are available by calling 263-SUNS. They play at Veterans Memorial Coliseum. For National Football League **Phoenix Cardinal** tickets, call 967-1402. The team plays at Arizona State University's Sun Devil Stadium in Tempe. For **Cactus League** spring training, see the box below.

MAPS • State highway maps are available from these sources: **Arizona Office of Tourism**, 1100 W. Washington St., Phoenix, AZ 85007, 542-TOUR; *Arizona Highways*, 2039 Lewis Ave., Phoenix, AZ 85009, 258-6641 or offices of the **Arizona Automobile Association** (for AAA members only). They're also distributed by most chambers of commerce and border inspection stations.

For a list of various city, county and other state maps, get a brochure from the **Department of Transportation**, Engineering Re-

CACTUS LEAGUE: SUN COUNTRY BASEBALL

Every March, shouts of "play ball!" echo through the cactus as eight members of the majors launch their spring training. The Valley of the Sun is the focal point, hosting five clubs—the Chicago Cubs, Milwaukee Brewers, Oakland A's, San Francisco Giants and Seattle Mariners. The Cleveland Indians work out in Tucson, the San Diego Padres set up shop in Yuma and the California Angels practice in Palm Springs, California.

Fans like the informality and vigor of Cactus League baseball, and the intimacy of the small stadiums. It's baseball played with enthusiasm, gusto—and mistakes; the way we played as kids on America's sandlots. They like the ticket prices, too: $5 to $7 for the best seats in the stands.

Many people come to Arizona specifically to watch these exhibition games. A recent survey showed that Three out of four spring training ticket-buyers are from out of state.

If you're one of these baseball junkies, here's where you can catch the action. Unless otherwise indicated, teams practice on their home fields. Tickets for most games are available through Dillard's box offices, or telephone 829-5555 in Arizona (293-1008 in Tucson area) and (800) 366-3269 out of state. All games start at 1 p.m.

Chicago Cubs play at HoHoKam Park, 1238 Center St. (near Brown Road) in Mesa; (602) 964-4467.

Cleveland Indians play at Hi Corbett Field in Reid Park, Tucson; (602) 293-1008. (The team moves to Florida in 1993, however.)

Milwaukee Brewers play at Compadre Stadium, 1425 W. Ocotillo Rd. (off Arizona Avenue), in Chandler; (602) 821-2200.

Oakland A's play at Phoenix Municipal Stadium, 5999 E. Van Buren (near Galvin Parkway in Papago Park), Phoenix. They practice at Scottsdale Community College, 9000 E. Chaparral Road in Scottsdale.

San Diego Padres play at Desert Sun Stadium, 1440 Desert Hills Dr. (off Avenue A), in Yuma; (602) 782-2567.

San Francisco Giants play at Scottsdale Stadium, 7408 E. Osborn Rd., Scottsdale; (602) 994-5123. They work out at Indian Bend Park, 4289 N. Hayden Road in Scottsdale, and in Scottsdale Stadium.

Seattle Mariners play at Diablo Stadium, 2200 W. Alameda (near Diablo Way), in Tempe; (602) 731-8381.

California Angels work out at Gene Autry Park, 4125 E. McKellips in Mesa, from mid-February to mid-March before adjourning to Angel Stadium in Palm Springs.

cords Services, 206 S. 17th Ave., Room 134-A, Phoenix, AZ 85007: 255-7011.

National Forest maps are available for $2 each from the **Southwest Regional Office**, U.S. Forest Service, 517 Gold Ave. S.W., Albuquerque, NM 87102; (505) 842-3292. Designate the particular national forest you want. Maps of BLM areas are available from the **Bureau of Land Management**, 3707 N. Seventh St., Phoenix AZ 85011; 241-5547. Topographical maps can be purchased from the **U.S. Geological Survey**, Denver Federal Building 41, Denver, CO 80225; (303) 236-7477.

MARRIAGE LICENSES • Although it isn't noted as a marriage mill, Arizona makes it easy to take the plunge. A license can be secured from any justice court for $22 and there's no waiting period or blood test requirement. Anyone from 18 to 22 years old must provide proof of age (a birth certificate or driver's license), and those 16 and 17 need parents' consent. Those under 16 need the court's consent, given only in special circumstances. To learn the location of the nearest **justice court**, dial 262-3361 in Phoenix or 792-8041 in Tucson.

MEXICO • See "Exploring south of the border" in Chapter 18.

MOBILE HOME PARKS • See "RV parks" below.

NON-SMOKING AREAS • Most cities restrict smoking to certain areas and many require restaurants to designate non-smoking sections. Many employers, either by law or voluntarily, provide non-smoking areas in the workplace.

NURSING HOMES • See "Health care" above.

ORGAN DONORS • You can indicate on your state driver's license if you want to donate organs or other usable parts in case of death. The program has an nice name: the Anatomical Gift Act.

PASSPORTS • No, you don't need a passport to enter Arizona, but you'll need one to go overseas from there. Call 262-3369 in Phoenix or 740-8333 in Pima County (Tucson) for details. Proof of citizenship such as a birth certificate or naturalization certificate is required, along with passport photos. Allow a week or more to obtain a passport.

POLITICAL PARTIES • Despite its conservative reputation, Arizona has more registered Democrats than Republicans—776,000 compared with 734,000 at last count. To become involved—should you wish—contact **Democratic State Headquarters**, 1509 N. Central Ave., Suite 100, Phoenix, AZ 85004; phone 257-9136 or **Arizona Republican Party**, 3501 N. 24th St., Phoenix, AZ 85016-6607; phone 957-7770. The state also has the usual splinter parties, plus a rather active Libertarian Party with 5,000 or more members. The address is: **Libertarian State Headquarters**, P.O. Box 501, Phoenix, AZ 85001; phone 248-8425.

PRIVATE SCHOOLS • Contact **Arizona Private School Association**, 420 W. Roosevelt St., Phoenix, AZ 85003; phone 265-8974.

PROFESSIONAL ORGANIZATIONS • See Chapter 5.

PUBLICATIONS • Copies of Arizona laws and other state publications can be obtained from the **Secretary of State** in the west wing of the capitol building, 1700 W. Washington St., Phoenix, AZ 85007;

phone 542-6169. If you don't know what to ask for, the office will send you a list of its publications.

RAINFALL • See individual community listings in Part Two.

RENTING • If you're a winter visitor looking for rentals, local chambers of commerce can be helpful. Tucson has a rent-finders service specifically for long-term winter visitors.

Regulations governing rentals are set down in the Arizona Residential Landlord and Tenant Act. Get a copy by contacting the **Secretary of State** in the west wing of the capitol building, 1700 W. Washington St., Phoenix, AZ 85007; phone 542-6169. Among its provisions are these:

• Final month's rent and deposits can't exceed one and a half times the monthly rent.

• Either the tenant or landlord must give 30 days notice prior to the rental due date before terminating a tenancy agreement.

• The agreement must state which deposits are refundable and which are not.

• Tenants must be told within two weeks of their departure from a rental of the disposition of all deposits. In other words, deposits must be returned or reasons given for their forfeiture.

• Landlords are required to provide trash removal containers, and to keep the property in compliance with building code that affect health and safety.

• If a landlord neglects to make repairs affecting health and safety—or repairs called for in the rental agreement—the tenant has several options. They include terminating the rental agreement, seeking temporary quarters and billing the landlord, or having the work done by a licensed contractor and deducting the cost from the rent. Generally, after receiving written notice from the tenant, the landlord has 14 days to make repairs.

• Landlords can't add surcharges to utility bills; they can collect only the actual amount of the bill from the tenant.

• Landlords must give two days notice of intention to enter the tenant's unit. However, they can enter immediately in the case of an emergency.

RETIREMENT COMMUNITIES • Dozens of retirement communities are located throughout the Arizona sunbelt, and we discuss them in greater detail in Chapter 6. Age limitations in some retirement communities are set by law, under provisions of Arizona Revised Statues 9-46201 A11. In other words, retirement communities can require that one member of a household (not necessarily the head of household) be a particular age or older.

RV PARKS • Towns and cities with RV parks that cater to long-term winter visitors are listed in Chapter 7. For a list of mobile home parks, send a check for $5 to **Arizona Mobile Housing Associa-**

tion, 2540 E. Thomas Rd., Suite I, Phoenix, AZ 85016; phone 955-4440. This doesn't include all the state's mobile home parks, but it does list 250 that are members of the association, describing the amenities, location and number of spaces in each.

SCHOOLS • For information on the state's public schools, contact the **Arizona Department of Education**, 1535 W. Jefferson St., Phoenix, AZ 85007. The department publishes a directory of all schools in the state, and results of periodic student testing. For details on the state's education system, see Chapter 4.

SENIOR COMMUNITIES • See "Retirement communities" above.

SENIOR SERVICES AND HEALTH CARE • See "Senior service agencies," listed in Chapter 6.

SMALL BUSINESSES • See Chapter 5 under "Starting a business."

SMALL CLAIMS • Residents can file for debt-collection for amounts up to $500 in Small Claims Court; filing fee is $2. Lawyers aren't permitted or required in Small Claims Court, unless both sides agree to legal representation. Although a judgment may be granted, courts do not assist in collecting. The ruling only confirms the debt, and you must take other steps to collect. Contact the **Small Claims Division** of the local court for specifics.

SKIING • See "Winter sports" below.

SOCIAL SECURITY OFFICES • For Social Security assistance, call (800) 234-5772. Offices are located in these Arizona communities:

Flagstaff—397 Malpais Lane (86001).

Glendale—5955 W. Myrtle Ave. (85301).

Mesa—1050 W. Main St. (85201).

Phoenix—1150 E. Washington St. (85034); and 3738 N. 16th St., Suite D (85016).

Scottsdale—11000 N. Scottsdale Rd. (85254).

Tucson—4601 E. Broadway (85711) and 2716 S. Sixth Ave. (85713).

SPEED LIMITS • Like the rest of the states, Arizona has a basic speed limit of 55 miles per hour, unless otherwise posted. Speed limit on most freeways outside metropolitan areas is 65. The maximum speed is 25 mph in residential districts and 15 mph at school crossings and in school zones when children are present. And yes, law enforcement officers—including the Arizona Highway Patrol—are equipped with radar.

TELEPHONE SERVICE • Area code is (602). Most of Arizona is served by USWEST Communications. The directory assistance number, statewide, is 1-411. For service, call toll-free 1-779-4700 (residential) or 1-438-5440 (business). To order white or yellow page directories, call (800) 422-8793.

TIME ZONES • Arizona is in the Mountain time zone and it's the only state in the Union that doesn't go on Daylight Saving Time. Why? Because those desert summer evenings are already long enough, thank you. The Navajo Reservation, however, does observe summer daylight time.

TRADE ORGANIZATIONS • See Chapter 5.

VETERANS' ASSISTANCE • The **Veterans Administration regional center** is at 3225 N. Central Ave., Phoenix, AZ 85012; 263-5411. Arizona has three veterans' hospitals—at Seventh Street and Indian School Road in Phoenix, at 3601 S. Sixth Street in Tucson and on Highway 89 North in Prescott; call (800) 352-0451 for details on the hospitals and other VA assistance.

Among the state's veterans groups are the **American Legion**, phone 241-2701; **American Veterans**, 241-2110; **Disabled American Veterans**, 241-2774; **Veterans of Foreign Wars**, 241-2719 and the **Paralyzed Veterans Association**, 241-2700.

VOTING • Arizona makes it easy to vote. You can register at any city clerk or county recorder's office, department of elections office, driver's license examining station, justice of the peace, political party headquarters or with any deputy registrar. The state embraces all federal voting requirements: You must be an 18-year-old American citizen who hasn't been convicted of treason or a felony, and you must be sane and not under mental guardianship. State residency requirement is 50 days. (Also see "Political parties" above.)

Absentee ballots are available to anyone who lives more than 15 miles from the polls, will be absent from their precinct on election day, is 65 or older or has a vision or physical defect.

WAGES • See Chapter 5 for details on wage ranges for various professions.

WEATHER • Arizona's legendary sunshine is perhaps the single most important impetus in the state's growth. For weather reports, tune to 162.4 or 162.55 on the VHF band, or telephone 957-8700. (Also see "Weather or not" in Chapter 1.)

WILLS AND THE RIGHT TO DIE • If you're 18 or older, you can make out a will, which must be witnessed by two other parties who aren't beneficiaries of the will. However, if it's hand-written, witnesses aren't required. Out-of-state wills are recognized, but you should check with an attorney to confirm that provisions of your will conform to Arizona law (bearing in mind the $500,000 inheritance tax exemption). Property should be placed in joint tenancy, so the surviving partner automatically inherits it.

Arizona is a "Right to die" state, which means that you can establish a living will that sets forth procedures for dealing with a terminal illness. Based on a 1987 court ruling, patients can refuse treatment if they are terminally ill. If patients are medically or mentally unable to make that decision and no living will has been made, courts can appoint a guardian to act on their behalf.

WINTER SPORTS ● Arizona offers these downhill ski areas: **Fairfield Snowbowl** above Flagstaff, 779-1951 or 800-352-3524 in Arizona and 800-526-1004 out of state; **Mount Lemmon Ski Valley** above Tucson, 576-1321; **Sunrise Ski Area**, an Apache-owned resort in central Arizona, 735-7669; and **Williams Ski Area** near Williams, 635-9330. The Snowbowl and Sunrise are the largest.

Groomed cross-country trails available are at the **Flagstaff Nordic Center**, 774-6216; **Mormon Lake Ski Center** near Flagstaff, 354-2240; **Montezuma Nordic Ski Center**, also near Flagstaff, 354-2221; and **Williams Ski Area**, 635-9330.

YELLOW PAGES ● Thumbing through a community's Yellow Pages can tell you a lot about your prospective home. Arizona's directories are particularly useful, with special sections containing local maps, lists of schools, nearby attractions and other information. To get phone directories for various communities, call **USWEST** at (800) 422-8793.

Chapter Four

SCHOOL DAYS NNNNNNNNNNNNNNNNN

ELEMENTARY AND HIGH SCHOOLS

If you're moving a family to Arizona, you'll be concerned about the quality of education in your future home town. You will be pleased to know that—overall—Arizona rates at or above the national average in most student test scores.

The state requires that all students be tested annually for their scholastic proficiency in reading, language and math. Elementary students take the Iowa Test of Basic Skills, while high school kids take either the Stanford Achievement Test (freshmen) or Stanford Test of Academic Skills (sophomore through seniors).

In tests administered in 1990, nearly all grades (one through twelve) scored higher than the national average in language. Most intermediate and high school grades also topped national scores in reading, while grades one through five scored slightly below. In math, most Arizona students scored at or just below the national average. Significantly, reading, language and math test scores for virtually all grades were higher in 1990 than in 1989.

You can obtain the latest testing results—both statewide and by school district—by contacting: **Arizona Department of Education,** 1535 W. Jefferson St., Phoenix, AZ 85007.

To encourage continued student proficiency, outstanding elementary and secondary schools are honored in an annual School Recognition Program. Among the criteria are effectiveness of instructional programs, community relations, student-teacher relations, academic goals, anti-drinking and drug programs and administrative leadership. The programs are sponsored by the Arizona Educational Foundation and Department of Education, with corporate participation by the Southland Corporation.

School attendance

Arizona's school attendance laws are pretty much the same as in other states. Parents or guardians of any child between eight and 16

39

must send the kid to school. Youngsters can leave school before age 16 only if they have finished the 10th grade or are 14 years old and are employed or in some sort of vocational or work training program.

These immunization shots are required for school children: measles, mumps, rubella, diphtheria, tetanus and polio. Proof of immunization must be provided by parents or guardians within 15 days after the child starts classes.

Private schooling

For a list of accredited private schools, contact: **Arizona Private School Association**, 420 W. Roosevelt St., Phoenix, AZ 85003; phone 265-8974.

Children can be taught at home if someone in the household has passed the Arizona Teacher Proficiency Examination within six months of the beginning of instruction. The child still must take state-required achievement tests. For specifics on home education, contact **Teacher Testing Unit, Arizona Department of Education**, 1535 W. Jefferson St., Phoenix, AZ 85007.

Some of the top public schools

Generally speaking, schools in the Phoenix and Tucson suburbs are among the state's leaders, based on results of annual student achievement tests. As a rule, suburban kids outscored their city-center peers.

According to the most recent testing results (1990), these were among Arizona's top-rated public schools. (This is not a precise analysis, but a general comparison of test scores.)

Elementary (grades one through eight)

St. David Unified District (Cochise County)—St. David School.

Flagstaff Unified District (Coconino County)—Knoles Elementary School.

Mesa Unified District (Maricopa County)—Alma School, Field School, Franklin School, Washington School, MacArthur School, Jordan School, Sirrine School, Ishikawa School, Kino Junior High, Poston Junior High, Rhodes Junior High, Taylor Junior High and Hendrix Junior High.

Peoria Unified District (Maricopa County)—Oakwood School, Kachina School, Heritage School, Pioneer School, Desert Palms School, Sahuaro School, Skyview Elementary School and Desert Valley School.

Scottsdale Unified District (Maricopa County)—Cochise School, Kiva School, Hopi School, Cherokee School, Anasazi School, Laguna School, Sequoya School, Zuni School, Mohave Middle School, Ingleside Middle School and Cocopah Middle School.

Paradise Valley Unified District (Maricopa County)—Mercury Mine School, Liberty School, Sandpiper School, Desert Springs School and Desert Shadows Middle School.

Chandler Unified District (Maricopa County)—Goodman Elementary School.

Washington Elementary District (Maricopa County)—Lookout Mountain School, Richard E. Miller School and Desert Foothills Middle School.

Alhambra Elementary District (Maricopa County)—Alhambra Traditional School.

Tucson Unified District (Pima County)—Fruchthendler School, Whitmore School, Gale School, Lineweaver School and Wrightstown School.

Tanque Verde Unified District (Pima County)—Tanque Verde School.

Catalina Foothills Unified District (Pima County)—Sunrise Drive School, Manzanita School, Canyon View School and Orange Grove Junior High. (Overall, Catalina Foothills was one of the highest-scoring districts in the state.)

Sonoita Elementary District (Santa Cruz County)—Elgin Elementary School.

Secondary (grades nine through twelve)

Flagstaff Unified District (Coconino County)—Coconino High School.

Mesa Unified District (Maricopa County)—Mountain View High School and Dobson High School.

Scottsdale Unified District (Maricopa County)—Arcadia High School, Saguaro High School and Chaparral High School.

Tempe Union High School District (Maricopa County)—Corona del Sol High School and Evening High School.

Tucson Unified District (Pima County)—University High School and Sabino High School. (University was one of the highest scoring high schools in the state.)

COLLEGES AND UNIVERSITIES

Arizona boasts some of America's leading institutes of higher education. They include the three-campus University of Arizona and a campus of America's only aeronautical university.

Since joining the Pacific Ten several years ago, Tucson's University of Arizona and Arizona State University in Tempe have earned national attention for their athletic teams, particularly in football and basketball. But that's just for fun and TV coverage. More importantly, they rank among America's leading state universities. Both have large, modern and handsome campuses with state-of-the-art learning facilities. They attract so many out of state students that officials have considered non-resident tuition adjustments to ensure that there's room for bright young Arizonans.

The state also supports a network of community colleges. These two-year schools provide broad-based science and liberal arts courses for high school graduates who've not yet decided on a major, or who need to tidy up their grades for four-year-school admission. They also provide vocational studies and career-change training to prepare people for the job market.

In the listings that follow, tuition, fees and room and board figures are per school year, unless indicated otherwise.

The state universities

University of Arizona • Tucson, AZ 85721; 621-3237. Arizona's oldest university, founded in 1885, it offers a broad base of undergraduate and graduate programs. Its colleges include agriculture, architecture, arts and science, business and public administration, education, engineering and mines, law, medicine, nursing and pharmacy. Special programs include anthropology, astronomy, classical archaeology, management information studies and arid land studies. Admission requirements: 3.0 or in top 25 percent of class. Tuition: $1,590 for residents and $7,046 for non-residents, plus fees. On-campus housing available, including family units; room and board $3,702. Number of students: 35,735.

Arizona State University • Tempe, AZ 85287; 965-9011. The state's largest university, ASU offers programs in a variety of fields. It specializes in architecture and environmental design (the campus theater was designed by Frank Lloyd Wright), engineering and applied sciences, accounting, graphic design, journalism and telecommunications, and such fine arts programs as dance, theater, art and music. Admission requirements: 2.5 for residents and 3.0 for non-residents. Tuition and fees: $1,590 for residents, $6,996 for non-residents. On-campus housing available; room and board averages $3,900 per year. About 43,000 students.

Northern Arizona University • P.O. Box 4084, Flagstaff, AZ 86001; 523-5511. NAU recently was rated by Money Magazine as one of the ten top university values in the country (quality of education for relatively low tuition). Its nine colleges offer programs in arts and sciences, business, education, forestry, health professions, hospitality management, engineering, social and behavioral sciences and creative and communication arts. Admission requirements: 2.50 grade point average. Tuition: $1,550 for residents, $6,245 for non-residents. On-campus housing available; room and board $2,800. About 16,000 students.

Other four-year colleges and universities

Arizona College of the Bible • 2045 W. Northern Ave., Phoenix, AZ 85021; 995-2670. Small campus offering bachelor of arts degrees in pre-seminary and various Christian studies. Admission requirements: 2.0 grade point average. Tuition: $4,370 for both residents and non-residents. On-campus housing available; lodging (no meals), $1,420. A hundred and twenty students.

DeVry Institute of Technology • 2149 W. Dunlap Ave., Phoenix, AZ 85021; 870-9201. A technical school offering courses in electronics engineering technology, electronics technician, computer information systems, business operations and accounting. Admission requirements: high school diploma or GED equivalent. Tuition: $5,335 per academic year for resident and non-resident. No on-campus housing; 2,700 students.

Embry Riddle Aeronautical University • 3200 Willow Creek Rd., Prescott, AZ 86301; 776-3728; or contact the Florida campus at Daytona Beach, FL 32014; (800) 111-ERAU. America's only university-level aeronautical school, it offers majors in aviation technology, aerospace engineering, aerospace science, aviation administration and related fields. The school has its own fleet of training planes at nearby Ernest A. Love Field. Admission requirements: high school diploma or equivalent. Tuition and fees: $4,630. Campus housing available; room and board $2,780. About 1,500 students.

Grand Canyon University • 3300 W. Camelback Rd., Phoenix, AZ 85061; (800) 266-2855 or locally 589-2855. A small Southern Baptist liberal arts school, it offers degrees in business administration, commerce, management, elementary education, nursing and several Christian studies. Graduate programs are offered in elementary and secondary education. Admission requirements: high school diploma with a 2.5 grade average. Tuition and fees: $5,016. On-campus housing available; room and board $3,050. About 1,800 students.

Prescott College • 220 Grove Ave., Prescott, AZ 86301; 778-2090. A small liberal arts school, it emphasizes experimental learning programs and field studies. Majors are environmental studies, cultural and religious studies, humanities, human development and outdoor action. Admission requirements: individual analysis; essay, review of transcripts. Tuition $7,800. No on-campus housing; 670 students.

Southwestern College • 2625 E. Cactus Rd., Phoenix, AZ 85032; 992-6101. A Conservative Baptist school, it focuses on biblical studies, elementary education, pastoral studies, theology and related subjects. Admission requirements: high school diploma or equivalent, plus a written essay. Tuition and fees: $3,720. On-campus housing; room and board about $1,700.

University of Phoenix • 4615 E. Elwood St., Phoenix, AZ 85040; 921-5332. This proprietary upper level institution offers graduate courses in business administration, management, commerce and nursing. Admission requirements: 2.0 grade point average and at least two years degree-related work experience. Tuition: $4,500 for business courses and $4,050 for nursing. No on-campus housing.

Western International University • 10202 N. 19th Ave., Phoenix, AZ 85021; 943-2311. It offers graduate and undergraduate business-oriented programs to employed professionals who want to further their educations. Fields of study include marketing, international business management, accounting, finance and management. Admission requirements: 3.0 for masters programs and 2.75 for bachelor programs. Tuition: $120 per unit for bachelor programs, $145 for masters. No on-campus housing; 1,500 students.

Two-year colleges and technical schools

Note: Arizona's community college program is open to anyone 18 years or older who "demonstrates evidence of potential success" in taking college classes. For some courses of study, there are additional requirements, such as a high school diploma, GED equivalency or college transfer credits. For more information, contact the Arizona Community College Board, 3225 N. Central Ave., Phoenix, AZ 85012; 255-4037.

Arizona Western College • Yuma, AZ 85364; 726-1050. Part of the state community college system, it offers associate of arts degrees in a variety of liberal arts and sciences subjects, plus vocational and continuing education programs. Admission requirements: open enrollment. Tuition and fees: $408 for residents, $3,768 for non-residents. No on-campus housing; 5,200 students.

Central Arizona College • Coolidge, AZ 85228; 723-4141. A county-supported college, offering assorted AA degrees; specializing in nursing. Admission requirements: open enrollment, except for nursing program which has prerequisites. Tuition and fees: $510 for residents, $4,296 for non-residents. On-campus housing; room and board $2,050. About 5,200 students.

Chaparral Career College • 4585 E. Speedway, #204, Tucson, AZ 85712; 327-6866. Two-year courses with associate in business degrees in computing, accounting, hospitality, administrative assistants and legal assistants. Admission requirements: high school graduate or GED equivalency; 2.0 grade-point average. Fees vary with the programs. No housing on campus; 400 students.

Cochise College • Route 1, Box 100, Douglas, AZ 85607; 364-7943; 364-7943. Community college offering AA degrees in a variety of subjects. Specialties include pilot training, aviation maintenance, computer sciences and nursing. Also vocational and continuing education programs. Admission requirements: high school education or GED equivalency. Tuition: $22 per semester unit for residents, $140 for out of state students. Men's and women's dorms and family housing apartments; room and board $1,367 per semester. About 4,900 students

Eastern Arizona College • 600 Church St., Thatcher, AZ 85552-0769; 428-8233. Community college offering AA degrees in a variety of subjects, plus vocational and continuing education programs. Admission requirements: high school graduate or GED equivalency. Tuition: $300 per semester of 12 units or more for residents, $1,862 for non-residents. Campus housing available; $505 for fall semester lodging, $337 for spring semester, plus $732 to $866 for meals. About 2,200 students.

Gateway Community College • 108 N. 40th St., Phoenix, AZ 85034; 275-8500. Part of the Maricopa Community College district; offering AA degrees in several subjects, plus vocational and continuing education courses. Open admission; requirements for some courses of study. Tuition: $656 within the area; $2,816 outside the area and $3,776 out of state. No on-campus housing; 3,831 students.

Glendale Community College • 6000 W. Olive Ave., Glendale, AZ 85302; 435-3000. Variety of lower division academic programs, plus occupational programs in automotive technology, business, computer design, drafting technology, electronics and other fields. Noted for its high-tech programs. Open admission. Tuition: $24 per credit unit for residents and $149 for non-resident. No on-campus housing; 18,500 students.

ITT Technical Institute • 4837 E. McDowell Rd., Phoenix, AZ 85008; 231-0871. Campus also at 1840 E. Benson Highway, Tucson, AZ 85714. One-year courses in computer science, electronics and computer engineering, drafting and computer-aided design. Admission requirements: high school graduate or GED equivalency. Tuition: $11,217 for full year, resident and non-resident. No on-campus housing but roommate assistance is available. About 315 students. Job-placement assistance during school and after graduation.

Lamson Junior College • Campuses at 1980 W. Main St., Mesa, AZ 85201; 2701 W. Bethany Home, Phoenix, AZ 85017; 1548-A W. Montebello, Phoenix, AZ 85015; and 4425 W. Olive Glendale, AZ 85302. Variety of lower division academic courses, plus trade and technical programs. Open enrollment, although some course require a high school diploma or equivalent. Tuition varies, about $15.50 per semester unit for Maricopa County residents, plus additional for out of area and out of state students.

Mesa Community College • 1833 W. Southern Ave., Mesa, AZ 85202; 461-7000. Variety of lower division academic programs, plus trade and technical programs; rated as one of America's leading vocational institutions. Admission requirements: open enrollment. Tuition: $15.50 per semester credit unit for Maricopa County residents, plus an additional $94 per semester for out of county and $125 per semester for out of state residents. No on-campus housing; the Office of Student Activities provides a free housing directory and roommate service.

Mohave Community College • Kingman, AZ 86401. Lower division academic programs in business, English, fine arts, general studies, science, mathematics, applied science, health science and technology. Admission requirements: high school diploma or GED equivalent. Tuition: $247 per semester for residents, $1,700 for non-residents. No on-campus housing; 5,600 students.

Navajo Community College • Tsaile, AZ 86558; 724-3311. Federally-supported college on the Navajo Indian Reservation. Offers a variety of lower-division liberal arts programs, including Native American studies. Admission requirements: high school diploma or equivalent. Tuition and fees: $410. On-campus housing; room and board $2,620. About 1,800 students; 88 percent are Native American.

Northland Pioneer College • Holbrook, AZ 86025; 524-6111. Part of the community college system, with programs in secretarial, office management, business administration, commerce and other liberal arts subjects, plus continuing education and vocational. Open admission. Tuition and fees: $120 for residents, $2,180 for non-residents. No on-campus housing; about 6,000 students.

Phoenix College • 1202 W. Thomas Rd., Phoenix, AZ 85013; 264-2492. Part of the Maricopa Community College system, offering a variety of lower division academic programs, plus trade, technical and continuing education programs. Open admission. Tuition and fees: $24 per semester credit unit for county residents, $118 for out of county and $149 for out of state residents. No on-campus housing.

Pima Community College • 2202 W. Anklam Rd., Tucson, AZ 85702; 884-6060. Variety of lower division academic studies, plus trade, technical and continuing education programs. Specialties include airframe repair, aviation mechanics, radiological and emergency medical technology. The school has the only EPA approved environmental training center in the West. Open admission. Tuition: $264 for residents, $1,287 for non-residents. No on-campus housing; 28,000 students.

Rio Salado Community College • 640 N. First Ave., Phoenix, AZ 85003; 223-4000. A non-campus college; part of the Maricopa Community College district offering a variety of lower division programs, continuing education and technical courses. Open admission. Tuition: $24 per credit hour for county residents and $26 for out of county and out of state. About 14,000 students.

Scottsdale Community College • 9000 E. Chaparral Rd., Scottsdale, AZ 85256; 432-6000. Part of the Maricopa Community College District, with a variety of liberal arts, technical and continuing education programs. Open admission; 2.0 grade point average for credit students. Tuition and fees; $24 per credit unit for county residents, $149 for out of state students. No on-campus housing; 10,150 students.

South Mountain Community College • 7050 S. 24th St., Phoenix, AZ 85040. Part of the Maricopa Community College District; AA programs include business administration, commerce, management and computer information systems. Open admission. Tuition and fees: $656 for county residents, $3,472 for other Arizonans and $4,432 for out of state. No on-campus housing; 2,648 students.

Yavapai College ● 1100 E. Sheldon St., Prescott, AZ 86301; 445-7300. Community college with a variety of science and liberal arts programs. Open admission. Tuition: $300 for residents, $2,000 for non-residents. On-campus housing; $1,100 room and board. About 3,800 students. Second campus in Clarkdale and extension programs in Flagstaff.

Chapter Five

THE JOB-SEEKERS ░░░░░░░░░░░░░░░░

ARIZONA'S EMPLOYMENT BASE

There's good and bad news in the Arizona employment picture, according to the Department of Economic Security's Job Service. Although job growth slumped toward the end of the Eighties, it appears to be picking up as we enter the new decade. Most Arizona watchers feel the state will continue to out-perform the rest of the nation. That's the good news.

The bad news is that, early in this decade, many professional and semi-skilled positions were still in over supply.

"Too many people are seeking too few jobs," says the Job Service. Also, wages in general are lower in Arizona than the national average, although that gap is improving.

Job-seekers should be "financially prepared to withstand a few months of unemployment," according to the Job Service, unless they've already lined something up.

The state's job growth chugged along at two percent a year toward the end of the last decade, but approached three percent in 1990. In Phoenix, the bellwether for growing Arizona, job growth is expected to out-gain population growth in the early Nineties. This guesstimate comes from Arizona State University's highly regarded Center for Business Research.

Tourism and other service industries lead the Arizona job market, employing half a million people and accounting for one of every four paychecks. The retail trade follows, comprising a fifth of all the employment force. Although manufacturing accounts for only 12 percent of Arizona's jobs, most are generated by desirable smokeless industries. The state has been very successful in attracting high tech plants, which provide 40 percent of the manufacturing payroll.

The highest-paying blue collar industry? Interestingly enough, it's mining, with an average weekly paycheck of $667.95. However, it's the smallest segment of the state's industry, employing only .8 percent of the work force, despite the fact that Arizona produces 60 percent of the nation's copper.

Twin plant manufacturing

One curious aspect of the Arizona job market is the so-called "twin plant" or "offshore" manufacturing operations. Working in concert with the Mexican government, several American firms have set up manufacturing plants near the Arizona-Mexico border to draw from Mexico's cheap labor pool. Often, plants are located on both sides of the border; thus the twin plant reference.

This helps American manufacturers compete against cheap overseas labor and it boosts Mexico's economy. However, it offers little for Arizona-bound job-hunters, other than a few management positions. Among the twin-plant communities are San Luis below Yuma, Naco south of Bisbee, Nogales-Nogales and Douglas-Agua Prieta.

Offshore manufacturing obviously has a major impact on the south side of the border. Agua Prieta's population leaped from 18,000 to more than 70,000 in the past ten years. Another example: With more than a hundred thousand residents, Nogales, Mexico, has nearly ten times the population of Arizona's Nogales. Those twin cities' twin plants employ 24,000. Nearly 50,000 Mexican nationals cross the border each day to work and shop.

Because of low wages and intense competition from hard-working Mexicans, we don't recommend job-hunting along the border.

Right to work

Arizona is a "right to work" state, which means that mandatory union membership is prohibited. Thus, there are no closed shops. Right to work laws create mixed blessings: They tend to attract businesses but suppress wages in fields that are generally unionized.

Predictably, union membership in Arizona is rather low, seven percent of the work force, compared with a national rate of 17 percent.

Employee rights

On the other side of the coin, Arizona is pro-labor when it comes to employee rights. If you switch jobs, the law requires that you receive copies of all communication between your present and prospective employers.

Blacklisting to prevent someone from getting a job is forbidden. Employers can exchange only specific information on job performance, qualifications, past experience, education and training.

WHERE THE JOBS ARE

Direct contact is the best way to land a job, and we discuss this toward the end of the chapter, under "Finding that job." Employment agencies, trade and professional organizations are useful tools, as well.

A good starting point is the Job Service. Its offices are scattered throughout the state. Like other state employment offices, they offer lists of local job openings, and they provide counseling to job-seekers. You'll find a complete list later in this chapter.

The department offers a variety of publications to aid your job search, including Arizona Occupational Employment Forecasts, Finding a Job in the Want Ads, Helpful Hints for Job Seekers, Applying for Government Jobs and current employment profiles for each county. Particularly useful is the monthly Labor Market Information Newsletter with statistics and up-to-date articles concerning the job market. For a list of the department's publications, contact: **Arizona Department of Economic Security**, occupational Employment Statistics, Dept. 733A, P.O. Box 6123, Phoenix, AZ 85005.

When we last checked, the statewide unemployment rate was a modest 5.9 percent. Of course, these conditions are certainly subject to change.The two most populous counties had the lowest rates: Maricopa (Phoenix) and Pima (Tucson), both with 4.7 percent. Also relatively low were Yavapai (Prescott), 5.4 and Coconino (Flagstaff-Sedona) with 7.1.

Highest unemployment rates were in Santa Cruz County (south central area, including Nogales), 13.1 percent and Yuma (southwest corner), 24.2 percent.

An excellent job-finding source is the Yellow Pages of the local phone directory, since it lists businesses and firms by type. **USWEST** provides phone service for all Arizona communities (except for a few hamlets), and you can order local directories by calling (800) 422-8793.

Phoenix obviously is the core of Arizona's employment market. The Valley of the Sun provides homes and jobs for more than half the state's population. Several major corporations are based here, including Greyhound, the fast-growing America West Airlines, Ramada Inns, U-Haul and Circle K Corporation. If you're seeking a large and diversified employment base, the Valley of the Sun is your best bet.

A useful job source for greater Phoenix is *The Book of Lists*, published annually by the Business Journal. Although it doesn't provide specific job listings, it publishes names, phone numbers and addresses of the area's largest companies. Listings include the type of work they do, what products they create and names of company principals. Other useful lists in the book includes leading radio and TV stations, scheduled airline service, car rental agencies, hotels and resorts, colleges and even women-owned firms. For a copy, send a check for $23.95 to: **The Business Journal**, 3737 N. Seventh St., Suite 200, Phoenix, AZ 85014. For more information on the Valley of the

Sun's employment base, try these contacts:

City of Phoenix Public Information Office, 251 W. Washington St., Phoenix, AZ 85003; 262-7176.

Phoenix Economic Growth Corporation, 400 N. Fifth St., Room 1625, Phoenix, AZ 8504; 253-9747 or (800) FOR-PHNX.

Phoenix Chamber of Commerce, 34 W. Monroe St., Suite 900, Phoenix, AZ 85003; 254-5521.

Greater Phoenix Economic Council, Two N. Central, Suite 210, Phoenix, AZ 85004; 256-7700.

Tucson, Arizona's number two city, obviously offers its second largest job market. Major employers include the University of Arizona, Davis-Monthan Air Force Base, Hughes Aircraft and National Semiconductor. To learn more about the city's economic and employment situation, contact the **Tucson Economic Development Corporation,** 465 W. St. Mary's Rd., Suite 200, Tucson, AZ 85701- 8268; phone 623-3673 or the **Tucson Metropolitan Chamber of Commerce,** P.O. Box 991 (same street address), phone 792-2250.

Job prospects diminish as you travel further from these two metropolitan areas. However, some smaller communities still offer fairly good prospects—particularly in tourism and the service sector. If you want to avoid urban congestion, you might try some of the fast-growing towns on the edge of the Valley of the Sun. What follows is a list of communities that offer average to better-than-average employment opportunities. You'll find more detail on these communities in Part Two.

Buckeye • A small town of 4,000, Buckeye is 30 miles west of Phoenix. The growing town is actively promoting light industry and now has four sizable manufacturing plants. Its labor force has jumped about 40 percent in the past ten years. **For information:** Town of Buckeye, P.O. Box 157 (508 Monroe St.), Buckeye, AZ 85326; 256-2488 or Buckeye Valley Chamber of Commerce, P.O. Box 717 (717 Monroe St., Buckeye, AZ 85326; 386-2727.

Bullhead City • Primarily a Snowbird community, it sits across the Colorado River from Laughlin, Nevada, a fast-growing gaming center whose casinos employ 10,000 people. And that's where most of the jobs are. Bullhead is a rather unlovely town, but it is growing. **For information:** City of Bullhead City, P.O. Box 1048, Bullhead City, AZ 86430; 763-9400 or Bullhead Area Chamber of Commerce, P.O. Box 66 (1251 Highway 95), Bullhead City, AZ 86430; 754-4121.

Casa Grande • Midway between Tucson and Phoenix, this small city actively seeking light industry, and has seen a 20 percent gain in its labor force since 1980. Its population is 18,610, up nearly 30 percent in the last decade. **For information:** Greater Casa Grande Valley Economic Development Foundation, 520 N. Marshall St., Casa Grande, AZ 85222; 836-6868.

Chandler • A growing city of about 90,000, southeast of Phoenix in the Valley of the Sun, Chandler offers a broad-based job market. Space age firms like Intel Corporation, Microchip Technology and Space Data Corporation offer potential on the high tech side. Manufacturing of all types accounts for one out of four jobs—one of the highest rates of any city in Arizona. **For information:** City of Chandler, 200 E. Commonwealth St., Chandler, AZ 85225; 786-2867 or Chandler Chamber of Commerce, 218 E. Arizona Ave., Chandler, AZ 85224; 963-4571.

Flagstaff • This is a vibrant, growing community just below the Grand Canyon. Its job count increased more than 30 percent in the past decade, from 17,841 to 23,412. Lumbering, tourism, science, high tech manufacturing and education are leading industries in this town of 44,000. It's home to Northern Arizona University and Lowell Observatory. **For information:** City of Flagstaff, 211 W. Aspen St., Flagstaff, AZ 86001; 774-5281 or Flagstaff Chamber of Commerce, 101 W. Santa Fe Ave., Flagstaff, AZ 86004; 774-4505.

Gilbert • Half an hour southeast of Phoenix, Gilbert jumped 500 percent in population and more than 40 percent in employment during the Eighties. Most jobs are in manufacturing and in a rapidly-expanding retail base. It also has one of the state's lowest unemployment rates—under three percent. Population is currently nearing 30,000. **For information:** Town of Gilbert, P.O. Box 837 (119 N. Gilbert Rd.), Gilbert, AZ 85234; 892-0800 or Gilbert Chamber of Commerce, P.O. Box 527 (1400 N. Gilbert Rd.), Gilbert, AZ 85234; 892-0056.

Glendale • Northeast of Phoenix, Glendale is a fast-growing city of 150,000, with job opportunities in aerospace, communications, precision metal work, chemicals, electronics and warehousing. Luke Air Force Base offers the potential of civil service jobs. **For information:** City of Glendale, 5850 W. Glendale Ave., Glendale, AZ 85301; 435-4169 or Glendale Chamber of Commerce, P.O. Box 249 (7105 N. 59th Ave.), Glendale, AZ 85311; 937-4754.

Goodyear • Half an hour west of Phoenix, this small community has diversified from its Goodyear Aircraft facility to lure such firms as McKesson, Rubbermaid and Intertec Aviation. Its population, now 5,500, nearly doubled in the Eighties and job availability increased more than 40 percent. **For information:** City of Goodyear, 119 N. Litchfield Rd., Goodyear, AZ 85338; 932-3494 or Tri-City West Chamber of Commerce, 501 W. Van Buren, Suite K, Avondale, AZ 85323; 932- 2260.

Kingman • It's a smaller version of Flagstaff, with chilly but mild winters, a population of 13,000 and a labor force that has almost doubled in the past decade. Although the job market wasn't too active in the early Nineties, it may pick up. Distribution centers and light manufacturing are drawn to this town on Interstate 40 near the California border. **For information:** Economic and Tourism Commission, City of Kingman, 310 N. Fourth St., Kingman, AZ 86401; 753-8130.

Litchfield Park • With a population of 4,300, it's a planned community 16 miles west of Phoenix. Like neighboring Goodyear, it offers a growing base of light manufacturing and service jobs, with an employment increase of nearly 45 percent in the past decade. **For information:** City of Litchfield Park, 214 W. Indian School Rd., Litchfield Park, AZ 85340 or Tri-City West Chamber of Commerce, 501 W. Van Buren, Avondale, AZ 85323; 932-2260.

Mesa • West of Tempe and Phoenix, Mesa is a thriving community with a low employment rate and a broad economic base. It's Arizona's third largest city, with a population nearing 300,000. Among major employers are McDonnell Douglas Helicopters, Rosarita Foods, General Motors Proving Grounds and Motorola. **For information:** City of Mesa, 55 N. Center St., Mesa, AZ 85201; 644-2181 or Mesa Chamber of Commerce, 120 N. Center St., Mesa, AZ 85201; 969-1307.

Peoria • It's just northwest of Glendale, with a population of 47,000. It offers employment potential in light manufacturing, the services industry and retailing. Nearly one job in four is in manufacturing. Also, one could commute to civil service work at Luke Air Force Base. **For information:** City of Peoria, P.O. Box 38 (8355 W. Peoria Ave.), Peoria, AZ 85380; 979-7325 or Peoria Economic Development Group, 8815 W. Peoria Ave., Suite 2, Peoria, AZ 85345; 486-2011.

Prescott • Handsomely situated in the pines of central Arizona, Prescott offers a mix of history (as the first capital), culture and steady economic growth. This town of 25,000 has a job force of nearly 13,000, up by a third in the Eighties. Its economic mix includes mining, ranching, light manufacturing and education—with three small colleges. **For information:** Prescott Area Economic Development Corporation, P.O. Box 671 (1500 E. Highway 69), Prescott, AZ 86302; 445-2290.

Sierra Vista • This is an Arizona surprise—the major population center of the southeastern corner (35,000), with a mild climate and a relatively large job force. Nearby Fort Huachuca Army base has nearly 12,000 military and civilian employees. Sierra Vista itself is working to attract more light industry. It offers the best job prospects in southeastern Arizona—which, realistically, is not as strong as the Phoenix, Tucson or Flagstaff areas. Overall work force has increased more than 25 percent in the past ten years. **For information:** Sierra Vista Economic Development Foundation, P.O. Box 2380, Sierra Vista, AZ 85635; 458-6948.

Tempe • With a population 150,000, it's home to Arizona State

University, one of the town's largest employers. Manufacturing provides about one in five Tempe jobs, with about 200 companies producing electronics, clothing, processed foods, prefabricated housing and machine products. **For information:** City of Tempe, 31 E. Fifth St., Tempe, AZ 85282; 968-8221 or Tempe Chamber of Commerce, 60 E. Fifth St., Room 3, Tempe, AZ 85281; 967-7891.

WHAT THE JOBS ARE

Few factory smokestacks smudge the state's sunny skies. Heavy industry, other than mining, is rare and most Arizonans prefer to keep it that way.

This means that the state offers little in the way of unskilled and semi-skilled employment, other than the usual service sector jobs. Most of the semi-skilled jobs have gone south, literally, to the offshore factories we mentioned above.

Of course the tourist industry absorbs a lot of workers: desk clerks, maids, culinary workers and waiters. As in the rest of the world, most of these pay little more than minimum wage. And the work is seasonal, unless you're lucky enough to get a job slinging hash at a Grand Canyon restaurant in the summer and in a fancy Phoenix resort in the winter.

The retail trade, which has little union representation in the state, also is low on the pay scale, with an average weekly wage of $240. Agriculture, forestry and fishing pays even worse, around $230 a week.

In other words, if you come to Arizona looking for work, it's best to bring a college degree, or at least a high school diploma and a trade. Most better-paying jobs are in the skilled clerical and professional ranks.

The 100 most-needed job skills

According to the Arizona Department of Economic Security, these are the among the job skills that will be most in demand during the Nineties. The percentage indicates projected growth in these specific occupations from 1990 to 1995.

Architects—22%
Artists and related workers—25%
Assemblers, precision, general—22%
Bartenders—21%
Bill and account collectors—21%
Brick and stonemason helpers—23%
Brick and masons—23%
Bus drivers—21%
Chemical technicians—23%

Civil engineer techs—22%
Clerks, counter and retail—25%
Concrete, terrazzo finishers—21%
Cooks, restaurant—22%
Cost estimators—21%
Data entry keypunchers—21%
Data processing equipment repair—22%
Dental assistants and hygienists—23%
Dentists—24%

Detectives, investigators—21%
Dietetic technicians—22%
Dispatchers, Police and fire—21%
Drywall installers—24%
Electrical, mechanical workers—23%
Electricians—21%
Electrician, powerline helpers—22%
Electromechanical equipment assemblers—23%
Engineers, various—22%
Flight attendants—24%
Food service and lodging managers—22%
Food and beverage workers—22%
Glaziers—24%
Guards and watchmen—25%
Hairdressers, hair stylists—21%
Heat, air condition, refrigeration installers—21%
Helpers, construction trades—22%
Home health aides—23%
Hostesses, restaurant, lounge—22%
Housekeepers—22%
Insulation workers—23%
Interior designers—21%
Interviewers, employment—24%
Interviewing clerks—24%
Lathers—25%
Laundry, drycleaning machine operators—21%
Legal secretaries—21%
Lithographic press setters—24%
Mail machine operators—21%
Managers, first line—24%
Manicurists—21%
Medical assistants—23%
Medical secretaries—24%
Medical, clinical lab techs—24%
Medicine, health service managers—23%
Messengers—22%
Nurses aids, orderlies and attendants—24%
Nurses, registered, practical—23%
Office machine operators—21%
Opticians, dispensing—23%

Painters, paperhangers—22%
Painter, paper hanger helpers—23%
Paralegal personnel—21%
Pest controllers, assistants—31%
Pharmacists—22%
Pharmacy assistants—21%
Photo processing machine operators—28%
Photographers—22%
Physical therapy assistants and aides—22%
Physicians and surgeons—22%
Pilots, flight engineers—23%
Plasterers, stucco masons—24%
Plastic molders, casters—24%
Plumbers, pipefitters, steamfitters—22%
Plumber, pipefitter helpers—24%
Printing press operators—24%
Property estate managers—21%
Physical therapists—24%
Radiological techs—23%
Receptionists and information clerks—22%
Reporters, correspondents—21%
Respiratory therapists—25%
Restaurant cooks—22%
Roofers—24%
Sales agents and reps—23%
Service supervisors—23%
Sheet metal installers—23%
Social workers—22%
Statistical clerks—21%
Street vendors and phone solicitors—24%
Structural metal workers—23%
Switchboard operators—23%
Tax preparers—21%
Taxi drivers, chauffeurs—22%
Technical writers—22%
Ticket agents—23%
Transportation agents—24%
Travel agents—21%
Typesetting, composing operators—23%
Waiters and waitresses—21%
Word processing typists—21%
Writers, editors—21%

White collar jobs and their salary ranges

A useful book called *The Phoenix Job Bank* describes the employment situation and salary ranges for dozens of occupations in Arizona. It lists major employers in Phoenix and Tucson, and tells readers which job skills will be most in demand during the Nineties. The book can be ordered through most bookstores, or contact **Phoenix Job Bank**, Bob Adams, Inc., 260 Center St., Holbrook, MA 02343; phone (800) USA-JOBS or (617) 767-8100. Cover price is $12.95.

According to the 1990 edition, these white collar jobs were expected to match or exceed overall job growth during the Nineties. Most salary ranges are quoted from a 1986 survey, so expect them to be higher by the time you read this.

Accounting and auditing pays from $20,000 to $70,000 a year in Arizona. During the Nineties, job openings for accountants and auditors is expected to increase much faster than for overall employment.

Advertising business is expected to increase faster than the average for other jobs, spurred by rapid growth in business and commercial sectors. Salaries range from $17,700 to more than $100,000 for the people who come up with that dynamite TV spot.

Architects can still find work, and expect to earn from $30,000 up, but the current building slump is dampening the demand. Business is expected to pick up toward the middle of the decade.

Attorneys—perhaps unfortunately—continue to be in demand in Arizona's increasingly complex socio-economic environment. But the competition for jobs is growing as law schools in the state and outside continue to pour out hopefuls.

Bank officers and managers jobs will increase at about the same pace as other white collar work during the Nineties. Salary range is from $20,000 to $50,000, and it goes higher for top-level management in major institutions.

Dietitians and nutritionists should find good job prospects. Entry-level salaries start at something over $21,000.

Economist job availability should grow faster than the average during the Nineties. Salaries for those with a bachelor's degree in economics starts around $23,000, with the median salary over $36,000.

Engineer job growth varies according to type. Chemical engineer, electrical engineer, industrial engineer, and mining engineer jobs are expected to keep pace with average employment. Civil engineer and metallurgical engineer jobs should grow faster than average, while aerospace and petroleum engineer jobs remain volatile, rising and falling with the economy, defense needs and events in the Middle East. Overall, engineers' pay in Arizona ranges from $30,000 to $80,000.

Financial Analysts will see job opportunities increase at an average pace. Pay scale ranges from $18,000 to $52,000.

Hotel managers and assistants will find good job prospects here, with employment growing much faster than average. Salaries averaged $34,500 in 1986, ranging between $21,000 and $87,000.

Industrial designers can anticipate job growth faster than the overall employment average, with salaries ranging from $17,000 to $34,000.

Insurance actuaries start at around $19,000 with a business degree and work up to $60,000. Job availability should grow much faster than for the overall employment market.

Insurance agents and claims adjusters will find good job prospects as Arizona's population continues to grow, and people continue to have mishaps. Pay scales range from $29,000 to $41,000 in the state's insurance industry.

Managers of retail stores, businesses and factories can anticipate average job growth. Salaries start at $20,000 and range beyond $50,000 with the median in 1986 at $34,000.

Newspaper reporters and editors will see average job growth, but mostly in smaller towns. Suburban papers usually do better than the big dailies. Pay is poor, however, starting around $10,000 and creeping up toward $50,000 for editors. Average is about $21,000.

Physicists with PH.D. degrees can anticipate good job prospects in the Nineties, with salaries ranging from over $31,000 to $50,000.

Public relations workers also can expect rapid job growth—much faster than the average for overall employment. Salaries range from $19,700 to $41,000.

Statisticians job growth will be above average for those with a bachelor's degree. Salaries range from $15,000 to $40,000.

Systems Analysts can anticipate good job prospects during this decade, with salaries ranging from $15,000 to $33,000.

Teachers' job availability varies—obviously—with the district. Check out the fastest-growing communities in "Where the Jobs Are" above. The Department of Education maintains a want-list for the state's various school districts. Contact: **Education Personnel Clearinghouse**, Arizona Department of Education, 1535 W. Jefferson St., Phoenix, AZ 85007; phone 542- 4550.

Underwriters' job prospects will continue to improve, along with the rest of the insurance industry. Salaries range from $22,000 to about $30,000.

Starting a business

Perhaps you're interested in creating jobs instead of getting one. With its pro-growth attitude, Arizona is very supportive of people and corporations wanting to go into business.

If you want to set up shop, begin by sending for the Guide to Establishing a Business in Arizona. It's available from the **Arizona Department of Commerce**, 3800 N. Central Ave., Suite 1400, Phoenix, AZ 85017; phone 280-1321. The same department offers Arizona Industrial Profiles, which are comprehensive studies of various communities that are interested in attracting new business.

For information on business licenses and taxes, contact the **Arizona Department of Revenue**, 1600 W. Monroe St., Phoenix, AZ 85007; phone 542-3572.

If you want to incorporate, contact the **Secretary of State**, 1700 W. Washington St., Phoenix, AZ 85007; phone 255-4285. For specific requirements of incorporation, contact the **Arizona Corporation Commission**, which has two offices:

1200 W. Washington St., Suite 102, Phoenix, AZ 85007; phone 542- 3135.

402 W. Congress St., Tucson, AZ 85701; phone 628-5284.

A particularly useful organization is the **Arizona Small Business Association,** 301 W. Osborn Rd., Room 104, Phoenix, AZ 85013; phone 265-4563 or 248-8856. It's a non-profit group set up to assist small business owners. Among its services are legislative representation, group medical and dental plans, a credit union and a group legal and accounting referral plan.

What business to open? Restaurants are the most commonly opened new businesses in the state, but they also have a high failure rate. Surveys show that these are among the businesses most in demand:

Accounting firms	Insurance agencies
Attorneys	Investment firms
Auto dealers (new, used)	Laundries, dry-cleaners
Beauty parlors	Management consultants
Clothing stores	Medical doctors
Computer stores	Mortgage companies
Furniture stores	Printers and copy shops
General contractors	Real estate companies
Housing developers	Travel agencies

Job service offices

Department of Economic Security Job Service Office are located in these communities:

Benson • 225 E. Fourth St., Benson, AZ 85602; 384-3583.

Bisbee • 207 Bisbee Rd., Bisbee, AZ 85603; 432-2206.

Casa Grande • 401 N. Marshall St. (P.O. Box 579), Casa Grande, AZ 85222; 426-3529.

Chinle • P.O. Box 2600, Chinle, AZ 86503; 674-5798.

Clifton • 300 N. Coronado, Clifton, AZ 85533; 359-2791.

Coolidge • 1155 N. Arizona Blvd., Coolidge, AZ 85228; 723-5351.

Cottonwood • 203 S. Candy Lane, Room 5, Cottonwood, AZ 86326; 634-3337.

Douglas • 1136 F St., Douglas, AZ 85607; 364-4446.

Duncan • P.O. Box 916, Duncan, AZ 85534; 359-2791.

Flagstaff • 397 Malpais Lane, Suite 9, Flagstaff, AZ 86001; 779-4513.

Fort Defiance • P.O. Drawer C, Fort Defiance, AZ 86504; 729-5076.

Globe • 605 S. Seventh St., Globe, AZ 85501; 425-3101.

Holbrook • 105 N. Fifth Ave., Holbrook, AZ 86025; 524-6835.

Kayenta • P.O. Box 708, Kayenta, AZ 86033; 697-3324.

Kingman • 301 Pine St., Kingman, AZ 86401; 753-4333.

Lake Havasu City • 278 London Bridge Rd., Lake Havasu City, AZ 86403; 855-9134.

Mesa • Seven S. Hibbert St., Mesa, AZ 85210; 834-7777.

Nogales • 473 Grand Ave., Nogales, AZ 85621; 287-4635.

Phoenix • seven offices:

815 N. 18th St., Phoenix, AZ 85006; 253-1133

1224 S. Seventh Ave, Phoenix, AZ 85007; 258-6611.

1202 S. Seventh Ave., Phoenix, AZ 85007; 255-4303.

438 W. Adams St., Phoenix, AZ 85003; 252-7771.

4635 S. Central Ave., Phoenix, AZ 85040; 276-5587.

9801 W. Seventh St. (P.O. Box 9369), Phoenix, AZ 85020; 861-0208.

3406 N. 51st Ave. (P.O. Box 14429), Phoenix, AZ 85031; 247-3304.

Payson • 112 W. Cedar St., Payson, AZ 85541; 474-4521.

Prescott • 234 N. Grove Ave., Prescott, AZ 86302; 445-5100.

Safford • 106 Eighth Ave., Safford, AZ 85546; 428-2911.

Show Low • 40 S. 11th St., Show Low, AZ 85901; 537-2948.

Sierra Vista • 2981 E. Tacoma St., Sierra Vista, AZ 85636; 458-4005.

Tuba City • P.O. Box 1140, Tuba City, AZ 86045; 283-4510.

Tucson • seven offices:

4525 E. Broadway, Tucson, AZ 85711; 628-5138.

10 E. Broadway, Tucson, AZ 85701; 628-5428.

195 W. Irvington Rd. (P.O. Box 12410), Tucson, AZ 85734; 628-5517.

1859 W. Grant St., Tucson, AZ 85745; 628-5398.

301 W. 22nd St., Tucson, AZ 85713; 628-5349.

55 N. Sixth Ave., Tucson, AZ 85701; 620-6626.

318 W. Fort Lowell Rd. (Box 5625), Tucson, AZ 85703; 293-1919.

Willcox • 104 S. Arizona Ave., Willcox, AZ 85643; 384-3583.

Winslow • 319 E. Third St., Winslow, AZ 86047; 289-2425.

Yuma • 201 S. Third Ave., Yuma, AZ 85364; 783-1221.

LICENSED OCCUPATIONS

Nearly a hundred professions require licensing or certification in Arizona. Some may have reciprocity with other states; check this out before starting your job hunt. These are the agencies that oversee the state's various regulated occupations.

Accounting • Arizona State Board of Accountancy, 3110 N. 19th Ave., Suite 140, Phoenix, AZ 85015; phone 255-3648.

Architect • Arizona State Board of Technical Registration, 1951 W. Camelback, Suite 250, Phoenix, AZ 85015; 255-4053.

Attorney • Executive Director, State Bar of Arizona, 363 N. First Ave., Phoenix, AZ 85003; 252- 4804.

Auctioneer • License and Registration Section, Department of Revenue, 1600 W. Monroe St., Phoenix, AZ 85007; phone 542-3572.

Aviation (mechanics, commercial pilots, flight instructors, crop-dusters, etc.) • Federal Aviation Administration, Flight Standards Office, 15041 N. Airport Dr., Scottsdale, AZ 85260; 640-2561.

Bail bondsman • Department of Insurance, 801 W. Jefferson St., Phoenix, AZ 85007; 255-5400.

Barber • Board of Barber Examiners, 1645 W. Jefferson St., Room 418, Phoenix, AZ 85007; 542-4498.

Boxer or wrestler • Arizona State Boxing Commission, 1645 W. Jefferson St., Room 212, Phoenix, AZ 85007; 255-1417.

Cemetery worker • Department of Real Estate, 202 E. Earll Drive, Suite 400, Phoenix, AZ 85012; 255-4345.

Chauffeur • Motor Vehicle Division, Department of Transportation, 1801 W. Jefferson St., Phoenix, AZ 85007; 255-7011, extension 7451.

Chiropractor • Board of Chiropractic Examiners, 5060 N. 19th Ave., Room 317, Phoenix, AZ 85015; 255-1444.

Collection agent • State Banking Department, 3225 N. Central Ave., Suite 815, Phoenix, AZ 85012; 255-4421.

Contractor • Registrar of Contractors, 800 W. Washington St., Phoenix, AZ 85007; 542-1525 and 416 W. Congress St., Tucson, AZ 85701; 628-6345.

Cosmetologist (including manicurist and hairdresser) • Board of Cosmetology, 1645 W. Jefferson St., Room 125, Phoenix, AZ 85007; 255-5301.

Dentist and dental hygienist • Board of Dental Examiners, 5060 N. 19th Ave., Suite 406, Phoenix, AZ 85015; 255-3696.

Escrow agent and mortgage broker • Banking Department, 3225 N. Central Ave., Suite 815, Phoenix, AZ 85012; 255-4421.

Funeral directors and embalmers • Board of Funeral Directors and Embalmers, 1645 W. Jefferson St., Room 410, Phoenix, AZ 85007; 542-3095.

Geologist • Arizona State Board of Technical Registration, 1951

W. Camelback, Suite 250, Phoenix, AZ 85015; 255-4053.

Driving instructor (private) • Motor Vehicle Division, Department of Transportation, 1801 W. Jefferson St., Phoenix, AZ 85007; 255-7011, extension 7451.

Driving instructor (high school) • Teachers Certification Office, State Board of Education, 1535 W. Jefferson St., Room 126, Phoenix, AZ 85007; 542-4367.

Emergency medical technician • Emergency Medical Services, Arizona Department of Health Services, 701 E. Jefferson St., Phoenix, AZ 85034-2249; 542-1000.

Engineer • Arizona State Board of Technical Registration, 1951 W. Camelback, Suite 250, Phoenix, AZ 85015; 255-4053.

Insurance agent (also broker and adjuster) • Department of Insurance, 801 E. Jefferson St., Phoenix, AZ 85007; 255-5400.

Midwife • Office of Maternal and Child Health, Arizona Department of Health Services, 1740 W. Adams St., Room 200, Phoenix, AZ 85007; 542-1870.

Naturopath • Board of Examiners, Naturopathic Physicians, 1645 W. Jefferson St., Room 410, Phoenix, AZ 85007; 542-3095.

Notary public • Secretary of State, 1700 W. Washington St., Phoenix, AZ 85007; 255-4285.

Nurse (all types) • Board of Nursing, 2001 W. Camelback Rd., Suite 350, Phoenix, AZ 85015; 255-5092.

Nursing care administrator • Board of Administrators, Nursing Care Institution, 1645 W. Jefferson St., Room 410, Phoenix, AZ 85007; 542-3095.

Optician (including opthamologist and optometrist) • Board of Optometry, 1645 W. Jefferson St., Room 410, Phoenix, AZ 85007; 542-3095.

Osteopath • Arizona Board of Osteopathic Examiners, 1830 W. Colter St., Suite Four, Phoenix, AZ 85015; 255-1747.

Pawnbroker • License and Registration Division, Department of Revenue, 1600 W. Monroe St., Phoenix, AZ 85007; phone 542-3572.

Pest control (agricultural) • Arizona Department of Agriculture, 1688 W. Adams St., Phoenix, AZ 85007; 542-4373.

Pest control (structural) • Structural Pest Control Board, 2207 S. 48th St., Suite M, Tempe, AZ 85282; 255-3664.

Pharmacist • State Board of Pharmacy, 5060 N. 19th Ave., Room 101, Phoenix, AZ 85015; 255- 5125.

Physician and surgeon (also physicians' assistants) • Board of Medical Examiners, 2001 W. Camelback Rd., Suite 300, Phoenix, AZ 85015; 255-3751.

Physical therapist • Board of Physical Therapy Examiners, 1645 W. Jefferson St., Room 410, Phoenix, AZ 85007; 542-3095.

Podiatrist • Board of Podiatry Examiners, 1645 W. Jefferson St.,

Room 410, Phoenix, AZ 85007; 542-3095.

Private investigator (also polygraph examiner) • Department of Public Safety, 2102 W. Encanto Blvd., Phoenix, AZ 85009; 223-2300.

Psychologist • Arizona State Board of Psychologist Examiners, 1645 W. Jefferson St., Room 410, Phoenix, AZ 85007; 542-3095.

Racetrack workers • Investigations and Licensing Division, Arizona Department of Racing, 800 W. Washington St., Room 500, Phoenix, AZ 85007; 542- 5151.

Radiology workers • Medical Radiological Technology, Board of Examiners, 4814 S. 40th St., Phoenix, AZ 85040; 255-4845.

Real Estate Broker (and real estate agents) • Department of Real Estate, 202 E. Earll Dr., Suite 400, Phoenix, AZ 85012; 255-3232.

Sanitation worker • Arizona Department of Environmental Quality, 2005 N. Central Ave., Phoenix, AZ 85004; 257-2300.

Securities dealer • Securities Division, Arizona Corporation Commission, 1200 W. Washington St., Suite 201, Phoenix, AZ 85007; 542-4242 or 402 W. Congress St., Tucson, AZ 85701; 628-5284.

Security guard • Department of Public Safety, 2102 W. Encanto Blvd., Phoenix, AZ 85009; 223- 2300.

Surveyor and assayer • Arizona State Board of Technical Registration, 1951 W. Camelback, Suite 250, Phoenix, AZ 85015; 255-4053.

Teacher (community college) • Community College Board, 3225 N. Central Ave., Suite 810, Phoenix, AZ 85012; 255-4037.

Teacher (elementary, high school) • Teachers Certification Office, State Board of Education, 1535 W. Jefferson St., Room 126, Phoenix, AZ 85007; 542-4367.

Travel agent • Department of Insurance, 801 W. Jefferson St., Phoenix, AZ 85007; 255-5606.

Veterinarian (and veterinary technician) • Veterinary Medical Examining Board, 1645 W. Jefferson St., Room 410, Phoenix, AZ 85007; 542- 3095.

Water treatment plant operator • See "Sanitation worker" above.

Weighmaster • Arizona State Department of Weights and Measures, 1951 W. North Lane, Phoenix, AZ 85021.

Well driller • Department of Water Resources, 15 S. 15th Ave., Phoenix, AZ 85004; 542-1550.

TRADE & PROFESSIONAL ORGANIZATIONS

For **union locals**, check the Yellow Pages of various communities under "Labor organizations."

ACCOUNTING • Arizona Society of Certified Public Accountants, 426 N. 44th St., Suite 250, Phoenix, AZ 85008; 273-0100.

Society of Practicing Accountants, c/o Elaine Hume, 6103 E. Grant Rd., Tucson, AZ 85715; phone 886-5793.

Institute of Internal Auditors, c/o Richard Simmonds, Western Savings and Loan, 3200 E. Camelback Rd., Suite 253, Phoenix, AZ 85018; phone 468-4100.

Association of Accountants, c/o Debbie Baldwin, 5301 N. Seventh St., Room 101, Phoenix, AZ 85014; 943-3137.

AIR CONDITIONING CONTRACTORS • See "Construction" below.

ADVERTISING, PUBLIC RELATIONS • American Marketing Association, c/o Lisa Stukel, 3136 W. Kimberly Way, Phoenix, AZ 85027.

Public Relations Society of America, c/o Judith E. Brown, P.O. Box 27210, Tucson, AZ 85726; 791-4401.

Public Relations Society of America, 1702 W. Camelback Rd., Room MF-1, Phoenix, AZ 85015-3347; 251-2482.

ARCHITECTS • American Institute of Architects, c/o Eleanor McNamara, 3738 N. 16th St., Suite F, Phoenix, AZ 85016; 279-0032.

AUTOMOBILE SERVICE • Service Station Dealers of Arizona, 714 N. Third St., Phoenix, AZ 85004; 254-0733.

BANKING, SAVINGS INSTITUTIONS • Arizona Bankers Association, 2700 N. Central Ave., Suite 620, Phoenix, AZ 85004; 222-5717.

• Institute of Financial Education, c/o Debbie Dishner, Southwest Savings and Loan, 2901 N. Campbell Ave., Tucson, AZ 85719.

BROADCASTING • Arizona Broadcasters Association, c/o Art Brooks, P.O. Box 654, Scottsdale, AZ 85252; 991-1700.

American Women in Radio and TV, P.O. Box 1109, Phoenix, AZ 85001

BUSINESS • See "Small businesses" below.

CHAMBERS OF COMMERCE • Arizona Chamber of Commerce, 1221 E. Osborn Rd., Phoenix, AZ 85014; 248- 9172

CHEMICAL • American Chemical Society, c/o Donald L. Anderson, Department of Geology, Arizona State University, Tempe, AZ 85281-1404.

American Institute of Chemical Engineering, c/o Neil Berman, Chemical Engineering Department, Arizona State University, Tempe, AZ 85287; 965-4113.

Arizona Water and Pollution Control Association, c/o Wayne Evans, City of Mesa, P.O. Box 1466, Mesa, AZ 85211-1466; 644-3229.

COMPUTERS, DATA PROCESSING • Data Processing Management Association, 3414 E. Thomas Rd., Phoenix, AZ 85018; 956-6423.

IEEE Computer Society, c/o Hemant Gorowara, 8550 McDowell Rd., Apt. H-118, Scottsdale, AZ 85257.

Association for Computer Science, P.O. Box 19027, Sacramento, CA 95819; (916) 421-9149.

CONSTRUCTION, CONTRACTORS • Arizona State District

Council of Carpenters, 2629 W. Orangewood, Phoenix, AZ 85021; 995-9240.

Associated General Contractors, 1825 W. Adams St., Phoenix, AZ 85007; 252-3926 and 1314 N. Third St., Phoenix, AZ 85004; 254-7025.

Home Builders of Central Arizona, 7301 N. 16th St., Suite 102, Phoenix, AZ 85020-5224; 274-6545.

Building Trades Council, 1841 N. 24th St., Phoenix, AZ 85008; 267-1179.

National Electrical Contractors Association, 4315 N. 12th St., Phoenix, AZ 85014; 263-0111.

Plumbing and Air Conditioning Contractors, 1616 E. Maryland St., Phoenix, AZ 85016; 277-2634.

Underground Contractors Association, 3101 N. Central Ave., Phoenix, AZ 85012; 265-1688.

DATA PROCESSING • See "Computers, data processing" above.

EDUCATION • Arizona Education Association, 2102 W. Indian School Rd., Phoenix, AZ 85015; 264- 1774.

Arizona Federation of Teachers, 4035 N. Reddell, Scottsdale, AZ 85251; 949-8261.

Arizona School Administrators, 3001 W. Fairmont Ave., Phoenix, AZ 85007; 277-0025.

ELECTRICAL and ELECTRONICS • Arizona Independent Electrical Contractors Association, 5134 N. Central Ave., Phoenix, AZ 85012; 265-9154.

Arizona State Electronics Association, 340 E. Carol Ann Way, Phoenix, AZ 85022; 942-0040.

Institute of Electrical and Electronics Engineers, c/o J.M. Wiestling, 8427 N. First Dr., Phoenix, AZ 85021; 371-6650.

ENGINEERING (also see "Construction" above) • American Society of Civil Engineers, c/o Thomas P. McGovern, MacVittie and Associates, 3505 N. Campbell Ave., Suite 501, Tucson, AZ 85719.

American Society of Plumbing Engineers, c/o Jonathan Lundstrom, 12675 N. 73rd Ave., Peoria, AZ 85345; 371-1333.

Arizona Society of Professional Engineers, 24 W. Camelback Rd., Suite M, Phoenix, AZ 85013-2530; 264-4871.

Structural Engineers Association, 100 W. Camelback Rd., Suite 100, Phoenix, AZ 85013; 277-0775.

FINANCIAL SERVICES • American Society of Appraisers, c/o Alfredo Molina, 1250 E. Missouri, Phoenix, AZ 85014; 265- 5001.

Association of Management Consultants, c/o Stanley Friedman, Coopers and Lybrand, 2500 Valley Bank Center, Phoenix, AZ 85073; 257-5000.

National Association of Credit Management, P.O. Box 13448, Phoenix, AZ 85002; 252-8866.

FOOD PRODUCTION AND DISTRIBUTION • Dairy Council of Arizona, 2008 S. Hardy Dr., Tempe, AZ 85282; 968-7814.

HEALTH CARE • American Occupational Therapy Association, c/o Patty Lamb, 2521 E. Malibu Dr., Tempe, AZ 85282; 994-9616.

American Society of Hospital Pharmacists, c/o Dennis Messier, 3661 N. Calle Agua Verde, Tucson, AZ 85715; 327-5461.

Arizona Association of Physician Assistants, P.O. Box 11666, Phoenix, AZ 85061.

Arizona Medical Association, 810 W. Bethany Home Rd., Phoenix, AZ 85013; 246-8901.

Arizona Pharmacy Association, 2207 Seventh St., Phoenix, AZ 85006; 258-8121.

Arizona Physical Therapy Association, 3875 N. 44th St., Suite 102, Phoenix, AZ 85018; 952-8637.

Chiropractic Association of Arizona, 605 N. Gilbert Rd., Mesa, AZ 85203; 890-2181.

HOTELS AND MOTELS • Arizona Hotel and Motel Association, 1110 E. Missouri St., Suite 720, Phoenix, AZ 85014; 624-6081.

INSURANCE • Phoenix Association of Life Underwriters, c/o Naomi Lionberger, 1612 W. Weldon Ave., Phoenix, AZ 85015; 274-3054.

JEWELERS • Arizona Jewelers Association, 2047 E. Camelback Rd., Phoenix, AZ 85016; 957-8539.

LEGAL SERVICES • Arizona State Bar Association, 363 N. First Ave., Phoenix, AZ 85003; 252-4804.

Association of Legal Administrators, c/o Ellen Moore, Jaburg and Wilk, Suite 100, 7600 N. 15th St., Phoenix, AZ 85020; 261-3261.

Federal Bar Association, c/o Peter N. Maydanis, 234 N. Central Ave., Suite 440, Phoenix, AZ 85004; 261-3261.

NEWSPAPERS • Arizona Press Women, 3734 E. Campbell Ave., Phoenix, AZ 85018; 955-5467.

Phoenix Newspaper Pressmen, 164 N. 74th St., Room 2104, Mesa, AZ 85207

OPTOMETRY • Arizona Optometric Association, 3625 N. 16th St., Suite 119, Phoenix, AZ 85016; 279-0055.

OSTEOPATHS • Arizona Osteopathic Association, 5057 E. Thomas Rd., Phoenix, AZ 85018; 840-0460.

PHARMACY • See "Health care" above.

PLUMBING • See "Construction" above.

PUBLIC EMPLOYEES • Arizona Public Employees, AFCME, 420 N. 15th Ave., Phoenix, AZ 85007; 252-6501.

PUBLIC RELATIONS • See "Advertising, public relations" above.

REAL ESTATE • Arizona Association of Realtors, 4414 N. 19th Ave., Phoenix, AZ 85041; 248-7787.

Building Owners and Managers Association, 3875 N. 44th St.,

Phoenix, AZ 85018; 952-8213.

International Association of Corporate Real Estate Executives, c/o Mike Little, Citibank, 3300 N. Central Ave., Suite 1510, Phoenix, AZ 85012; 263-6302.

Tucson Association of Realtors, 1622 N. Swan Road, Tucson, AZ 85712; 327-4218.

RESTAURANTS • Arizona Restaurant Association, 2701 N. 16th St., Phoenix, AZ 85006; 234-0701.

SMALL BUSINESSES • Arizona Small Business Association, 301 W. Osborn Rd., Room 104, Phoenix, AZ 85013; 265-4563 or 248-8856.

SOCIAL WORKERS • National Association of Social Workers, 610 W. Broadway, Tempe, AZ 85282; 968-4595.

STRUCTURAL ENGINEERS • See "Construction" and "Engineers" above.

TRAVEL • American Society of Travel Agents, Seven Continents Travel, 4351 W. Indian School Rd., Phoenix, AZ 85031; 272-5634.

TRUCKING • Arizona Motor Transport Association, 2111 W. Mc-Dowell Rd., Phoenix, AZ 85009; 252-7559.

UTILITIES • American Water Works Association, c/o Wayne Evans, City of Mesa, P.O. Box 1466, Mesa, AZ 85211; 644-3229.

VETERINARIANS • Arizona Veterinary Medical Association, 810 W. Bethany Home Rd., Suite 109, Phoenix, AZ 85013; 242-7936.

WOMEN'S PROFESSIONAL GROUPS • American Women in Radio and TV, P.O. Box 1109, Phoenix, AZ 85001

Women in Communication, P.O. Box 33131, Phoenix, AZ 85067; 256-3998.

Women in Construction, 2600 W. Central Ave., Phoenix, AZ 85004; 263-7405.

Women in Design, P.O. Box 61631, Phoenix, AZ 85082

HOW TO LAND THAT JOB

The day after I graduated from a little high school in southwestern Idaho, I hit the road, seeking fortune if not fame.

With only a high school diploma and no specific skill, I found neither. But I did find out how to get a job. After wandering around the western states for several months, I took shelter at the home of a favorite uncle in southern Oregon. I was broke and needed work.

Uncle Clark took me to a pear packing shed and asked the foreman if he could use a hard-working, skinny seventeen-year-old. Unfortunately, all the jobs were taken. My uncle then pointed to a stack of empty pallets.

"I'm gonna sit this kid over there," he told the foreman. "Sooner or later, one of your crew will get mad and quit, or he'll get lazy and you'll fire him. And when that happens, here's your replacement."

I was put to work shortly after lunch.

My point is simple: to find a job, go where the jobs are. Direct contact with a prospective employer is the best way to get work, whether you're looking for something glamorous, highly skilled or mundane.

I realize that my pear packing plant experience is a bit simplistic. You'll want to be more professional than that—developing a list of prospective companies, finding out who to contact, and then making appointments to see them.

Even with today's emphasis on college degrees and vocational skills, employers still admire job-hunters with drive and spunk. It suggests that they'll be enterprising and hard-working once they get the job. If two people are equally qualified for a position, the one who makes a personal appearance often gains the edge.

Besides, there's the advantage of timing. If you wait for a job opening to show up in the want-ads, there'll be a dozen people after it by the time you send in your resume. But if you canvas the industry with resumes, then follow up with personal visits, you just might wind up in the right place at the right time.

That's how it worked after I'd gone from pear packing to a stint in the Marine Corps to newspaper reporting. When I decided I was ready to advance to a better job, I'd write to every paper in the area where I was interested in working. I'd include a resume and a cover letter saying that I'd be in the area in a few days. Then I'd follow up with a phone call, asking if I could make an appointment—at a time convenient for the editor, of course.

A couple of times, I got a job almost before an editor knew he had an opening.

According to The Phoenix Job Market, job-seekers who use direct contact are twice as successful as those who rely on the want-ads or an employment agency.

That isn't to suggest that you should ignore the other two sources. Perhaps the best approach is to employ all three. Incidentally, the Sunday edition of a newspaper generally has the most help wanted ads. Also, some trade and professional organizations offer employment services for their members.

Finding prospective employers

But how do you determine which employers to contact? Several resources are available to you. Trade and professional groups and unions may have lists of affiliated companies. The Phoenix Job Market, the book we mentioned above, is particularly useful. To get a copy, check the nearest bookstore or contact Bob Adams, Inc., 260 Center St., Holbrook, MA 02343; phone (800) USA-JOBS or (617) 767-8100. Cover price is $12.95.

Also useful is the Phoenix Business Journal's Book of Lists, which shows many of the city's largest firms. To get one, send a check for

$23.95 to The Business Journal, 3737 N. Seventh St., Suite 200, Phoenix, AZ 85014.

As we also mentioned above, try the good old Yellow Pages. Call USWEST at (800) 422-8793 to order directories for various Arizona communities. You'll find addresses but not ZIP codes, so pick up a **U.S. Postal Service ZIP Code Directory** at your local post office for $12.

Once you've compiled a list, narrow it down to the firms that interest you, and those most likely to be hiring. Next, find out who to contact. A simple phone call to the company personnel department should work. Never send a job query without addressing it to a specific person. If you do, it'll likely end up in the wastebasket with the rest of the junk mail.

Now, armed with a list of companies and a contact in each, prepare your cover letter and resume. Both should be brief, yet complete, convincing and to the point. Don't give a busy personnel manager or foreman too much to read. Also, avoid corporate doublespeak, redundancy and verbosity. Write about yourself confidently, without sounding pompous. Don't brag; let the facts of your background make your case. And avoid cliches like the plague.

Resumes can be cranked out by a copy shop but the cover letter should be personalized. That doesn't mean it must be painfully pecked out by hand. If you have access to computer programs such as Wordstar's Mailmerge, you can create a letter that's both personalized and mass-produced. Many firms now specialize in preparing and producing resumes and cover letters.

Above all else, neatness counts. From the look of your cover letter to the style of your tie and the shine on your shoes, you will be judged by appearance. When you go in for an interview, you go in as a stranger. Your prospective employer can evaluate you only go by the facts you present and the way you present yourself.

A well-organized appearance suggests a competent, well-organized individual. In reality, that isn't always true. In the writing business, in fact, it tends to be the exception. Some of the best, most creative and aggressive reporters I've ever known usually came to work looking like they'd just fallen out of bed. (Some probably had.) However, get the job and prove your worth before revealing your scruffy side.

Experts disagree on the style and content of cover letters and resumes. And in reality, there is no best style, since the personalities of the recipients differ. Some personnel managers get off on symphonic prose that oozes buzz words and corporate jargon. Others are no-nonsense types who want you to state your case directly and concisely.

I've found that a simple, to-the-point style works best. Save the details and adjectives for the job interview. As we said above, cover letters should at least look typewritten, even if you've cheated with Mailmerge, while resumes can be a copy shop product.

Here's a tip: In your letter, write as if you know the territory. It suggests that you've done your homework; that you've studied up on your home-to-be. Use words and phrases familiar to locals, such as "Valley of the Sun" instead of "Phoenix and vicinity." But don't overdo it; only guidebook authors are supposed to say "the glorious Grand Canyon State."

Sample cover letter

Robin R. Righteous
1494 Confidence Lane
North Chicago, IL 60064
Phone (708) 123-4567

January 15, 1991

Scrooge McTaxbite, Personnel Manager
Moneygrub and Nickelsqueeze, Inc.
1010 Taxshelter Way
Phoenix, AZ 85007

Dear Mr. McTaxbite:

After several years as an accountant with a major Chicago firm, I have decided to move my family to the Valley of the Sun. My research tells me that Moneygrub and Nickelsqueeze is one of Arizona's more aggressive and successful accounting houses. And that's the kind of firm I'm seeking.

You will note in my enclosed resume that I have considerable experience in tax accounting, slush fund concealment and computer-generated windfall spreadsheets. These are skills that can be useful in your operation.

I thrive in a competitive work environment and I need the kind of challenge offered by an aggressive company in a growing state such as Arizona.

I'm coming to your area in early March. Can we set up an appointment to discuss the contributions I can offer Moneygrub and Nickelsqueeze? You can contact me at the above phone number and address.

Thank you for your attention,

Robin R. Righteous

Sample resume

Resumes can have a variety of approaches. If the job you seek is skill-intensive, the resume should emphasize your qualifications and work experience. If you're seeking management opportunities, a chronological resume would be best, showing how you've worked up through the ranks. Obviously, if you're just starting out, the resume should stress your educational accomplishments and career goals.

I also like to toss in a little "Mister Good Citizen" community service stuff.

Although some resume-writers disagree, I prefer to give a reason for leaving each job—a positive reason, obviously. Here's how I'd do my resume—if I didn't already own the company:

Don W. Martin
987 Europa Court
Walnut Creek, CA 95310
(415) 456-7890

Professional experience

March 1979 to present: Associate editor of Motorland, the travel magazine of the California State Automobile Association. Responsible for much of the editorial operation, working with staff writers and editorial assistants in planning, writing and editing copy. Also research and write travel stories, along with automotive, safety and other technical articles. Coordinate editorial activities with production department, helping direct copy flow, proofing and layout. Had complete charge of the magazine during a two-month illness of the editor.

March 1976 to February 1979: Managing editor of the Petaluma (California) Argus-Courier, a small daily newspaper north of San Francisco. Directed a news, sports, society and photo staff of eight. Also responsible for planning and layout of the newspaper, and wrote some copy. Left to enter the field of travel magazine editing and writing.

June 1963 to February 1976: Sunday magazine editor of the Oxnard Press-Courier, a mid-sized daily newspaper in southern California. Began as copy editor on the city desk, then spent four years as editor of the Sunday feature magazine and daily entertainment page. Left to accept the challenge of newspaper management.

May 1960 to May 1963: Various editorial posts for the Oceanside Blade-Tribune, a small daily newspaper in southern California. Began as a police beat reporter and was promoted to assistant sports editor, then copy editor and editorial page editor. Left to accept a post on a larger newspaper.

Other employment, 1950 to 1960: Began career as a printer's devil for the weekly Wilder (Idaho) Herald at age 16, while still in high school; also was editor of the high school newspaper. Served with the Marine Corps public information service as editor of several base newspapers and as a correspondent in Korea, Japan and Taiwan.

Other job experience: Have sold dozens of free-lance articles and photos to newspapers and magazines. Co-authored with my wife *The Best of San Francisco*, a guidebook published by Chronicle Books in 1986 and revised in 1990.

Professional skills

Familiar with IBM Wordstar and Ventura desktop publishing program; type 90 words per minute. Proficient with 35mm camera.

Education

Wilder (Idaho) High School, graduated in 1951
Naval Journalists' School, Great Lakes, Ill., graduated in 1956.
Have taken evening college courses in English, journalism, political science and history.

Awards and community service

Won two Department of Defense awards and one Marine Corps Journalism award for excellence in editing military newspapers. Also, four California Press Photographers Association awards for feature photo layouts. Earned the Ventura County (California) Diane Seeley award for promoting the arts. Served as founding president of the Ventura County Theater Council, was a board member of the Ventura County Forum of the Arts and a member of the Petaluma (California) Kiwanis Club and Daly City (California) Junior Chamber of Commerce.

Personal information

In excellent health; married to Betty Woo Martin, PharmD, real estate broker and co-author of guidebooks.
Born April 22, 1934, in Grants Pass, Oregon. Listed in Marquis' Who's Who in the West and Contemporary Authors.

References, both professional and personal, are available on request.

Hmmm... Sounds pretty good. Think I'll hire the guy.

Chapter Six

THE RETIREES

A PLACE UNDER ARIZONA'S SUN

Contrary to what you've seen on the evening news, most retired folks aren't spending their golden years in a home for the aged, or sitting in a creaking rocking chair on the front porch.

The majority of them are upbeat, active people who've saved their money and perhaps paid off their homes. They look forward to some of the best years of their lives.

Our life expectancy is approaching 70 for men and 75 for women. More than 30 million Americans are now retired. Further, many people are retiring at a younger age—adding more numbers to these growing ranks. Equally important, with today's emphasis on physical fitness, most older people are healthier than their parents. We are thus creating a new socio-economic order—a great legion of people who retire earlier and live longer. Some spend as many years in retirement as they did raising their families.

A recent survey indicated that more than 70 percent of retirees feel they are secure economically. This security leads to mobility, and that leads us into this chapter of *Coming to Arizona.*

Today's seniors are less inclined to keep the old family roost after their kids have flown the coop. And the kids tend to scatter more, leaving their home towns in search of greener pastures and greener paychecks.

Since the brood has left, why put up with another frigid February or urban traffic jam? Why deal with all that gardening and house-cleaning? Why worry about high crime rates and higher taxes? With the emphasis on physical fitness, today's retirees want to get out and do things. They don't want to trudge through snow to reach the tennis courts or be chased off the golf course by a chilling rain.

So why not go someplace that's warm, safe, secure and affordable?

Like Arizona, for instance.

Although specific numbers are hard to find, Arizona probably attracts more migrating seniors than any other state, except for Florida and California. It's ahead of Texas and New Mexico, the other two leading sunbelt states.

Where are they drawn from? Although figures aren't broken down by age, most newcomers are from the Midwest. Illinois loses more citizens to Arizona than any other state, perhaps ten thousand a year. Ohio is a distant second, with about half as many migrants going south. An equal number come from Michigan.

Surprisingly, California sends nearly as many emigrants to Arizona as Michigan does, although they aren't necessarily retirees. Job opportunities and lower housing prices lure many Californians to the state next door. Other leading sources for migrants—in order of numbers—are Colorado, New York, Wisconsin, Minnesota, Iowa and Indiana.

Like most states, Arizona allows apartment, condo and subdivision owners to designate a minimum age for residents. This, of course, defines the "retirement complex." They range from full-care apartments and condos to planned developments with golf courses, swimming pools, tennis courts and other active-life amenities.

Mobile home parks are popular with year-around retirees, as well as wintertime Snowbirds. In fact, one in ten Arizona residents lives in mobile housing—one of the highest ratios in the Nation. Adults-only parks are particularly numerous along the Colorado River corridor.

If you're considering the purchase of a home or condo in a retirement community, remember that the age requirement limits your market and thus may inhibit its resale value. Except in a few highly-desirable communities, retirement homes tend to bring less on the resale market than comparable family houses. Also, bear in mind that mobile homes generally depreciate while fixed homes increase in value.

The Phoenix Yellow Pages contains seven pages of listings for "Retirement & Life Care Communities & Homes." Tucson's phone book offers a three and a half page selection. Both have extensive adult mobile home park listings as well.

What kind of retirement?

Once you've made the decision to come to Arizona, you need to determine which retirement facilities are best suited to you. Basically, they fit into five categories. In the first two, one usually has the option of purchasing, leasing or renting, while the final three are usually on a month-to-month basis, with the cost of care and perhaps meals included in the price. Some advanced-care units can be purchased, however.

Independent living ● As the name suggests, this is retirement in a conventional family community. Some seniors, particularly more active ones, prefer this. They like the mix of young and old, which is more akin to the city they left behind. Arizona offers a host of planned all-age communities with the same amenities as retirement villages— golf, tennis, swimming and planned activities.

Planned adult community • Like any planned complex, the adult village offers a variety of activities, plus the advantage of facilities geared to older people. Ease of mobility is considered in room layouts; even wall plugs are mounted higher in some homes. And you won't have to worry about a teen-age rap party next door. Dwellings range from detached homes and townhouses to condos and apartments.

Independent retirement complex • These facilities, usually offered on a lease plan, are for fully ambulatory people who don't want the bother of housekeeping. They usually offer maid service, planned activities and special outings. Meals may be included, or they can be an option offered at a central dining area. One might compare it with living in a hotel, or perhaps a motel with a kitchenette. They're usually set up as townhouses, condos or apartments.

Residential facility for the elderly • These offer a higher level of care than the independent complex. Full housekeeping and meal service generally are provided, and aides are on hand to help with mobility problems and perhaps to monitor medications. However, they don't generally have on-site nursing care. Most are apartments or condos. Group outings are offered for those who are unable to drive or who prefer not to.

Life care facility • These complexes are best for those with impaired mobility or a debilitating illness. Also, some still-ambulatory seniors prefer to turn all their day-to-day decisions and responsibilities over to someone else. Facilities range from apartments to furnished rooms. On-site lifetime medical care is part of the program. All housekeeping and meals are furnished, and full-time nursing care is available for those in need. The most comprehensive level of life care facilities are nursing homes and convalescent hospitals.

Senior service agencies

Several agencies in Arizona offer advice, assistance and information for seniors. If you're interested in extended health care, the **Office of Long Term Health Care** of the Arizona Department of Health Services will send you A Guide to Selecting Long Term Health Care Services for the Elderly and Disabled It also offers a directory of all state-licensed nursing care facilities. Contact either of these offices:

Phoenix area • 701 E. Jefferson St., Phoenix, AZ 8534; phone 263-8856.

Tucson area • 402 W. Congress St., Tucson, AZ 85701; phone 323-1303.

For a directory of nursing homes and related services, contact **Ari-**

zona Nursing Home Association, 1817 N. Third St., Suite 200, Phoenix, AZ 85004; 258-8996.

Another useful organization is the **Governor's Advisory Council on Aging,** 1717 W. Jefferson St., Phoenix, AZ 85007, phone 262-7486.

Area offices of Arizona's **Agency on Aging** provide a variety of services for people 60 and over. They function as activity and information centers for seniors and even offer delivery services for those who can't get about. Offices are in these communities:

Phoenix area • 1366 E. Thomas Rd., Suite 108 Phoenix, AZ 85014; phone 264-2255.

Northwestern Arizona • P.O. Box 57, Flagstaff, AZ 86002; phone 774-1895.

Southwestern Arizona • 100 Maple Ave., Yuma, AZ 85364; 782-1886.

Central Arizona • P.O. Box 1129 (512 E. Butte St.), Florence, AZ 85232; phone 868-4166.

Tucson area • 2955 E. Broadway, Tucson, AZ 85716; phone 795-5800.

Southeastern Arizona • 118 Arizona St., Bisbee, AZ 85603; phone 432-5301.

THE RETIREMENT TOWNS

Planned retirement communities were invented in Arizona. No, Sun City wasn't the first. A place appropriately called Youngtown is the nation's, and probably the world's, original senior village. Located just west of Phoenix, it was created in 1954 by the Youngtown Land and Development Company. It still thrives as a busy little city of about 2,600.

Del E. Webb started Sun City, next door to Youngtown, in 1960. It has become America's largest retirement community, with a population nearing 45,000. A satellite, Sun City West, was started in 1978, and it now has 19,000 residents. A third Del Webb retirement complex, Sun City Vistoso, is just north of Tucson.

We offer below a list of some of Arizona's major planned retirement villages. A letter or phone call to each will earn you a quick packet of information. (Incidentally, some of these commercial retirement villages have evolved into incorporated communities, so they may be listed elsewhere in this book.)

Fountain of the Sun • 8001 E. Broadway, Mesa, AZ 85208; 984-0165.

Leisure World • 908 S. Power Rd., Mesa, AZ 85026; 832-3232.

SaddleBrooke Country Club • 64518 E. SaddleBrooke Blvd., Tucson, AZ 85737; (800) 733-4050 or (602) 791-7464 locally.

SunBird Golf Resort • 6250 SunBird Blvd., Chandler, AZ 85249; (800) 523-6664 or locally (602) 732-1000.

Sun City Vistoso • 13990 N. Desert Butte Dr., Sun City Vistoso (Tucson), AZ 85704; (800) 442-8483.

Sun City West • 13323 Meeker Blvd., Sun City West, AZ 85375; (800) 341-6121 outside Arizona; (800) 453-7167 in Arizona; (800) 341-6121 outside and (602) 546-5126 locally.

Sun Lakes Country Clubs • 25025 S. EJ Robson Blvd., Sun Lakes, AZ 85248; (800) 321-8643 or locally (602) 895-9600.

Westbrook Village • 9721 W. Rockwood Dr., Peoria, AZ 85345; 933-0181.

Retirement areas

Maricopa (Phoenix) and Pima (Tucson) counties are home to most of Arizona's retirees. Not all these folks live in planned villages like Sun City, of course. Smaller senior complexes are scattered throughout the Valley of the Sun and greater Tucson area. Some planned communities have both senior and family sections, with separate-but-equal facilities for each age group.

About one in four Maricopa and Pima county residents are over fifty. However, several other counties have more seniors per capita. Yavapai County, whose main city is Prescott, has the highest ratio of folks over fifty—41 percent. Mohave County along the Colorado River is second with 33 percent.

The Colorado River corridor ranks third behind Phoenix and Tucson in the total number of retirees. Most are in the communities of Yuma, Parker, Lake Havasu City and Bullhead City. The river towns offer two big advantages—access to water sports and cheaper home prices than Phoenix-Tucson. But they have disadvantages as well. For one thing, they're hotter than the hinges of Hades in summer. Phoenix and Tucson, at much higher elevations, are cooler. Also, the river communities don't offer a lot of cultural lures.

And no, we don't regard Lake Havasu City's London Bridge as a cultural lure.

If you're considering an Arizona retirement, don't restrict yourself to the sunbelt. Communities such as Flagstaff, Sedona and Prescott to the north and Sierra Vista in the southeast have retirement facilities as well. Small mountain towns north and east of Phoenix offer a mix of retirement and recreational opportunities.

Most of these places are more than 4,000 feet high, so they get occasional snow dustings, but the weather is never harsh. Compared with Toronto, Buffalo or Chicago, winters are downright mild. Annual snowfall in Prescott, for instance, is 24 inches. Sierra Vista's is a mere ten inches and the average January low temperature is 35 to 40.

Some retirees are drawn to these higher-elevation towns because they miss the four seasons back home. In Prescott, Flagstaff and Se-

WHERE THE SENIORS LIVE (by percentage)

Source: Population Statistics Unit, Arizona Department of Economic Security

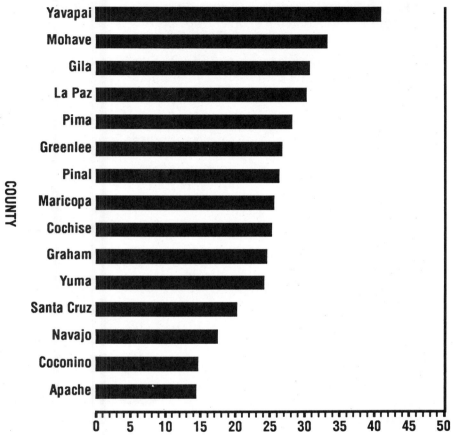

COUNTY

Yavapai
Mohave
Gila
La Paz
Pima
Greenlee
Pinal
Maricopa
Cochise
Graham
Yuma
Santa Cruz
Navajo
Coconino
Apache

0   5   10   15   20   25   30   35   40   45   50

PERCENTAGE OF POPULATION OVER 50

Yavapai County, which contains Prescott and south Sedona, has Arizona's highest ratio of residents over fifty--more than 40 percent. They aren't all retired, of course, but the county is very popular with retirees. Mohave County on the Colorado River Corridor is second in senior ratio.

dona, you even get piney woods and fall color.

If we were considering coming to Arizona as retirees, we'd pick one of the places listed below. We don't suggest any of the heavily urbanized cities of the Valley of the Sun, since there's no reason for a retiree to get tangled up in the commute rush.

However, if you don't mind a little congestion and you want to be close to downtown Phoenix, you might consider such places as Mesa,

Chandler, Tempe (with Arizona State University on your doorstep), Glendale or Peoria.

You'll find more detailed descriptions of the state's various communities in Part Two. We discuss their advantages and disadvantages, average winter and summer temperatures, growth rates and other essentials. Meanwhile, we offer a list of possible retirement towns.

CENTRAL ARIZONA

If you want to be near the business, economic and social hub of Arizona, set your sights on the Valley of the Sun. Although it's beginning resemble Los Angeles with its sprawl, you can find your cactus patch on the outer fringes and escape the congestion. Phoenix is served by a growing network of freeways and the heart of the city is easily reached during off-commute hours.

Even during the morning rush, delays are nothing compared with those you'll encounter in most Eastern cities or the Los Angeles and San Francisco Bay areas. When we were exploring the Phoenix-Scottsdale area for *The Best of Arizona*, we stayed at an RV park near Goodyear, about 20 miles out. By 9 a.m., we could breeze into the heart of town in half an hour.

Scottsdale and Paradise Valley were once somewhat isolated by suburban sprawl, but a new cross-town freeway is quickly penetrating that northeastern edge of the Valley of the Sun.

If you'd like to get a bit further out and still be within dinner range, we'd recommend places such as Apache Junction on the eastern edge of the valley or Arizona City and Florence to the south. The latter two are in the busy north-south Interstate 10 corridor, providing easy access to both Phoenix and Tucson.

Apache Junction • This city of 17,000 is set against the rough backdrop of the Superstition Mountains, southeast of Phoenix. It offers several mobile home parks and a few planned developments. It's within a short drive of Phoenix, yet well beyond the urban congestion. We particularly like its topography. The terrain is high desert, and the forested hills and reservoirs of the Salt River Canyon are a short drive away. **For information:** *Apache Junction Chamber of Commerce, P.O. Box 1747, Apache Junction, AZ 85217; phone 982-3141.*

Arizona City • The agricultural setting isn't particularly interesting, but the weather's nice and so is the location, midway between Phoenix and Tucson. This planned community of 2,000 was established in 1960, and it offers amenities such as a fake lake, golf course and several parks. **For information:** *Arizona City Chamber of Commerce, P.O. Box 5, Arizona City, AZ 85223; 466-5141.*

Carefree and Cave Creek • Take your pick of these two small towns, located in the rugged desert northeast of Scottsdale. Carefree is a somewhat upscale planned community while Cave Creek is on the rustic side, preserving remnants of an old mining town. Population of Carefree is about 2,000 while Cave Creek is twice that. They both offer good locations: close to Phoenix yet on the uncluttered outer edge of the Valley of the Sun. **For information:** *Carefree/Cave Creek Chamber of Commerce, P.O. Box 734, Carefree, AZ 85377; 488-3381.*

Florence • You don't hear much about it, but Florence is a fine place for retirement, with an historic downtown section and some modern subdivisions around the edges. In Pinal County midway between Phoenix and Tucson, it has a rather mild climate. It's in an agricultural valley, so you won't get any desert scenery. **For information:** *Florence Chamber of Commerce, P.O. Box 929 (291 Bailey St.), Florence, AZ 85232; 868-5837.*

Fountain Hills • This planned community of 11,000 is on the northeastern rim of the Valley of the Sun. Established in 1970 by the creators of Lake Havasu City, it's a modern town set in attractive high desert terrain. It offers a mix of planned subdivisions and shopping centers. There's no London Bridge, however. **For information:** *Fountain Hills Chamber of Commerce, P.O. Box 17598 (12635 N. Saguaro Blvd.), Fountain Hills, AZ 85628; 837-1654.*

Paradise Valley • If you can afford it, Paradise Valley is a great place to retire. Just beyond the reach of Phoenix and Scottsdale's congestion, it's a community of elegant homes set in a ruggedly handsome desert, surrounded by equally rugged mountains. Most lodgings are individual homes; there are few planned retirement complexes. Expect the summers to be hot. **For information:** *Greater Paradise Valley Chamber of Commerce, 16042 N. 32nd St., Suite C-2, Phoenix, AZ 85032; 482-3344.*

Scottsdale • Upscale and expensive, Scottsdale sits against dramatic Camelback peak in high desert on the edge of Phoenix. Now rather urbanized, it has lost much of its original Old West charm. However, it offers some of Arizona's finest planned developments, upscale shopping centers and luxury resorts. **For information:** *Scottsdale Chamber of Commerce, P.O. Box 130 (7333 Scottsdale Mall), Scottsdale, AZ 85252; 945-8481.*

Sun City and Sun City West • Large Sun City offers a complete assortment of leisure amenities. Lodgings range from detached homes to townhouses and condos. Sun City West is newer, smaller and a bit more modern. With a combined population of 63,000, the twin communities provide extensive shopping and business facilities. They're on the outer edge of the Valley of the Sun, convenient to Phoenix but beyond the sprawl. **For information:** *Del E. Webb Development Company, 13323 W. Meeker Blvd., Sun City, AZ 85375; 975-2270 or Northwest Valley Chamber of Commerce, 12211 W. Bell Rd., Suite 204, Surprise, AZ 85374; 583-0692.*

Wickenburg • Wickenburg just loves to play cowboy. Western shops line its streets, half a dozen dude ranches are nearby and real cowboys herd real dogies in the surrounding desert. It's fifty miles northwest of Phoenix, well beyond that suburban scatter. Indeed, it feels like another place in another time, "out Wickenburg way." There aren't a lot of retirement facilities here, but if you love old Roy Rogers movies, this is your place. **For information:** *Wickenburg Chamber of Commerce, P.O. Drawer CC (215 Frontier St.), Wickenburg, AZ 85358; 684-5479.*

Youngtown • This where it all began, in America's very first retirement town. It has the requisite senior leisure facilities—a clubhouse, fake lake, tennis and six golf courses. Another eighteen are within five miles. No longer in a remote desert, Youngtown is now rimmed by Sun City, Peoria and El Mirage. **For information:** *Town of Youngtown, 12030 Clubhouse Square, Youngtown, AZ 85363; 933-8286.*

NORTH CENTRAL ARIZONA

If you want pine trees and four seasons in your retirement picture, pick one of these north central Arizona towns. Some, like Flagstaff and Prescott, are more than a mile high. They offer occasional winter snows but severe storms are rare. The Sedona-Oak Creek Canyon-Verde Valley area are noted for their fall color, so you transplanted New Englanders will feel right at home.

Cottonwood • Although it's a rather ordinary-looking town without fancy subdivisions, Cottonwood offers a fine location, just below beautiful Oak Creek Canyon and Sedona. A relatively mild climate, proximity to a variety of tourist attractions and low housing cost have lured a lot of retirees. One of four residents is over 65. **For information:** *Verde Valley Chamber of Commerce, 1010 S. Main St., Cottonwood, AZ 86326; 634-7593.*

Flagstaff • One of our favorite Arizona communities, it offers a balance of culture, educational facilities and location. Home to Northern Arizona University, Flagstaff sits at the base of the towering San Francisco Peaks, about 70 miles southeast of the Grand Canyon. With a population of 44,000, it offers all the services and amenities a retiree would need. It can get cold in winter, however. Not Chicago cold, but the average low in January is 15 degrees and it gets about 84 inches of snow. **For information:** *Flagstaff Chamber of Commerce, 101 W. Santa Fe, Flagstaff, AZ 86004; 774-4505.*

Lake Montezuma • Lake what? Lake Montezuma, Rimrock and McGuireville are little known outside Arizona. They're three planned villages in the higher reaches of the Verde Valley, with terrain ranging from prairie to forest. These hamlets are popular with retirees who like the surrounding national forest and don't mind the temperature getting a bit chilly in winter. Snowfall is rare. **For information:** *Verde Valley Chamber of Commerce, 1010 S. Main St., Cottonwood, AZ*

86326; 634-7593.

Payson • This is another woodsy place, a town of 9,000, sitting a mile high, 78 miles northeast of Phoenix. It offers a mix of "Swiss alpine, old west and contemporary ambiance," insists the chamber of commerce. Sixty percent of its populous is retired, and the community sponsors several active senior programs. You'll get the four seasons, although winters are mild, with maybe two feet of snow. **For information:** *Payson Chamber of Commerce, P.O. Box 1380, Payson, AZ 85547; 474-4515.*

Pine and Strawberry • Essentially vacation and retirement towns, these villages are in the east-central Arizona woods north of Payson. Many Valley of the Sun residents spend weekends here to escape desert heat; some maintain second homes among the pines. The area is more than a mile up, so winters are chilly but not harsh. Figure on a couple of feet of snow. **For information:** *Pine-Strawberry Chamber of Commerce, P.O. Box 333, Pine, AZ 85544; 476-3547.*

Prescott • Like Flagstaff, Prescott offers a mix of culture, education and scenery, located in the west central Arizona woods. It has extensive senior programs and good medical facilities; one in four residents is retired. This is four-seasons country, getting about two feet of snow. The ambiance and attitude are Old West, although the town has a sturdy red-brick New England look. Incidentally, it's pronounced "PRESS-kit," partner. **For information:** *Prescott Chamber of Commerce, P.O. Box 1147 (117 W. Goodwin St.), Prescott, AZ 86302; 445-2000.*

Sedona • If we could afford it, we'd be tempted to retire to Sedona and watch those glorious sunsets against the redrock peaks of Oak Creek Canyon. One of the most dramatically-located towns in America, it's a haven for tourists, artists and an occasional music festival. Shops, galleries and boutiques abound. Several planned communities extend south, some tucked into their own awesome redrock niches. At 4,300 feet, Sedona offers mild year-around climate and glorious fall color. **For information:** *Sedona/Oak Creek Canyon Chamber of Commerce, P.O. Box 478, Sedona, AZ 86336; 282-7722.*

Verde Village • This planned complex, next door to Cottonwood in west central Arizona, has about 5,000 residents and two-thirds of them are retired. It's in an agricultural valley, between the spectacular setting of Oak Creek Canyon and the pine forests of the Prescott area. **For information:** *Verde Valley Chamber of Commerce, 1010 S. Main St., Cottonwood, AZ 86326; 634-7593.*

COLORADO RIVER CORRIDOR

Prepare for extreme summer heat if you choose the Colorado River Corridor as your retirement home. This area is noted mostly as a Snowbird haven, but many people crank up their air conditioners and stay the year-around. The Colorado River has so many dams that it's now a virtual chain of lakes, so cooling water sports are always available.

Bullhead City ● Sprawled over 43 square miles along the Colorado River corridor, Bullhead is an unlovely city, but it offers great winter climate. Further, if you like those one-armed bandits, the fast-growing Nevada gaming center of Laughlin is just across the pond. Summers get very hot here, sometimes topping the national charts. Bullhead has many mobile home parks and a few planned residential communities. **For information:** *Bullhead Area Chamber of Commerce, P.O. Box 1048, Bullhead City, AZ 86430; 763-9400.*

Lake Havasu City ● This city of 20,000 was started by developer Robert P. McCulloch, who hauled the London Bridge over here (in pieces, of course) as a focal point. Reassembling the British bridge in the desert got him the headlines he needed; the town has been growing ever since. It offers a good mix of retirement villages, all-age subdivisions and mobile home parks. The lake offers assorted water sports and a gimmick English village has been built around the bridge. **For information:** *Lake Havasu Area Chamber of Commerce, 1930 Mesquite Ave., Suite Three, Lake Havasu City, AZ 86403; 453-3444.*

Yuma ● If you like living far from the rest of civilization, consider Yuma. With a population topping 50,000, it offers all the basic essentials, and an abundance of water recreation on the adjacent Colorado River. Not a fancy place, it's an honest workingperson's town. It's rich in history, as the site of Yuma Crossing, on the first trail to California. That trail is now Interstate 8, so access to this remote mini-metropolis is easy. Like the other Colorado River corridor towns, Yuma's biggest disadvantage for year-around retirement is summer heat. **For information:** *Yuma County Chamber of Commerce, P.O. Box 6468, Yuma, AZ 85366; 344-3800.*

SOUTHERN ARIZONA

The Tucson-to-Nogales corridor is rapidly gaining favor with year-around retirees. Averaging more than a thousand feet higher than Phoenix, towns here aren't quite as hot in summer as their big sister to the north. Another choice is southeastern Arizona, the state's undiscovered corner. It's a mix of high desert, prairie country and mountains. Winters are relatively mild. Bisbee, Sierra Vista, Pearce and Sunsites are rather temperate all year.

Bisbee ● This old copper mining town of 8,000 people isn't well-known as a retirement haven. But we like its funky look and sense of history, and the climate is rather mild. Summer highs are in the upper eighties and winter lows in the mid-thirties. There's virtually no snowfall. Bisbee is in southeastern Arizona, about six miles from the Mexican border. **For information:** *Bisbee Chamber of Commerce, P.O.*

The transplanted London Bridge is a focal point of the planned desert community of Lake Havasu City in the Colorado River Corridor.

Drawer BA (Seven Naco Rd.), Bisbee, AZ 85603; 432-2141.

Catalina • Twelve miles north of Tucson, Catalina is home to a pair of major retirement communities, Sun City Vistoso and Saddle-Brooke. Established in the 1950s, it's situated in foothills of the Catalina Mountains. Although it's in the desert, the elevation is 3,000 feet, so summers are relatively mild—five to ten degrees cooler than Tucson. **For information:** *Greater Catalina/Golder Ranch Village Council, P.O. Box 8674 CRB, Tucson, AZ 85738.*

Green Valley • Like Sun City, Green Valley was planned as a retirement community, so it has complete senior facilities: golf, tennis, swimming and such. We like its location, midway between Tucson and the Mexican border. The terrain is rolling desert, not really attractive but the climate's great in winter. Temperatures nudge 100 in the summer, but that's why air conditioning was invented. **For information:** *Green Valley Chamber of Commerce, P.O. Box 566 (108 W. Continental Rd., Suite 178), Green Valley, AZ 85622; 625-7575.*

Sierra Vista • Looking more like a suburb than a city, Sierra Vista is an orderly sprawl of subdivisions and shopping centers in southeastern Arizona. The elevation is 4,623 feet, creating a mild year-around climate. While not really handsome, this town of 35,000 is clean, well-planned and convenient, with several modern housing developments. Historic Fort Huachuca, a still-active Army post, is just to the south. **For information:** *Sierra Vista Chamber of Commerce, 77 Calle Portal, A-2140, Sierra Vista, AZ 458-6940.*

Tubac • If you like history and artistic funk with your retirement, check out this weathered little town, 40 miles south of Tucson and 23 miles north of Nogales. With a population under a thousand—two-thirds of them retired—Tubac offers several galleries and boutiques and a very laid-back lifestyle. Several artists-in-residence provide the proper local color. Tubac State Historic Park and Tumacacori Mission National Monument are in the neighborhood. The terrain is high desert. **For information:** *Tubac Chamber of Commerce, Kino Park, Tubac, AZ 85621; 398-2704.*

Tucson • Since we didn't recommend Phoenix as a retirement town, why Tucson? Because it's half the size, not quite as sprawling and less congested. While the greater Valley of the Sun has more than two million residents, Tucson's population is only half a million. (Only?) Further, it's higher and slightly cooler than Phoenix and it's in a dramatic setting, surrounded by craggy desert mountains. Several retirement complexes are in and about the city. **For information:** *Tucson Convention and Visitors Bureau, 130 S. Scott Ave., Tucson, AZ 85701; 624-1889.*

Chapter Seven

THE SNOWBIRDS

FEATHERING YOUR WINTER NEST

While hundreds of thousands of retirees snip their roots and nestle here permanently, an even larger number of seniors come to Arizona only to enjoy the winter sunshine.

They embrace the best of both worlds: heading south before the first snow flies, then returning home in the spring to keep their ties with family and friends. It's no wonder that they've earned the nickname "Snowbird."

Arizona ranks second to Florida and ahead of California and Texas as America's leading Snowbird retreat. It draws as many as a million winter visitors each year.

A recent Arizona State University survey indicated that most Valley of the Sun winter visitors arrive in November (32 percent) and depart in April (55 percent). Sunbelt chambers of commerce report similar trends.

The ASU survey revealed some surprising statistics. Despite their image as RV enthusiasts, at least half of Arizona's Snowbirds check into apartments and condos, and many own winter homes here. Of those who do occupy RV or mobile home parks, 70 percent leave their rigs there year-around. Only 30 percent tow a trailer or drive an RV to the state, and they often return to the same park. So it's evident that most of these visitors, like other migrating birds, like to return to the same nest year after year.

And Snowbirds definitely are migrants. While the state lures tens of thousands of permanent retirees, 95 percent of the winter visitors responding to the ASU survey said they planned to fly back home in the spring. The average length of winter stay is between four and five months. Two thirds have been doing the Snowbird bit for five or more years.

Where do most of the Snowbirds roost? Along the Colorado River Corridor and in the greater Phoenix area. Many Rio Colorado towns see their populations increase many-fold each winter. The Phoenix

Convention and Visitors Bureau estimates that as many as 200,000 Snowbirds flock into the Valley of the Sun.

Where do they come from? A surprising 20 percent are from Canada. Most American Snowbirds come from the chilly Midwest, but not from Michigan, as do the permanent retirees. In fact, Michigan doesn't even finish in the top ten. After Canada, Minnesota sends the most winter visitors with 13 percent. Iowa and Washington are tied with eleven. North Dakota is next with seven percent, an amazing figure, since it has a population of less than 700,000. Others in the top ten are Colorado, six percent and Illinois, four percent; California, Oregon and Wisconsin all have three percent.

Winter visitors don't come just for suntans and golf. Three out of four Arizona's Cactus Baseball League ticket-buyers are from another state. Two-thirds of the fans say they head south *specifically* for spring hardball.

For those interested in finding winter apartments and condos, Tucson, Phoenix and some other cities list short-term lodgings in their accommodations guides. Both citys' visitors guides have apartment and condo listings and Tucson's convention and visitor's bureau has an apartment-finder service.

Most Arizona RV parks offer special rates for long-term visitors. Many are elaborate resorts, with swimming pools, golf courses, marinas, recreation centers, social programs, group outings and other amenities.

Incidentally, whether you plan to winter in Arizona for two weeks or six months, remember to bring your sweater—perhaps even a down jacket. Compared with Bismark, North Dakota, and Edmonton, Ontario, much of Arizona is a winter paradise. But nighttime temperatures sometimes dip down to freezing in the Phoenix and Tucson areas. Days generally are in the balmy 60s, often climbing into the 70s. Tucson is more than a thousand feet higher than Phoenix and therefore slightly cooler.

If you require toastier winter nights, the Colorado River corridor is warmer than the higher desert interior. Bullhead City, for instance, boasts an average January low of 37 and a high of 80. Yuma, Parker and Bullhead often report the nation's highest temperatures, in both winter and summer.

Although higher-elevation places like Flagstaff, Sedona, Prescott and the mountain regions northeast of Phoenix attract many year-around retirees, few Snowbirds choose to fly there. Therefore, our list of recommended roosts is focused on cactus country. Colorado River towns offer a plenitude of RV and mobile home parks, while their selection of condo and apartment rentals is rather limited. So if you want a solid roof over your winter roost, you'll find a much better selection in the Valley of the Sun and Tucson.

THE BEST SNOWBIRD ROOSTS

Our list ranges from cosmopolitan Phoenix to dusty Quartzsite, and it includes some sun-country places you may not be aware of. Some of our selections also are suggested as retirement towns in the previous chapter, so expect to trip over some repetition.

To learn more about these cities, towns and villages, move along to Part Two of *Coming to Arizona.* We discuss population growth, advantages and disadvantages, summer-winter climate and other essentials.

CENTRAL ARIZONA

This, as we said in the last chapter, is the beating heart of Arizona—its business, social and population hub. You can winter in the busy Valley of the Sun or park on the fringes, away from the crowds. If we had a choice, we'd probably pick our first listing—Apache Junction. Carefree and Cave Creek would be close seconds.

Apache Junction ● Forty miles southeast of Phoenix in the Superstition Mountain foothills, Apache Junction is popular with winter visitors as well as permanent retirees. With more than a hundred RV parks and resorts, this community of 17,000 people draws about 40,000 winter visitors. We particularly like its setting in a handsomely rugged desert. It's a short drive to Salt River Canyon, whose reservoirs offer a bit of aquatic recreation. Pine-clad mountains are just beyond. And Phoenix is less than an hour in the other direction. **For information:** *Apache Junction Chamber of Commerce, P.O. Box 1747, Apache Junction, AZ 85217; phone 982-3141.*

Cave Creek and Carefree ● With a combined population of about 6,000, these hamlets are 25 miles north of Phoenix. Cave Creek is a deliberately rustic Western-style town; the planned community of Carefree is more contemporary. They sit side-by-side in an attractive, rough-hewn desert. The only disadvantage we can see is that the area has a limited number of RV parks. However, more are a-building. If you want a Carefree (sorry about that) or Cave Creek winter vacation, better book up early. **For information:** *Carefree-Cave Creek Chamber of Commerce, P.O. Box 734, Carefree, AZ 85377; 488-3381.*

Casa Grande ● Midway between Phoenix and Tucson, this town of 16,000 doesn't attract a lot of winter folk. It's in a farm belt, and the area can get a bit windy. However, if you like to be within an hour's drive of both major urban centers, you might check it out. Winters are temperate, with warm days and cool to chilly evenings. A few RV parks are in the area and more are being built. **For information:** *Greater Casa Grande Chamber of Commerce, 575 N. Marshall, Casa Grande, AZ 85222; 836-2125.*

Mesa-Tempe ● In the southeastern part of the Valley of the Sun, these large communities offer all your basic needs. Access to next-door

Phoenix and Scottsdale is easy and the towns have their own cultural lures as well. Both offer fine museums, and Tempe is home to Arizona State University. They're primarily bedroom communities, but they do have several RV resorts and parks. Apartments may be a bit scarce because of the presence of ASU; all those students need winter roosts as well. **For information:** *Mesa Convention & Visitors Bureau, 120 N. Center St., Mesa, AZ 85201; 969-1307* and *Tempe Chamber of Commerce, 60 E. Fifth St., Suite 3, Tempe, AZ 85281; 894-8158.*

Phoenix-Scottsdale • You say you want to be in the middle of the action, with a great choice of cultural offerings, restaurants and classy resorts? Phoenix and Scottsdale *are* the Valley of the sun, containing most of its population and its finest resorts. Most of the RV parks are on the outskirts, while apartment and condo rentals are scattered throughout the area. The Yellow Pages will help you find a place to roost. If you're a preseason baseball fan, fly no further. Five of the eight Cactus League clubs conduct spring training in and about Phoenix. Expect Phoenix-Scottsdale accommodations to be on the pricey side, compared with much of the rest of Arizona.

For information: *Phoenix & Valley of the Sun Convention and Visitors Bureau, 505 N. Second St., Suite 300, Phoenix, AZ 85004-3998; 254-6500* and *Scottsdale Chamber of Commerce, P.O. Box 130 (7333 Scottsdale Mall), Scottsdale, AZ 85251-4498; 945-8481.*

COLORADO RIVER CORRIDOR

If you love water sports and balmy January nights, head for the river. Although the mighty Colorado has its roots in the 10,000 foot ramparts of the Rocky Mountains, it has dropped to nearly sea level by the time it reaches the Arizona-Nevada-California border. This is the warmest part of Arizona, too hot for some in summer but great for just about everyone in winter.

The corridor is primarily RV territory. Hundreds of RV and mobile home parks and resorts line the Colorado River. The strange dusty desert town of Quartzsite draws great caravans of motorhomes and travel trailers during its annual swap meet and gem and mineral show. Estimates run into the hundreds of thousands.

Bullhead City • Fast-growing Bullhead City offers toasty winter climate and less than four inches of rain a year. An added bonus is the rising new casino town of Laughlin, just across the water. In fact, some casinos offer free shuttles to hurry you over from the non-gambling Arizona shore. Bullhead isn't attractive. It's a hastily-assembled town of 13,600 residents, scattered along a dozen miles of shoreline. However, it offers an abundance of water recreation on Lake Mohave. Dozens of RV parks rim the river, mostly on the Arizona side, with a few on the Nevada shore. **For information:** *Bullhead Area Chamber of Commerce, P.O. Box 1048, Bullhead City, AZ 86430; 763-9400.*

Lake Havasu City • The home of the misplaced London Bridge is the first and still the largest of the Colorado River's planned winter resort communities. It has many year-around residents as well. Adjacent Lake Havasu offers an abundance of water sports. Many RV parks are in the area, including a new full-service resort on Lake Havasu Peninsula. **For information:** *Lake Havasu City Area Chamber of Commerce, 1930 Mesquite Ave., Suite 3, Lake Havasu City, AZ 86403; 855-4115.*

Lake Mead National Recreation Area • We'll give this listing more detail than the others in this chapter, since it's not covered in our communities section in Part Two.

If you're a water sports buff, this is your place. Lake Mead NRA offers hundreds of miles of shoreline along Lake Mead and Lake Mojave. For those dazzled by statistics, the two reservoirs have more total shoreline than California.

There's no town on the Arizona side of the lake, but Boulder City, Nevada (population 12,000), offers all the essentials. It's an attractive community laid out in the 1930s as the construction town for Hoover Dam, which creates Lake Mead. Curiously, Boulder City is the only town in Nevada that prohibits gambling. However, there are plenty of casinos nearby, including one between Boulder City and the Arizona border. Las Vegas is a mere 30 miles away.

This area is primarily RV country, unless you want to check into a motel room or resort for the winter. Nine marinas occupy the Lake Mojave and Lake Mead shorelines. Most have campgrounds or RV parks with long-term rental spaces. Some offer resort lodges as well. In addition, there are several RV parks and motels in Boulder City.

The climate here is similar to Bullhead City to the south. Winters are warm and dry with cool evenings, and rainfall is less than four inches a year. (Most of that little dab falls in the summer.) The average January high is 80 and the low is 38. In summer, the mercury rockets past 100.

For information: *To get a list of marinas and other details about the NRA, contact Lake Mead National Recreation Area, 601 Nevada Highway, Boulder City, NV 89005-2426; (702) 293-8907. For area information, contact: Boulder City Chamber of Commerce, 1497 Nevada Highway, Boulder City, NV 89005; (702) 293-2034.*

Parker • Surrounded by the Colorado River Indian Reservation, Parker is a friendly mix of Native Americans and whites. It has a quiet, small-town aura, with a population around 3,000. While not a fancy resort town, it's one of the least expensive places on the river. The area offers a huge selection of RV parking places. The 20-mile "Parker Strip" between the town and Parker Dam is practically wall-to-wall RV parks and resorts. They line both the Arizona and California shores. **For information:** *Parker Area Chamber of Commerce, P.O. Box 627, Parker, AZ 85344; 669-2174.*

Quartzsite • This curious place is 21 miles east of the Colorado River, on I-10. The good news is that it offers the cheapest RV park rates in the state. The bad news is that it's hound-dog homely. Quartzsite isn't quite a town; it's a scraped-away patch of desert that has become one huge RV facility. Retail business is limited, with only a handful of restaurants and stores. However, hundreds of temporary shops set up in tents during the winter. You'll do your essential shopping by driving 25 miles west to Blythe, California. **For information:** *Quartzsite Chamber of Commerce, P.O. Box 85, Quartzsite, AZ 85346; 927-5600.*

Yuma • Snowbirds nearly double Yuma's population of 50,000 each winter. It's not a fancy resort town, but more of a simple Main Street USA that happens to be sitting in the middle of the desert. It's rich in history, as well, occupying the site of Yuma Crossing, on the first cross-country trail to California. The southernmost of the corridor towns, Yuma also is the driest, with an annual rainfall under three inches. Although it rims the river, most of its RV resorts are inland, along I-8 to the east. Others are across the stream, in Winterhaven, California. **For information:** *Yuma County Chamber of Commerce, P.O. Box 6468, Yuma, AZ 85366; 344-3800.*

SOUTHERN ARIZONA

Tucson and the area south to Nogales offer fine Snowbird climate. We also recommend Sierra Vista, a bit farther east. It's located in a rather interesting area.

Sierra Vista • This sprawling but well-planned town of 34,000 is an appealing winter roost if you don't mind chilly evenings. January nights get frosty, and you may get an sporadic dusting of snow. We like its location in southeastern Arizona's "Cowboy Corner." It's close to historic Tombstone and Fort Huachuca, Chiricahua National Monument and several mountain wilderness areas. Tucson is but 70 miles away, and the Mexican border is close as well. Seasonal apartments are scarce; most winter accommodations are in RV parks, which are rather inexpensive. Several are concentrated in nearby Huachuca City. **For information:** *Sierra Vista Chamber of Commerce, 77 Calle Portal, #140-A, Sierra Vista, AZ 85635; 458-6940.*

Tubac • A bit warmer than Sierra Vista, Tubac is a tiny, pleasantly funky art colony 40 miles south of Tucson. It's rich in history as Arizona's oldest non-Indian settlement. Assuming you like historic-artistic funk, Tubac has only one major drawback: its winter visitor facilities are minimal. There are only a few RV parks in the area and apartment/condo rentals are rare. **For information:** *Tubac Chamber of Commerce, P.O. Box 1866 (Kino Park), Tubac, AZ 85646; 398-2704.*

Tucson • With fine cultural offerings, good restaurants, desert gardens, excellent museums and galleries, Tucson is a great Snowbird roost. It offers a good assortment of RV parks and resorts, winter apartments and condos. The visitor's bureau has an apartment-locator service. Another plus: Arizona's best Mexican border shopping is just 63 miles south, in Nogales.

Think of Tucson as a flat San Francisco with warm sunshine. It's a bit cooler than the Colorado River corridor towns, of course, but January's average daytime high is a pleasant 66. **For information:** *Metropolitan Tucson Convention & Visitors Bureau, 130 S. Scott Ave., Tucson, AZ 85701; 624-1817.*

JOINING THE RV CLAN?

If retirement is just down the road, you may be considering the purchase of a travel trailer or motorhome. They're a great boon to Snowbirds, offering most of the comforts of home in a more or less portable package. And of course, you can shift easily from place to place.

Virtually every sunbelt chamber of commerce has lists of RV parks and mobile home resorts catering to long-term visitors. Incidentally, the best place to find mobile home park and campground guidebooks is in rec vehicle and camper supply stores, not in bookstores.

The **Arizona Travel Planner**, published by the state's office of tourism, also lists RV parks. For a free copy, along with other good stuff about the state, contact: **Arizona Office of Tourism**, 1100 W. Washington St., Phoenix, AZ 85007; phone 542-TOUR.

Another source is the **Arizona Mobile Housing Association,** 2540 E. Thomas Rd., Suite I, Phoenix, AZ 85016; phone 955-4440. You can request a free directory that lists about 250 mobile home and RV parks that are members of the association. The Yellow Pages list rec vehicle spaces under "Recreational Vehicle Parks", "Mobile Home Parks" and "Campgrounds." To order phone books for various communities, call **USWEST** at (800) 422-8793.

The **American Automobile Association** lists assorted Arizona campgrounds and RV parks in its *Southwestern CampBook.* **Woodalls North American Campground Directory** is a thick, comprehensive guide to RV parks and campsites in the U.S. and Canada. Also useful is **Trailer Life's RVing America's Backroads: Arizona.** It's not a campground directory, but a full-color hardcover travel guide. The text is directed toward the RV set, with travel tips, attractions, activities and maps of suggested tours.

You probably already know that mobile home parks are set up primarily for permanently parked units and RV campgrounds are more for short-term visitors. But in Arizona, both types often make exceptions and accommodate RVers and trailer-towers for the winter. In fact, many of the places we used while researching *The Best of Arizona* and *Coming to Arizona* had a combination of overnight spaces, long-term spaces and permanently parked mobile homes.

Important note: Many RV parks with long-term rates—particularly those near metropolitan areas—book up early, so make your plans as soon as possible.

Types of rec vehicles

We've had considerable experience with RV living, since we use a camper to research our travel books. Of course, our rig is a bit snug for Snowbirding to Arizona; it's a 1979 Volkswagen camper named Ickybod. You'll want something more roomy for your four to six months under the Arizona sun.

Rec vehicles come in seven basic types, and we'll review each to help you make your choice. A major consideration is mobility once you get to your Snowbird roost. Some folks tow a "tag-along" vehicle. Others lean toward travel trailers or fifth-wheel units, so they can use the towing rig to get about. Here's a simple solution if you're both willing to drive: take the family car along with the motorhome.

If you tow a tag-along, check with the car dealer first. Some vehicle's drive-trains are lubricated only when the engine is running. A solution is to get a two-wheel towing dolly that keeps the drive wheels off the ground.

Now, a review of your RV choices:

Pickup-mounted campers

This was America's original motorhome—a housing shell mounted on a pickup or truck bed.

Advantages • Obviously, it's your best buy if you already own a pickup. Some camper units are even equipped with jacks so you can drive out from under the shell and have the use of your vehicle. Today's fancy pickups come with all the trimmings and are fairly easy to drive. They have a reasonably short wheelbase and aren't too difficult to park.

Disadvantages • You can't move between the driving and passenger compartment without pulling over. Campers have a rather high center of gravity and tend to be unstable in winds. Also, most are a bit small for long-term residence.

Motorhomes

These are built from the wheels up, onto a ready-made chassis.

Advantages • Motorhomes are the vehicles of choice for most Snowbirds. They come in all sizes from little 18-footers to 50-foot castles on wheels with all the amenities. You have direct access between the driving and living area. And they're easy to set up. Pull up and park, and you're home.

Disadvantages • The larger and more comfortable they are, they more difficult they are to drive. Of course, they have power steering and brakes and the better ones have adequate horsepower. Still, the long wheelbase makes them tricky to maneuver. And forget about parallel parking. Motorhomes generally are the most expensive RV rigs, foot for foot.

Chassis mount

They're similar to motorhomes, but the unit is built onto the body of a van, utilizing the original cab. Most have long rear overhangs to provide more interior room on a relatively short wheelbase.

Advantages ● They're usually a bit less expensive than a motorhome, since the maker buys mass-produced van chassis-cab units. Otherwise, they offer the same advantages.

Disadvantages ● The van wheelbase limits their size, and some of the larger ones have ridiculously long rear overhangs. You have to be careful not to swat a sign or passer-by when you make a tight turn.

Travel trailers

These are the oldest RVs, tracing their ancestry back hundreds of years to horse-drawn gypsy carts and shepherd wagons.

Advantages ● If you like to nest in the same place all winter, travel trailers may be your best bet. They're much less expensive per foot, since you aren't buying a motor vehicle. And of course, you have your towing rig free to run around once you get settled in.

Disadvantages ● Speed is limited to 55 mph in most states, even on freeways posted at 65 for cars. Also, passengers aren't allowed to ride in travel trailers. The rigs tend to be unstable in high crosswinds and winding roads. Your ride will be rougher, since the hitch telegraphs bumps to the car.

Fifth-wheel unit

This is a hybrid between a travel trailer and camper, which is attached to a special gizmo in the bed of a pickup. Fifth- wheelers cost about the same, foot-per-foot, as a travel trailer. If we were Snowbirding, this would be our choice for a rec vehicle.

Advantages ● They're more stable than a travel trailer and some states allow passengers to ride in them. They're easy to unhook and set up at a campground, freeing the tow vehicle. You can get very large rigs with all the comforts, providing you have a pickup hefty enough to pull it. Fifth-wheelers are much easier to maneuver than trailers.

Disadvantages ● Once you've parked the rig, you're stuck with a truck for transportation. Also, fifth-wheelers share some of a trailer's disadvantages in maneuvering and parking.

Tent trailers

If you're on a tight budget, or if you have a light-duty towing vehicle, folding tent trailers may be the way to go.

Advantages • They're a cut above a tent, and relatively cheap. Some of the better tent trailers even have bathrooms and showers, in addition to full kitchens. They tow much easier than a travel trailer. Their compact, fold-down design offers little wind resistance and doesn't block rear vision.

Disadvantages • They offer little insulation from temperature and campground noises. Although they're easy to set up, their fold-down design limits kitchen and bathroom amenities.

Van conversion

This is similar to a chassis mount, except that the living area is built into the original body shell of the van.

Advantages • They're small enough to maneuver and park in towns. In fact, we use Ickybod as our second car when we're not on the road. Van conversions obviously get better gas mileage than the big rigs. Pop-top versions are reasonably comfortable, once you get settled in a campground.

Disadvantages • Face it, folks. Do you want to live for several months without an on-board pottie? (Some have tiny bathrooms, but they sacrifice space elsewhere.) Vans have limited storage and living area, and you have to fold down the bed every night. They're not practical for long-term use, except for a single person who doesn't mind padding to the campground pottie. (Ickybod loses a lot of his appeal at 3 o'clock in the morning.)

Trailer regulations

All rec vehicles require special handling skills. This is particularly true for trailers. Because of the inherent instability of towed vehicles, most states have special laws governing them. They're fairly uniform from state-to-state and usually include these requirements:

• Safety chains are mandatory and they should be long enough to permit turning. They also must be short enough to keep the trailer's tongue from digging into the ground if the hitch fails.

• Passengers aren't allowed to ride in travel trailers in most states, although Arizona permits them in both trailers and fifth-wheelers.

• Size limits of trailers vary from state to state. In Arizona, a trailer can't be more than 40 feet long, eight feet wide and 13.5 feet high. Combined length of a trailer and towing vehicle is 65 feet.

• Outside mirrors are required on both sides of a towing vehicle if the trailer obstructs rear vision, which all but small camp trailers do.

• Towed rigs must have the same lighting system as your car: taillights, stoplights and turn indicators.

• Towing more than one vehicle, such as a travel trailer and a boat, is a no-no.

• The speed limit is the same for towed vehicles as for large trucks: 55 mph, even on freeways posted at 65.

● In Arizona, separate braking systems are required on trailers with a gross weight over 1,500 pounds. (It varies from 1,500 to 3,000 pounds in other states.) Trailer brakes are always a good idea, where required or not. They help prevent jackknifing and they keep the trailer from shoving the car ahead in a sudden stop.

Handle with care

Whether you're driving a motorhome or towing a trailer, follow these tips to ensure that your new home on the road stays there:

● If you're a first-timer, practice stopping and turning on familiar roads before you head south. RVs handle differently than cars. Most have a rather high center of gravity and their weight hinders acceleration. Give yourself plenty of leeway when passing. They require longer stopping distances than cars, particularly trailers and fifth-wheel units.

● Shift into a lower gear when you're going downhill. The added weight will push you faster than you think.

● A trailer tow bar pushes down on your vehicle's rear wheels, making it less stable. Also, it can tilt your headlights into the eyes of oncoming drivers. If you're pulling a heavy rig, get a special towing package that includes beefed-up rear suspension.

● Remember that your rear vision will be restricted and side-view mirrors usually have blind spots. Signal well in advance and change lanes slowly, to give vehicles around you time to react.

● Don't overload your rig. Water and fuel weigh about eight pounds per gallon, adding hundreds of pounds to the vehicle weight. Check with the dealer for the gross vehicle rate rating, which is the maximum allowable load, including people and cargo. If you exceed this, lots of things can happen and they're all bad. You may have a blowout; your rig will lurch on curves and accelerate on downgrades; your stopping distance will be increased; and you won't have adequate pickup for safe passing.

● Balance your load and keep your RVs center of gravity as low as possible. Don't put heavy objects in higher shelves or cab-over bunks.

● Be very careful of fire! Check all gas fittings and carry dry chemical extinguishers. Bear in mind that you're traveling with several gallons of Propane and gasoline. Check evacuation routes. Today's RVs are required to have at least two exits; learn where they are. (One may be a break-away window).

● Don't give your RV a headache. The average car is just over four feet high, but most RVs top out at seven feet or more.

● Finally, and this is for courtesy as well as safety, stay in the right-hand lane except for passing. You're required to do so in some states. On two-lane roads, pull over whenever possible to let faster traffic pass. Again, some state laws require it. An RVs width makes it difficult for those behind to see oncoming vehicles.

Nothing is more exasperating that trundling behind a big motor-home. And no, we're not amused by that rear bumper sticker that says: "We're spending our children's inheritance." Don't force a cranky motorist into a dangerous pass. You may be the first at the scene of the accident, as a participant.

RV support groups

When you join the RV set, you join a fraternity that has its own jamborees, caravans and clubs. You'll find that its members are a gregarious lot, quick to share opinions, advice, assistance and friendship. Making friends at RV parks and campgrounds is easy; just stop by and borrow a cup of coffee. Many RV parks, particularly those catering to long-term visitors, sponsor dances and other social functions.

If you're widowed, don't be shy about hitting the road alone. Many second-time-around romances have bloomed over a campground barbecue pit or bingo party.

Some RV makers, like Airstream, promote social and other programs for their vehicle buyers.

A particularly useful organization for the Snowbird set is the **Good Sam Club,** operated by TL Enterprises of Agoura, California. Membership is $19 per year (less for multiple years). You can join sending a check to: Good Sam Club, P.O. Box 500, Agoura, CA 91301. If you have a VISA or MasterCard, you can sign up by calling (800) 234-3450.

Membership benefits include 10 percent discounts on camping, parts, accessories and Propane at participating RV parks, campgrounds and RV dealers. Members also get free trip routing service and travelers checks, and 50 percent off subscriptions to *Trailer Life* and *Motorhome* magazines. Members receive a free newsletter which lists upcoming caravans, camporees and other news of the RV world.

The club also has a travel agency offering discounts on cruises and air fares. Mail forwarding and messenger services are provided for a fee. Thick campground directories listing Good Sam member and non-member parks can be purchased.

This all sounds like a commercial, but it's unsolicited. (We even pay for our own membership.) We just think the organization does a good job.

PART TWO

THE COMMUNITIES

To create a complete relocation guide, we've ridden off in three directions, with special sections for job-seekers, permanent retirees and Snowbirds.

We've already touched on some communities that offer good job prospects, senior facilities or winter roosts. What follows is a more detailed look at the state's cities and towns. We don't attempt to cover every hamlet. We review only those which we feel hold special potential—and appeal—for those contemplating a move to Arizona.

In the listings that follow, property taxes are based on 1989 figures supplied by the Arizona Department of Commerce. Population figures are from 1989 estimates or the 1990 census, whichever was available at press time. Most unemployment figures are from 1989, although some communities have provided more recent data.

97

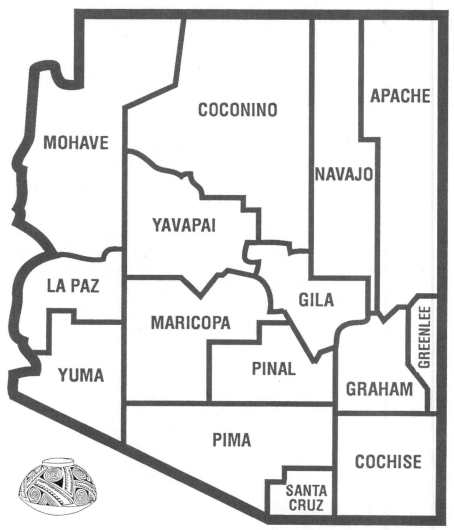

Arizona's population is focused in the communities of two counties—Maricopa (Phoenix) and Pima (Tucson). More than two-thirds of the state's residents live in one or the other. Both counties also have extensive wilderness areas; Pima stretches west across untracked desert, nearly reaching the California border. Huge Coconino County, covering 18,629 square miles, embraces much of the Grand Canyon and the ponderosa uplands above the Mogollon Rim. Its seat is Flagstaff, the largest community in northwestern Arizona, with a population of 43,780.

Chapter Eight

THE WESTERN EDGE

THE COLORADO RIVER CORRIDOR

This section covers communities bordering the Colorado River, that watery divide between Arizona, Nevada and California. We also mention towns that are a few miles inland.

Rio Colorado isn't really a river in this area, however. With seven dams between the Grand Canyon and the Mexican border, it's more of a chain of lakes. These reservoirs provide unlimited water recreation, and that's one of the area's chief lures.

THE WAY IT WAS ● The Colorado is one of the most harnessed rivers in the world. Indeed, its muddy water is the lifeblood of southwestern Arizona and much of California and Nevada.

It ran wild and free for untold centuries, carving the majestic Grand Canyon above and carrying rich red soil south into the Gulf of California. Like all wild things, Rio Colorado was unpredictable. For centuries Native Americans tried to farm along its rich riverbottom banks, only to be flooded out one year and wilted by drought the next.

European and American explorers began coming upriver from the Sea of Cortez in the early 1800s; others passed this way during the 1849 California Gold Rush. Some chose to stay; they pushed the Indians off their land and took up farming. Suffering the same water-flow frustrations as their predecessors, these newcomers decided that the great river needed to be put into harness.

The first efforts came in 1901, when water was diverted into the Imperial Canal near Yuma to irrigate the dry but rich soils of California's Imperial Valley. However, Rio Colorado didn't take to harness easily. A flood breached the canal in 1905 and the wild river changed course. For 16 months, it flowed unchecked into the Salton Basin, 235 feet below sea level. By the time the breach was finally closed in 1907,

Hoover Dam, completed in 1935, put the Colorado River into harness.

the runaway river had created the 40-mile-long Salton Sea, which still exists.

Men were more determined than ever to control Big Red. In 1909, the Laguna Dam was completed just north of Yuma. It provided desert irrigation, but brought an end to river navigation. Until this time, paddlewheelers had chugged as much as 300 miles upstream to service riverside communities.

Laguna Dam was too far downstream for effective river control, and spring thaws continued to bring muddy floods. To put an end to Rio Colorado's mischief, the U.S. Bureau of Reclamation launched history's most challenging dam project, in the narrow and rocky walls of Black Canyon. In 1935, the completion of Hoover Dam—the world's highest—marked the end of the free-flowing Colorado.

Meanwhile, in another time and place, air conditioning was being perfected. In 1906, Willis S. Carrier of Buffalo, New York, developed a "dew-point control air washer," passing air through temperature-controlled water pipes. Better refrigerants were developed in the 1920s and the true air conditioner was born. The first public use of air conditioning was in a movie theater in 1922. By the 1930s, small and relatively efficient units were being produced.

For Arizona, they couldn't have come at a better time.

THE WAY IT IS • Air conditioners and reservoirs have spawned a string of skinny communities along the banks of Rio Colorado. They stretch from Hoover Dam south to Yuma and on into Mexico.

Most of the riverside towns are unplanned and not very pretty. The subtle beauty of the desert suffers under the weight of asphalt and the glare of neon. They are lively places, however, where glossy speed-boats skim over placid reservoirs and retirees live out their American dream of a winter place in the sun.

The corridor isn't strictly for the Snowbirds. Some folks crank up their air conditioners and retire here permanently. But it's much more popular with winter visitors. Yuma, the largest of the river towns, nearly doubles its population in winter, and scruffy little Quartzsite balloons from 900 to upwards of 200,000. If you plan to settle the year-around along Arizona's western edge, stay close to your air conditioner in July, when the average daytime high is around 108!

BULLHEAD CITY

Elevation • 504 feet

Location • In Mohave County on State Route 95, across the Colorado River from Laughlin, Nevada.

Climate • Warm, dry winters with cool evenings; hot, dry summers. July average high 108.2, low 79.1; January average high 62.2, low 41.8. Rainfall 4.19 inches; no snowfall.

Population • 13,600

Population trend • Gained 10.2 percent per year from 1980 to 1989.

Property tax • $11.17 per $100 valuation (assessed at 10 percent of real value).

Unemployment rate (1989) • 5.2 percent.

Bullhead city sits just above the triangle where the Arizona, Nevada and California borders merge. Named for a promontory now submerged into Lake Mohave, it's a low-rise scatter of housing tracts, modular homes and mobile home parks. This sun-warmed jumble of hasty settlement is the northernmost of that string of towns along Rio Colorado's desert shoreline.

South along State Route 95, unincorporated communities of Riviera, Fort Mohave and Golden Shores stretch Bullhead's outskirts to I-40. Much of this are is encompassed in the Fort Mohave Indian Reservation.

Bullhead City wasn't incorporated until 1984, but its roots go back to the 1945, when it was the construction camp for Davis Dam, immediately north. A mere 504 feet above sea level, it often earns the dubious honor as America's summer hot spot. Tourist officials wish people wouldn't talk about that. In winter, thousands of Snowbirds triple the town's population. About 20 RV and mobile home parks line the river's shores.

Laughlin, Nevada, across the reservoir, is another reason for Bullhead's popularity. A few years ago, entrepreneur Don Laughlin guessed that winter vacationers might like to pass the time pulling a few slot machine handles. He built a casino, more followed, and a sudden city blossomed in the desert. Laughlin immodestly named it for himself.

Nearly a dozen gaming halls now line the Nevada side, beguiling Bullhead folks with the seductive glitter of neon. To make things easier, large parking lots have been paved at Bullhead City's north end, where launches provide free casino shuttles.

Economy • Tourism fuels Bullhead's economic fires, and of course Snowbirds bring their retirement checks. Booming Laughlin employs 10,000 people and new casinos seem to blossom every month. The Mohave Generating Station, a cooperative of four utilities, also is a major employer.

Job prospects • The services sector, including tourism, employs nearly 40 percent of Bullhead's work force. Retail trade is second with 20 percent and construction third with 14 percent (1989 figures). Job availability, according to the chamber of commerce, is about average.

Real estate • The area has several planned subdivisions with amenities such as pools and tennis courts, along with conventional homes and a few condos. A typical new three-bedroom home averages $95,000. Much of Bullhead's housing, both permanent and temporary, is in mobile home parks.

The media • Three newspapers—the tri-weekly *Mohave Valley News*, biweekly *Booster/Laughlin Leader* and the weekly combined *Laughlin Gambler-Bullhead City Bee*. One TV station, plus cable with 22 channels.

Medical services • One 68-bed hospital, one 120-bed extended care facility and a mental health clinic.

Industrial facilities • A 190-acre industrial park near the airport.

Transportation • Served by Greyhound. Bullhead City Airport has a 5,000 foot runway; scheduled flights by feeder lines.

Education • Bullhead City campus of Mohave Community College, plus one elementary, intermediate and high school.

Local government • Incorporated in 1984; mayor, six council members and a city manager.

Places to stay • Twenty-five motels, 21 RV parks and nine mobile home parks.

Leisure facilities • Three parks, one 18-hole and four nine-hole golf courses.

Tourist lures • The biggest lure, of course, is Lake Mohave, offering assorted water sports. Gaming is available across the pond in

Laughlin. The Black Mountains to the east provide outdoor pursuits such as hiking, picnicking and off-roading. The historic gold mining towns of Oatman and Goldroad are in this area.

Contacts • Bullhead Area Chamber of Commerce, P.O. Box 66 (1251 Highway 95), Bullhead City, AZ 86430; 754-4121.

City of Bullhead City, P.O. Box 1048, Bullhead City, AZ 86430; 763-9400.

Bullhead/Laughlin Airport Industrial Park, P.O. Box 570, Bullhead City, AZ 86430; 754-2829.

KINGMAN

Elevation • 3,225 feet

Location • In Mohave County on In-terstate 40, about 50 miles northeast of the Colorado River.

Climate • More temperate in summer than the river towns because of its higher elevation. July average high 97.4, low 67.2; January average high 55.3, low 31.4. Rainfall 9.35 inches; snowfall 3.4 inches.

Population • 12,795

Population trend • Gained 3.7 percent a year from 1980 to 1989.

Property tax • $11.39 per $100 assessed valuation.

Unemployment rate (1991) • 5.7 percent

This community of 11,000 occupies an attractive valley of eroded cliffs and buttes at the junction of I-40 and U.S. 93. Dating from 1882, it was named for surveyor Lewis Kingman, who was plotting a rail route between Needles, California, and Albuquerque, New Mexico. But it was silver and copper discoveries in the surrounding hills that kept the town on the map.

Mining declined during the 1930s and was virtually shut down by World War II. The surrounding countryside is dotted with ghost towns and semi-ghost towns worthy of exploring. They include Chloride, Cerbat, Mineral Park, Goldroad, Old Trails and Oatman.

While those towns withered, Kingman survived as a provisioning center for travelers on the Santa Fe railway and historic Route 66. The first path through here dates back to 1859, when Army Lt. Edward Beale's construction crew carved a wagon road that eventually led from Arkansas to Los Angeles. It was the first federally-funded road in the Southwest; old U.S. 66 roughly follows its course.

Kingman is still an important crossroad and a popular pausing place for motorists hurrying along I-40. Incidentally, the town's favor-ite son isn't Surveyor Kingman or a former mining baron. It's the late, gravel-voiced actor Andy Devine, who was born in nearby Flagstaff and grew up here. The main street is named for him, and he's featured in a special exhibit at the local museum.

The turn-of-the-century downtown looks a bit sleepy these days, since most of the business has shifted to suburban shopping centers. There's a fair amount of action in these suburbs as the town enjoys a modestly growth surge.

Economy • Kingman is the regional trade center for northwestern Arizona. With I-40 and the Santa Fe railway passing through town, it's an important warehousing and distribution area. Light manufacturing is growing, particularly at an airport industrial park.

Job prospects • They're about average, according to the local Job Service office. The best prospects are in construction, manufacturing, retail sales, tourism and other services. More than one job in four jobs is in wholesale and retail trade, with 22.6 percent in the services sector. Manufacturing is growing, accounting for 13.4 percent of the work force.

Real estate • The housing market includes a mix of older homes and new subdivisions, with the average price of a three-bedroom detached home around $65,000.

The media • One daily newspaper, *The Mohave County Miner* and a weekly, the *Kingman Booster*. One local TV station plus feeds of four stations from Phoenix and two from Las Vegas; also 28-channel cable service.

Medical services • An 83-bed regional hospital, one medical clinic, a mental health clinic, a spinal rehabilitation center and two nursing homes.

Industrial facilities • Kingman Airport Industrial Park with 4,000 acres, plus various other industrial and warehousing sites.

Transportation • Served by Greyhound, Las Vegas-Tonopah-Reno Stage (bus) and Amtrak. Kingman Airport has two 6,800-foot lighted runways; America West provides scheduled service.

Education • Mohave Community College, five elementary schools, a junior high and high school.

Local government • Seat of Mohave County since 1887. Incorporated in 1952; mayor, six council members and a city manager.

Places to stay • Thirty-four motels and four RV parks.

Leisure facilities • Nine parks, three aerobic centers, a senior center and Elderhostel, three public pools and two golf courses, plus tennis, racquetball and shuffleboard courts.

Tourist lures • Hualapai Mountain Park and the Cerbat Mountains offer picnicking, camping and hiking. A downtown historic district includes turn-of-the-century buildings, Locomotive Park, a walking tour and the Mohave Museum of History and Arts.

Contacts • Kingman Area Chamber of Commerce, P.O. Box 1150 (333 W. Andy Devine Ave.), Kingman, AZ 86402-1150; 753-6106.

Economic & Tourism Development Commission, City of Kingman, 310 N. Fourth St., Kingman, AZ 86401; 753-8130.

Kingman 2000 and Mohave County Airport Authority, 7000 Flightline Dr., Kingman, AZ 86401; 757-2005.

LAKE HAVASU CITY

Elevation • 482 feet

Location • In Mohave County, 19 miles south of I-40 on State Highway 95.

Climate • Warm, dry winters with cool evenings; hot, dry summers. July average high 108.6, low 78.8; January average high 67.3, low 37.1. Rainfall 3.82 inches, no snowfall.

Population • 22,835

Population trend • Gained 4.1 percent per year from 1980 to 1989.

Property tax • $14.57 per $100 assessed valuation.

Unemployment rate (1991) • 6.6%

• FLAGSTAFF

• PHOENIX

• TUCSON

You've likely heard the story by now. The London Bridge, while not falling down, was too old and narrow to handle modern traffic, so city officials put it up for sale. They didn't really expect any buyers, but entrepreneur Robert P. McCulloch offered $2,460,000 in 1968. He said he wanted to move it to the Arizona desert, where he'd purchased a piece of Lake Havasu shoreline.

The Arizona desert? The London Bridge?

About $9 million later, McCulloch had accomplished the ridiculous. The bridge was dismantled stone by stone and reconstructed over an Arizona sandpile. Then the sand was scooped out to create a channel between the mainland and a peninsula in Lake Havasu.

Voile! McCulloch had the centerpiece for his planned city in the desert. Incidentally, there were some bridge pieces left over, and you can buy them at local souvenir shops.

Lake Havasu City is the largest of the new communities along Rio Colorado, and it's also the best-planned. Local officials say "The Bridge" is Arizona's second most-visited attraction. However, its adjoining English Village is a tacky tourist trap instead of an authentic British, style attraction. It does have an English pub and a nice import shop. Out on the pond, paddleboats paddle in and about the bridge and Miss Havasu II takes visitors on an historical tour of Lake Havasu.

Historical? Lake Havasu?

Economy • Tourists and retirees are the main contributors to Havasu's economy. Officials estimate that the bridge lures 35 million tourist dollars a year. Light manufacturing is gaining ground, particularly in a city-owned industrial park.

Job prospects • They were below average to poor at this writing, with rather low wages, according to the local Job Service office. Best possibilities are in light manufacturing, tourism and other service jobs.

Real estate • Planned subdivisions offer some of the best housing variety along the Colorado River. Prices begin around $70,000.

The media • One twice-weekly newspaper, *The Herald* and a tri-weekly, *Today on the Colorado River.* The area is served by Kingman's daily *Mohave County Miner.* Two local TV stations and eight others by feed; cable TV with 14 channels.

Medical services • One 99-bed hospital and a 120-bed nursing home.

Industrial facilities • A city-owned industrial park and another being planned near the airport.

Transportation • Served by Greyhound; feeder and charter lines operate out of Lake Havasu Airport.

Education • Lake Havasu campus of Mohave Community College, plus five elementary, one junior high and one high school.

Local government • Incorporated in 1978; mayor, six council members and a city manager.

Places to stay • Twenty-two motels and resort hotels, short-term apartment and condo rentals, five mobile home parks and five camp-grounds.

Leisure facilities • Four 18-hole golf courses, three parks, swimming beaches on Lake Havasu, several tennis courts.

Tourist lures • The bridge and its English Village are the main draw, of course. Water sports are popular on Lake Havasu and the beaches of Lake Havasu State Park.

Contacts • Lake Havasu Area Chamber of Commerce, 1930 Mesquite Ave., Suite 3, Lake Havasu City, AZ 86403; 855-4115 and 453-3444.

Economic Development Officer, Lake Havasu City, 1795 Civic Center Blvd., Lake Havasu City, AZ 86403; 453-4152.

PARKER

Elevation • 450 feet

Location • In La Paz County, on the Colorado River, midway between interstates 10 and 40 on State Route 95.

Climate • Warm, dry winters with cool evenings; hot, dry summers. July average high 108.6, low 78.8; January average high 67.3, low 37.1. Rainfall 3.82 inches, no snowfall.

Population • 3,025

Population trend • Gained 2 percent per year from 1980 to 1989.

• FLAGSTAFF

• PHOENIX

• TUCSON

Property tax • $9.2 percent per $100 valuation.
Unemployment rate (1989) • 4.1 percent

Parker is a folksy little riverside town surrounded by the Colorado River Indian Reservation. It's not exclusively an Indian community, but a town with an affable ethnic mix of Native Americans and whites.

While it's not a glamorous resort, Parker offers the advantage of inexpensive home prices and some of the cheapest RV parks in Arizona. In fact, it's the RV capital of the Colorado River corridor.

The "Parker Strip" stretching ten miles north from the town to Parker Dam is side-by-side RV parks, on both the Arizona and California shores. The reservoir here has the typical Native American name of Lake Moovalya. It's one of the busiest boating, water-skiing and fishing lakes on the river.

Economy • Like everything else in Parker, the economy is rather water-oriented. Most of area's income is derived from tourism, retail sales and retirees.

Job prospects • Although its unemployment rate is low, Parker is one of the river corridor's slowest-growing towns. It's not a good market for job-hunters. A third of the jobs are in tourism and other services; 21.1 percent are in retail trades.

Real estate • The market is moderately active, with home prices a good buy. Figure on $50,000 for a three-bedroom detached house.

The media • One weekly newspaper, *The Parker Pioneer*. Two local TV stations, plus feeds from Yuma and Phoenix; also a cable TV company.

Medical services • One 39-bed hospital.

Industrial facilities • A 100-acre industrial park, owned by the Colorado River Indian tribe.

Transportation • Served by Greyhound. Avi-Suquilla Airport has a 4,800-foot lighted runway; no scheduled air service.

Education • Elementary and high schools only; extension courses available from Yuma's Arizona Western College.

Local government • Became seat of La Paz County when it was separated from northern Yuma County in 1983. Incorporated in 1948; mayor, six council members and a city manager.

Places to stay • Twenty-three motels, 49 mobile home and RV parks on the Arizona side and probably an equal number on the California shore.

Leisure facilities • Six parks, one public swimming pool, a senior citizens' center and an 18-hole golf course.

Tourist lures • Water sports abound, of course. The Colorado River Tribes Indian Museum offers stuff on Indian culture, plus a gift shop and library. Nearby Buckskin State Park (eleven miles north),

River Island State Park and La Paz County Park (eight miles north) offer camping, boat launching, water sports and picnicking.

Contacts • Parker Area Chamber of Commerce, P.O. Box 1217 (1217 California Ave.), Parker, AZ 85344; 669-2174.

Town of Parker, P.O. Box 6509 (1314 11th St.) Parker, AZ 85344; 669-9265.

Colorado River Tribal Council, Parker, AZ 85344; 669-9211.

QUARTZSITE

Elevation • 879 feet

Location • In La Paz County, 21 miles west of the Colorado River on I-10.

Climate • Warm, dry winters with balmy evenings; sizzling, dry summers. July average high 108.6, low 81; January average high 65, low 36.8. Rainfall 4.37 inches; no snowfall.

Population • 3,300 (probably lower in summer)

Population trend • Gained 12 percent a year from 1980 to 1989.

Property tax • $10.93 per $100 assessed valuation.

Unemployment rate (1989) • 5.8 percent

We probably should be more kind, but we said in the introduction that this book is straightforward and honest. And let's face it, folks. Quartzsite is the ugliest town in Arizona.

Actually, it isn't exactly a town, but more of a collection of RV parks in the desert.

It dates back to 1856 when one Charles Tyson built a civilian fort and stage stop. Today, it resembles a huge traveling show that's about to pull up stakes. Although a few businesses are anchored to the desert dirt, most of the trade is conducted out of tents and shade ramadas. And most of this happens in winter. When the mercury starts to rise, Quartzsite shrinks from as many as 200,000 to fewer than a thousand souls.

This dusty desert village has no town government, no sewer or water system, no schools, police department or zoning regulations. What it has is a mobile population who's median age is somewhere between Social Security and infinity. They're having the time of their lives with barbecues, potluck dinners and dances. Some merely unfold camp chairs on a swatch of Astroturf beside their RVs and breathe the clean desert air. At Stardusty Ballroom, which has only a floor—no walls or ceiling—oldsters fox-trot to music of the swinging years. "Dance at your own risk," a sign warns.

Cheap rent is the town's main attraction. With dozens of RV parks competing for customers, space rent is the lowest in Arizona. Further, the Bureau of Land Management will let you park at La Posa Recreation Area for just $25 for six months. Located south of I-10, La Posa has no utilities, not even water, but you can't beat the rates.

The town's winter visitor count is estimated as high as 200,000, although that may be an exaggeration. It swells to nearly half a million during the Quartzsite Gemboree, a monster gem and mineral show, flea market and RV rendezvous held each winter. During the show, folks say you can walk from one end of town to the other over the rooftops of RVs.

Economy ● Tourism is the only basis for Quartzsite's economy and most of that comes between November and April.

Job prospects ● They're virtually nil, except for seasonal retail jobs. Sales and services account for half of the employment. The largest employer is a truck stop, so you get the idea.

A RIVER BE DAMMED

Dams of the lower Colorado River Reclamation Project provide water for 11 million people in Arizona, California and Nevada. They generate 5.7 billion kilowatt-hours of electricity each year. Reading from north to south, these are the dams of the lower Colorado and their functions:

Hoover Dam ● Completed in 1935, it's the keystone to the project, providing flood control, water storage and hydroelectric power. It's a concrete arch dam, holding back Lake Mead, capable of storing 30 million acre-feet of water.

Davis Dam ● This earth and rock-fill dam was completed in 1953 and is used primarily to store water for delivery, via lower dams, to Mexico under the Mexican Water Treaty. It also generates electricity. Its reservoir, Lake Mohave, can store 1.8 million acre-feet of water.

Parker Dam ● An earth and rock-fill near-twin to Davis, it was completed in 1938 to provide water storage and hydroelectric power. Water from its 1.5 million acre-foot Lake Havasu goes primarily to Southern California.

Palo Verde Diversion Dam ● This earth and rock-fill structure was completed in 1957 to divert water to California's Palo Verde Valley.

Senator Wash Dam ● It's an earthfill embankment designed to store excess water in a small 12,250 acre-foot reservoir for later use. After release, the water passes through hydroelectric turbines.

Imperial Dam ● Two miles below Senator Wash, this concrete dam was completed in 1938. It provides water for southwestern Arizona through the Yuma Project and to southern California through the All-American Canal.

Laguna Dam ● The granddaddy of the project, Laguna was completed in 1909 and now augments water deliveries of Imperial Dam, five miles upstream.

Real estate • Little is happening in the way of housing development; most of the action is in mobile home parks.

The media • No local publications or TV stations. TV feeds from Yuma and Phoenix, plus a 14-channel cable system.

Medical services • Part-time medical centers only; nearest full service is in Blythe, California, 22 miles west.

Industrial facilities • None.

Transportation • Greyhound; nearest airports are in Parker and Blythe.

Education • No schools in Quartzsite; elementary school in Ehrenburg, 20 miles west and high school in Salome, 36 miles east.

Local government • Incorporated in 1989; mayor, town council and town manager.

Places to stay • Three motels and scores of RV and mobile home parks.

Leisure facilities • You mean other than sitting on a patch of Astroturf in front of your RV, sipping a martini? There's one nine-hole golf course, a senior center and 22 shuffleboard courts. Some mobile parks have pools, not open to the public.

Tourist lures • Other than a small, rather scruffy museum, there isn't much. People are lured into the surrounding hills for excellent rockhounding.

Contacts • Town of Quartzsite, P.O. Box 58, Quartzsite, AZ 85346; 927-4333. Quartzsite Chamber of Commerce, P.O. Box 85, Quartzsite, AZ 85346; 927-5600.

YUMA

Elevation • 138 feet

Location • In Yuma County, on Interstate 8 along the Colorado River, 25 miles from the Mexican border.

Climate • Warm, dry winters with cool evenings; hot, dry summers. July average high 106.6, low 73.6; January average high 68.4, low 36.8. Rainfall 2.99 inches; no snowfall.

Population • 51,575

Population trend • Gained 2.2 percent per year in the 1980s.

Property tax • $14.44 per $100 assessed valuation.

Unemployment rate (1991) • 24 percent.

It isn't handsome, but Yuma is a lively town that offers modest home prices and a lot of history. With a high unemployment rate, the town appeals mostly to retirees and to Snowbirds, who come by the thousands in winter.

Arizona's first explorers saw more barrier than beauty in the Colorado River. Then in 1699, mission-founder Father Eusebio Kino found a fording place where the Gila and Colorado merge. "Yuma Crossing" thus became an important link in the first trails west. Kino, incidentally, is credited with naming the Colorado for its reddish, silt-laden waters.

In 1779, Father Francisco Tomas Garces established two missions along the river. A presidio was built to protect Mission la Purisima Concepcion, on what is now the California side. The entire settlement, including the good padre, was wiped out in a bloody Quechan Indian uprising two years later. That finished things for the Spanish at Yuma Crossing.

Colonel Stephen Watts Kearny and frontier scout Kit Carson forded the river here in 1846, headed west to snatch California from Mexico. During California's gold rush, many argonauts used this southern route. A few returned to this area, attracted by nearby gold strikes and the agricultural potential along the Colorado's bottomlands.

The hamlet of Colorado City was established here in 1854. Historians tell us, with a sly grin, that the town's first permanent resident was a shady lady named Sarah Bowman, who ran a combined restaurant, bar and bawdy house. The river flexed its muscles in 1862, washing Colorado City into the Sea of Cortez, bordello and all. Another town, called Arizona City, was built on higher ground. Later, the name was changed to Yuma, after the local Indians.

Water diversion from the Colorado River provided an agricultural base for Yuma's economy and the town took hold. The military was attracted by the area's cloud-free days and wide open spaces during World War II. Two outfits are still there, a Marine Corps Air Station and the U.S. Army Yuma Proving Ground.

If you approach Yuma from California, you'll pass through a sand dune area right out of Lawrence of Arabia. In fact, several films have been shot here, including desert scenes from Star Wars. From fall through spring, hundreds of RVers camp along a frontage road and run their dune buggies over this slice of California Sahara.

Economy • It's a mixed bag, from military bases to Snowbirds to agriculture. More than 166,000 acres of crops are watered by the Colorado River. The town also is an important stop for cross-country travelers, who pause for a tank of gas and a six-pack of Mountain Dew.

Job prospects • They're limited. Our hard-working Mexican neighbors take most of the field work. A few light industries are being drawn here, so the high unemployment rate may have lowered by the time you read this.

Real estate • A typical three-bedroom house goes for $50,000 to $80,000.

The media • The *Yuma Daily Sun* and weekly *Valley Foothills News*. Two local TV stations plus cable.

Medical services • One 283-bed hospital and an emergency care unit; six extended care units.

Industrial facilities • Several industrial parks are available as Yuma pushes to attract more light manufacturing.

Transportation • Greyhound and Amtrak stop here. Yuma International Airport is served by America West and some feeder lines.

Education • Arizona Western College, six vocational schools, five private schools, 21 public elementary and three high schools.

Local government • The seat of Yuma County. Incorporated in 1873; mayor, six council members and a city administrator.

Places to stay • Thirty motels and more than a dozen RV parks. Some parks are in town, others along the river and some to the east along I-8.

Leisure facilities • Eight parks, four golf courses, three public pools, an adult center, plus bowling alleys, tennis courts and such. The San Diego Padres conduct their spring training here.

Tourist lures • Yuma offers three museums (see Part Three), plus the Yuma Territorial Prison historic park, a newly-developing Yuma Crossing State Park and Fort Yuma on the California side of the river.

Contacts • Yuma County Chamber of Commerce, P.O. Box 230 (377 S. Main St.), Yuma, AZ 85366-8230; 782-2567.

City of Yuma, 180 W. First St., Yuma, AZ 85364; 783-1271.

Yuma Economic Development Corporation, P.O. Box 1750 (377 Main St., Suite 202), Yuma, AZ 85366-9750; 783-0193.

Chapter Nine

NORTHWESTERN ARIZONA

BENEATH THE MOGOLLON RIM

If you travel about northwestern Arizona in search of a possible future home site, you may think you've taken a wrong turn and wound up in the Pacific Northwest. Approaching Flagstaff, the area's largest city, you'll see great stands of ponderosa pines carpeting Coconino National Forest. On the horizon, the serrated San Francisco Peaks thrust more than 12,000 feet skyward.

The great Colorado Plateau occupies much of northwestern Arizona. The Grand Canyon was created when this tableland gradually uplifted while the Colorado River carved down through its layered rock. That's a simplistic explanation which won't satisfy any self-respecting geologist, but it's adequate for our purposes.

This tableland, 4,000 to 8,000 feet high, extends down from the Grand Canyon and drops off abruptly at the 200-mile-long Mogollon Rim. It's a wonderfully mixed land of alpine lakes, volcanic peaks and red rock canyons.

THE WAY IT WAS ● The area's first settlers were the true natives, drawn to these high, cool pine forests around 15,000 to 20,000 years ago. They shared the land with antelope, bison and camels, migrating with the seasons to hunt and forage. About 4,000 years ago, they began rudimentary agriculture, growing a balanced protein diet of corn, squash and beans.

From these early tribes evolved the Sinagua (*si-NAU-wa*), who settled around present-day Flagstaff and south through Oak Creek Canyon around 1000 A.D. Although they occupied much of the forested Colorado Plateau, their name in Spanish means "without water." It was a reference to the porous, leaky volcanic soil in the eastern region of the plateau, where their abandoned villages were first noted by Spanish explorers. An advanced society, the Sinagua farmed, built irrigation canals and constructed elaborate adobe pueblos above ground and in the niches of protective cliffs.

113

Then curiously, by the time those Spanish travelers passed through here in the 16th century, the Sinagua had gone. Were they driven out by drought, disease or the arrival of warlike Athabaskans from the north? Archaeologists can only speculate. Thousands of ruins have been found to prove they were here; nothing has been found to confirm why they left.

White migration to the region didn't begin until the middle 1800s. Settlers were drawn by minerals, harvestable forests and rich farmlands. The first permanent community was Prescott, selected as the site for Arizona's territorial capital in 1863. Four years later, it lost the capital to Tucson and finally to Phoenix, but mining and lumbering continued to draw settlers.

From Prescott, settlement spread northward, through the fertile Verde Valley, Sedona's beautiful Oak Creek Canyon and to the pine fringes of Flagstaff.

THE WAY IT IS • Despite its beauty, few people live in the extreme reaches of northwestern Arizona. Grand Canyon National Park and several Indian reservations occupy much of it. An area north of the canyon—and therefore isolated by it—is called the Arizona Strip. It's home to a few hardy Mormon settlements, high prairie ranches, some fine stands of pine and not much else.

However, the lower reaches of the Colorado Plateau are quite popular, particularly along the base of the Mogollon Rim. Even though this is still timber country, winters are relatively mild, while summers are sunny and warm.

Northwestern Arizona's lower reaches offer good potential for relocating families and year-around retirees who don't mind an occasional snowfall and chilly winter nights.

CAMP VERDE

Elevation • 3,133 feet

Location • In Yavapai County, just off I-17, 86 miles north of Phoenix.

Climate • Warm to hot summers; cool winters. July average high 107, low 60.5; January average high 56.5, low 29. Rainfall 19.24 inches; snowfall five inches.

Population • 6,420

Population trend • Gained 5.9 percent per year during the Eighties.

Property tax • $13.81 per $100 valuation (assessed at 10 percent real value).

Unemployment rate (1989) • 4.5 percent

Centuries ago, Sinagua Indians built a compex society in northwestern Arizona, such as the so-called Montezuma's Castle near Camp Verde. Then they mysteriously disappeared around the 14th century.

If you like small town living, you may like to retire in historic Camp Verde. The oldest settlement in the Verde Valley, it was established in 1865 as an Army fort to protect settlers from Indian raids. Remnants of the garrison are preserved in Fort Verde State Park.

The town is rather ordinary looking, but it's in a good location, just off a major interstate highway and within a short drive of an assortment of tourist lures. It's popular with the horsy set.

Economy • Construction, tourism and light industry form Camp Verde's rather limited economic base.

Job prospects • They're below average, according to the Camp Verde Chamber of commerce. Most residents commute to Cottonwood and Sedona to work, since this isn't a commercial center.

Real estate • Homes are rather inexpensive, perhaps $50,000 for a typical three-bedroom. A few new subdivisions are being built in the Verde Valley. A 42-unit low income senior housing project is available for retirees.

The media • One weekly newspaper, the *Journal*. TV via relay from Flagstaff and Phoenix.

Medical services • Most are in Cottonwood.

Industrial facilities • Five small industrial sites are available.

Transportation • Nearby I-17 brings Greyhound and Arizona Central lines. The local airport has a 4,000-foot unpaved runway; no lights or fuel.

Education • Elementary and high schools only.

Local government • Incorporated in 1986; mayor, six council members and a town manager.

Places to stay • Three motels and three campgrounds.

Leisure facilities • A recreation center, large senior center, tennis courts and a horse arena.

Tourist lures • Fort Verde State Historic Park, plus the other Verde Valley attractions (see Cottonwood below).

Contacts • Camp Verde Chamber of Commerce, P.O. Box 1665, Camp Verde, AZ 86322; phone 567-9294.

Town of Camp Verde, P.O. Box 710, Camp Verde, AZ 86322; 567-6631.

COTTONWOOD

Elevation • 3,300 feet

Location • In Yavapai County, in the heart of the Verde Valley, about 20 miles southwest of Sedona.

Climate • Warm summers, mild to chilly winters. July average high 98.4, low 66; January average high 58.2, low 28.4. Rainfall 12.21 inches; snowfall five inches.

Population • 5,770

Population trend • Gained 2.7 percent per year in the Eighties.

Property tax • $11.18 per $100 assessed valuation.

Unemployment rate (1989) • 5.9 percent

Although not very large, Cottonwood is the commercial center of the Verde Valley. It's actually a town with two faces. Newer Cottonwood is a typical collection of small shopping centers and subdivisions, while Old Cottonwood offers a handful of false front stores housing Indian crafts shops, antique stores and a couple of curio shops.

The town dates from the 1870s when soldiers from nearby Camp Verde were stationed here. Settlers followed, and named their hamlet for a nearby stand of cottonwoods.

Clarkdale is a smaller town just to the south, with an oldstyle business district. It was built as a model company town in 1914 to house workers for a large smelter that processed copper ore from nearby Jerome. The smelter has shut down and Clarkdale today is a quiet little place with an old-fashioned Main Street USA feel. Interestingly, another model community—Verde Valley Ranch—is being built nearby. A project of the Phelps Dodge Corporation, it will feature 1,700 homes, a golf course, a lake and river access.

Economy • Since Cottonwood is the trade center for the Verde

Valley, its economy is rooted in retail and service areas. Retired people make up 25 percent of the Cottonwood-Clarkdale population.

Job prospects • Cottonwood offers a rather tepid employment market, according to the local Job Service office. Most positions are in retail sales, tourism and other service areas. Some residents commute to motel, restaurant and sales jobs in Sedona.

Real estate • Cottonwood-Clarkdale are bedroom communities for service workers Sedona; three-bedroom home prices range from $60,000 to $80,000.

The media • Biweekly *Verde Independent*. TV via feeds from Flagstaff and Phoenix, plus 12-channel cable.

Medical services • A 104-bed hospital.

Industrial facilities • Two industrial parks near the airport.

Transportation • Greyhound at Camp Verde, 15 miles away. Cottonwood Airport with 4,250-foot paved, lighted runway; charter service and rental cars.

Education • Verde Campus of Yavapai College, plus elementary, junior high and high schools.

Local government • Incorporated in 1960; mayor, six council members and a city manager.

Places to stay • Seven motels, offering an inexpensive alternative to Sedona's resorts, a few campgrounds and RV parks.

Leisure facilities • Four parks, a recreation center, golf course, a public pool and the usual bowling alleys, tennis courts and such.

Tourist lures • Cottonwood is a good base for exploring nearby attractions such as Sedona-Oak Creek Canyon, Tuzigoot National Monument, Montezuma's Castle National Monument, Fort Verde State Historic Park and the historic mining town of Jerome.

Contacts • Verde Valley Chamber of Commerce, 1010 S. Main St., Cottonwood, AZ 86326; 864-7593.

City of Cottonwood, 827 N. Main St., Cottonwood, AZ 86326; 864-5526.

FLAGSTAFF

Elevation • 6,905 feet

Location • In Coconino County, on I-40 and I-17, midway between Arizona's eastern and western borders.

Climate • Warm summers, cool to cold winters. July average high 81.1, low 50.6; January average high 42.2, low 14.6. Rainfall 19.8 inches; snowfall 84.4 inches.

Population • 43,780

Population trend • Gained 2.6 percent per year in the Eighties.

Property tax • $9.77 per $100 assessed valuation.
Unemployment rate (1991) • nine percent.

Flagstaff is the most versatile small city in Arizona, both for visitors and new residents. Northern Arizona University provides cultural opportunities, while fine museums and historic buildings preserve the area's past. Its population base is large enough to provide all the essential services. The nearby San Francisco Peaks offer alpine lures.

It does get nippy in winter, since it's the highest and most northern of northwestern Arizona's larger towns. However, severe storms are rare and winters are mild if you compare them with the Midwest.

If you like the great outdoors, you'll find it in abundance. Flagstaff is the seat of Coconino County, the largest in the United States. More than 92 percent of its 11,896,720 acres are within a national forest, monument, park (including the Grand Canyon) or other federal preserve. Nearly half the county's 96,000 residents live in Flagstaff.

The city's downtown is a mix of turn-of-the-century and modern buildings. Although most retail business has moved to the suburbs, old Flagstaff remains active and attractive.

Flagstaff was settled in the late 1870s by sheepmen. The railroad came through in 1882, providing an outlet for a growing lumbering industry. The odd name comes from a flagpole that may have been erected to guide westbound travelers. Some historians say limbs were stripped from a tall pine tree and a flag was hoisted on July 4, 1876, to honor America's centennial. The town was named in 1881 and incorporated three years later.

Economy • Although tourism is the main industry, lumbering, light manufacturing and education are important as well. With the presence of Lowell Observatory and a U.S. Geological Survey office, space sciences also figure in the economic picture.

Job prospects • The employment situation is "very competitive," according to the local Job Service office. Best prospects are in construction, retail sales, tourism and other service jobs.

Real estate • Three-bedroom home prices range from $70,000 up. A good selection is available in older homes, new subdivisions, townhouses and condos. The market is "very active," according to the local board of realtors.

The media • One daily, *The Arizona Sun* and a weekly, *The Nava-Hopi Observer*. TV feeds from Phoenix and Los Angeles, plus a cable system.

Medical services • A 110-bed hospital and two convalescent hospitals.

Industrial facilities • Four major industrial parks.

Transportation • Served by Greyhound, Nava-Hopi Bus Lines and Amtrak. Pulliam Airport has a 7,000-foot runway, with daily service by America West and Sky West airlines.

Education • Northern Arizona University, Yavapai Community College, eight private schools, 13 elementary, two junior high and three high schools.

Local government • Seat of Coconino County since 1891. Incorporated in 1894; mayor, six council members and a city manager.

Places to stay • Sixty-two motels, a youth hostel and seven RV parks and campgrounds.

Leisure facilities • Three public pools, an ice rink, symphony orchestra, four recreation centers, 20 parks, three golf courses and the usual bowling alleys, tennis courts and such.

Tourist lures • Flagstaff is Arizona's best-located city for sightseeing. It's a short drive to Grand Canyon National Park, Oak Creek Canyon, the outdoor lures of the San Francisco Peaks, Fairfield Snowbowl and Sunset Crater, Wupatki, Tuzigoot, Montezuma's Castle and Walnut Canyon national monuments. Local lures include several museums, Riordan State Historic Park and Lowell Observatory.

Contacts • Flagstaff Chamber of Commerce, 101 W. Santa Fe., Flagstaff, AZ 86004; 774-4505.

Community Development Office, City of Flagstaff, 211 W. Aspen St., Flagstaff, AZ 86001; 774-5281.

JEROME

Elevation • 5,248 feet

Location • In Yavapai County, on the slopes of Mingus Mountain in the Verde Valley west of Cottonwood.

Climate • Warm summers, cool to chilly winters. July average high 89.2, low 67.1; January average high 49.8, low 32.3. Rainfall 17.95 inches; snowfall 24.9 inches.

Population • 495

Population trend • Gained 1.8 percent per year in the Eighties.

Property tax • $13.55 per $100 assessed valuation.

Unemployment rate (1989) • 6.4 percent

If you like an idle pace and historic funk, you might consider Jerome for retirement. Don't go there looking for work, however. Although it was once a boomtown of copper production, things are pretty quiet these days. It's basically a scruffy hillside town frozen in time, popular with history buffs and tourists.

Historians say Jerome never was pretty. Cantilevered into the slopes of Cleopatra Hill, halfway up Mingus Mountain, it was one of Arizona's largest and wildest mining camps. In 1903, a visiting New York Sun reporter called it "the wickedest town in America."

Its terraced streets were lined with saloons and bawdy houses. Homes were so steeply terraced, claim old-timers, that you could look down your neighbor's chimney. Slides were common and the town jail skidded several dozen feet downhill, where it remains to this day.

The first claim was filed on Mingus Mountain in 1876. In 1883 the United Verde Copper Company built a smelter and the boom began. At its peak, Jerome bustled with 15,000 citizens. In less than 80 years, a billion dollars worth of copper, gold, silver, lead and zinc was rooted from the ground. Alternately leveled by fire and rebuilt, the town thrived until 1953, when the last copper mine was shut down.

Jerome has become a mecca for visitors fascinated by its wicked past. It has attracted a rather youthful population of artists and shop-keepers, as well. Instead of old miners dozing in the sun, one is more likely to see pretty young entrepreneurs who would look more at home in a bikini on Malibu Beach.

The business district, properly scruffy, is terraced on three levels as the highway switchbacks through town. Galleries, curio shops and an-tique stores occupy many of its old buildings. Red and green scars are still evident in the hillsides, where miners dug for gold, silver and cop-per.

Economy • Tourism.

Job prospects • There aren't many, unless you want to open a boutique or work in one.

Real estate • Three-bedroom home prices start around $50,000. If you're interested in restoration, an occasional turn-of-the-century fixer-upper reaches the market. Real oldies can go as high as $175,000.

The media • No local newspaper; three TV stations arrive by re-lay—one each from Phoenix, Flagstaff and Prescott.

Medical services • The nearest are in Cottonwood.

Industrial facilities • No industrial parks.

Transportation • Nearest facilities are in Cottonwood.

Education • One elementary and one high school.

Local government • Incorporated in 1899; mayor, six council members.

Places to stay • Two motels and three bed and breakfast inns.

Leisure facilities • Three parks and an archives research center.

Tourist lures • Jerome is the tourist lure, with three museums, a state historic park, three art galleries, several boutiques and period restaurants.

Contacts • Jerome Chamber of Commerce, P.O. Box K, Jerome, AZ 86331; 634-5105.

Jerome Historical Society, P.O. Box 156, Jerome, AZ 86331; 634-5477.

Town of Jerome, P.O. Box 335, Jerome, AZ 86331; 634-7943.

PAGE

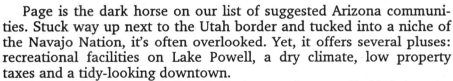

Elevation • 4,380 feet

Location • In Coconino County, near the Arizona-Utah border on the edge of the Navajo reservation.

Climate • Very dry; warm to hot summers, chilly to cold winters. July average high 97, low 71; January average high 45, low 24. Rainfall 4.78 inches; snowfall 4.9 inches.

Population • 7,285

Population trend • Gained 4.5 percent per year in the Eighties.

Property tax • $7.12 per $100 assessed valuation.

Unemployment rate (1989) • 4.2 percent

Page is the dark horse on our list of suggested Arizona communities. Stuck way up next to the Utah border and tucked into a niche of the Navajo Nation, it's often overlooked. Yet, it offers several pluses: recreational facilities on Lake Powell, a dry climate, low property taxes and a tidy-looking downtown.

Sitting high on a red dirt shelf above Lake Powell, it thrives on tourist business lured by Glen Canyon National Recreation Area. Neither Page nor its high plateau surroundings are particularly attractive, being rather devoid of shrubbery. But this planned community has a nice swept-clean look. It was created as the construction town for Glen Canyon Dam, with features such as underground utilities and a cluster of public schools rimmed by the main residential area.

East of Page is the core of the local economy—the huge coal-fed Navajo Generating Plant, operated by Phoenix' Salt River Project. It's currently the target of an environmental battle, accused of polluting the skies above the Grand Canyon. Consuming 24,000 tons of coal a day brought by rail from nearby mines, it produces enough electricity for a city of three million.

Economy • Tourism and public utilities balance the local economy. An estimated 3.5 million people visit Lake Powell National Recreation Area each year.

Job prospects • They're good only in tourism and public utilities. Seventy percent of the jobs are tied to these sources. The Page/Lake Powell Chamber of Commerce says overall job prospects are "about average."

Real estate • Three-bedroom houses average $90,000, according to the chamber of commerce.

The media • Two weeklies, the *Lake Powell Chronicle* and *Navajo-Hopi Observer*. TV feeds from Phoenix and Salt Lake, plus cable.

Medical services • One 25-bed hospital, two medical clinics and a mental health clinic.

Industrial facilities • A 102-acre industrial park.

Transportation • Page Airport, with a lighted 5,500-foot runway, is served by Sky West Airlines, plus charter lines.

Education • Extension courses from Yavapai Community College; two elementary schools, two junior highs and one high school.

Local government • Incorporated in 1975; mayor, six council members and a city manager.

Places to stay • Ten motels, including waterside resorts on Lake Powell; several private and national recreation area campgrounds and RV parks.

Leisure facilities • Three parks, a nine-hole golf course, senior citizen center, recreation center, public pool, bowling alleys and tennis courts.

Tourist lures • Glen Canyon National Recreation Area embraces adjacent Lake Powell and Glen Canyon Dam, offering boating, camping, picnicking, fishing and such. The Navajo Indian Reservation is next door, and both rims of the Grand Canyon are a few hours' drive.

Contacts • Page/Lake Powell Chamber of Commerce, 716 Rimview Dr., Page, AZ 86040; 645-2741.

City of Page, P.O. Box HH, Page, AZ 86040; 645-8861.

PAYSON

Elevation • 4,930 feet

Location • In Gila County, 94 miles northeast of Phoenix on State Route 87.

Climate • Warm summers, cool to chilly winters. July average high 92.5, low 58.5; January average high 53.1, low 23.7. Rainfall 20.77 inches; snowfall 25.1 inches.

• FLAGSTAFF

• PHOENIX

• TUCSON

Population • 8,370

Population trend • Gained 5.7 percent per year in the Eighties.

Property tax • $12.55 per $100 assessed valuation.

Unemployment rate (1991) • about nine percent.

Payson is tucked into a woodsy setting below the Mogollon Rim. This scenic mountain retreat might tempt you if you don't mind getting wet and maybe a bit chilly in winter. It's similar in setting to Flagstaff, but without the job potential or wide economic base, so it's a better bet for retired folk.

Well off Arizona's main traveled routes, it's popular as a summer retreat for Phoenicians fleeing the desert sizzle.

The town first saw life when prospectors found a bit of gold in the creek bottoms in 1881. They didn't find much, but the town grew anyway, as a ranching center. Author Zane Grey loved the timbered land below the Mogollon Rim. He built a hunting cabin northeast of town, where he wrote many of his books.

Downtown Payson's Old Main Street section recalls its cowboy past.

Economy ● Retirement and tourism provide Payson's economic base. More than 60 percent of its population is retired. The community has an active senior center and senior recreation program.

Job prospects ● Payson's Economic Development Corporation is working to attract light industry, although job prospects at this writing were below average. Best bets, says the local Job Service office, are in retail sales, tourism and other service jobs.

Real estate ● Housing ranges from older homes in downtown Payson to a several woodsy subdivisions and summer cabins. Prices for a three-bedroom start around $60,000 to $70,000.

The media ● Three weeklies, the *Mogollon Advisor, Rim Country News* and *Payson Roundup*. One local TV station, plus six from Phoenix and a 12-channel cable system.

Medical services ● One 44-bed hospital and three nursing homes.

Industrial facilities ● Two industrial parks.

Transportation ● Payson Airport has a lighted 5,000-foot runway.

Education ● A community college, two elementary schools, a junior high and high school.

Local government ● Incorporated in 1973; mayor, six council members and a town manager.

Places to stay ● Sixteen motels, nine RV parks and five campgrounds, plus others in the surrounding Tonto National Forest.

Leisure facilities ● Senior center, golf course, two parks, small zoo, bowling alleys and tennis courts.

Tourist lures ● Tonto National Forest provides the usual hiking, camping, picnicking and stuff. Tonto Natural Bridge, Zane Grey Cabin and Old Main Street draw visitors as well.

Contacts ● Payson Chamber of Commerce, P.O. Box 1380, Payson, AZ 85547; 474-4515.

Town of Payson, 303 N. Beeline Hwy., Payson, AZ 85547; 474-5242.

Payson Economic Development Corporation, 613 S. Beeline Hwy., Payson, AZ 85547; 474-5921.

PINE/STRAWBERRY

Elevation • Pine 5,448 feet; Strawberry 6,047 feet

Location • In Gila County, 15 miles northwest of Payson

Climate • Warm summers, cool to chilly winters. July average high 92.5, low 58.5; January average high 53.1, low 23.7. Rainfall 20.77 inches; snowfall 25.1 inches.

Combined population • 3,900

Population trend • Gained 12.3 percent per year in the Eighties.

Property tax • $11.77 per $100 assessed valuation.

Unemployment rate (1989) • 10.7 percent

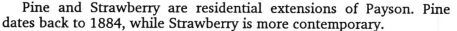

Pine and Strawberry are residential extensions of Payson. Pine dates back to 1884, while Strawberry is more contemporary.

Both are fast-growing, although their economy depends heavily on weekend visitors and second-home dwellers from Phoenix. The twin communities are popular with retirees. An active senior center provides camaraderie, social functions and such.

Economy • Primarily tourism and recreation.

Job prospects • Very limited; the few service jobs available are quite seasonal, since Pine and Strawberry are primarily summer retreats for desert dwellers. They offer better prospects for retirement than employment.

Real estate • Three-bedroom home prices range from $75,000 to $100,000, according to the local chamber of commerce.

The media • The weekly *Payson Roundup*. TV relays from Phoenix, Tucson and Prescott, plus 11-channel cable.

Medical services • One clinic; other facilities in Payson.

Industrial facilities • None.

Transportation • Shuttle bus service to Phoenix; Payson Airport is 15 miles away.

Education • One elementary school; high school in Payson.

Local government • Unincorporated; services provided by the Gila County Board of Supervisors.

Places to stay • Six motels and four RV parks in the area.

Leisure facilities • See Payson listing above.

Tourist lures • See Payson listing.

Contacts • Pine/Strawberry Chamber of Commerce, P.O. Box 333, Pine, AZ 85544; 476-3547.

Gila County Board of Supervisors, 1400 E. Ash St., Globe, AZ 85501; 425-5763.

PRESCOTT

Elevation • 5,347 feet

Location • In Yavapai County, on State Route 89, about midway between Phoenix and Flagstaff.

Climate • Warm summers, cool to chilly winters. July average high 88.9, low 56.9; January average high 50.1, low 21.5. Rainfall 18.1 inches; snowfall 23.7 inches.

Population • 25,040

Population trend • Gained 2.6 percent per year in the Eighties.

Property tax • $12.13 per $100 assessed valuation.

Unemployment rate (1989) • 4.7 percent

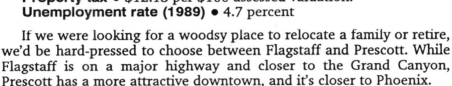

If we were looking for a woodsy place to relocate a family or retire, we'd be hard-pressed to choose between Flagstaff and Prescott. While Flagstaff is on a major highway and closer to the Grand Canyon, Prescott has a more attractive downtown, and it's closer to Phoenix.

So, flip a coin.

Friendly natives may gently correct you when you say "Pres-kott." It's "PRESS-kit," with the last syllable bitten off quickly. Even local radio announcers, alleged guardians of proper pronunciation, say it that way.

Once you've learned the language, townsfolk will boast of PRESS-kit's idyllic location, between the dry high desert and the cool pines of PRESS-kit National Forest. The town has several art galleries and an active performing arts center. Two colleges and a highly-respected aeronautical university provide an academic base. It also has a few museums, several antique shops and the Bradshaw Mountains for a playground. History? Why, PRESS-kit is where it all began!

When Arizona was sliced free from New Mexico in 1863 to become its own territory, the mineral-rich central highlands was selected as the site for a capital. It was first located at nearby Fort Whipple, then in Prescott itself. A town was laid out in a neat grid and a sturdy log and whipsaw-board governor's mansion was constructed. In 1867, before something fancier could be built, the capital was shifted to Tucson, and eventually wound up in Phoenix. But the town has done just fine without it, as a trading, ranching and lumbering center.

Prescott looks more like a vintage New England village than a Southwestern community. Early American homes and occasional Victorians line streets shaded by mature trees. Many business buildings are of red brick. But don't be fooled. The town is decidedly Western, with several cowboy shops and galleries. Locals claim that their annual Frontier Days is America's oldest rodeo, dating back to 1888.

Economy • Prescott offers a good economic balance of tourism, education, light manufacturing and retail sales.

Job prospects • Most in demand are skilled trades and clerical jobs. Four out of ten positions are in the services area, mostly tourism, while retail trade is second and construction is third. Manufacturing, in fourth place, is gaining quickly as more light industries are drawn to the area.

Real estate • Older homes and new planned developments comprise Prescott's realty mix. Average price of a three-bedroom home is $80,000 to $125,000.

The media • One daily, *The Prescott Courier* and a twice-weekly, *The Prescott Sun.* Two local TV stations, five channels from Phoenix and cable service.

Medical services • A 208-bed hospital, a 129-bed regional medical center, 208-bed veterans' hospital and domiciliary, five nursing homes and an adult day care center.

Industrial facilities • Five industrial parks.

Transportation • Served by Greyhound. Ernest A. Love Field has two runways, with scheduled flights by Mesa Airlines.

Education • Embry Riddle Aeronautical University, Yavapai Community College, Prescott College (four-year liberal arts), five private schools, six public elementary, two middle and one high school.

Local government • Seat of Yavapai County. Incorporated in 1881; mayor, six council members and a city manager.

Places to stay • Twenty-five motels and hotels, seven national forest campgrounds, six private campgrounds and RV parks.

Leisure facilities • Several public parks, zoo, three public pools, two golf courses, four art galleries, roller skating rink, plus tennis courts, racquetball courts, bowling alleys and such.

Tourist lures • Surrounding Prescott National Forest offers the usual outdoor pursuits. The town has five museums including the excellent Sharlot Hall Museum that includes the original territorial governor's mansion.

Contacts • Prescott Chamber of Commerce, P.O. Box 1147 (117 W. Goodwin St.), Prescott, AZ 86302; 445-2000.

City of Prescott, P.O. Box 2059 (201 S. Cortez St.) Prescott, AZ 86302; 445-3500.

Prescott Area Economic Development Commission, P.O. Box 671 (1500 E. Highway 69), Prescott, AZ 86302; 445-2290.

SEDONA

Elevation • 4,240 feet

Location • In Oak Creek Canyon, 27 miles south of Flagstaff; divided between Coconino and Yavapai counties.

Climate • Warm summers; temperate winters; occasional frost. July average high 95.1, low 65.1; January average high 55, low 29.7. Rainfall 17.15 inches; snowfall 8.8 inches.

Population • 14,000

Population trend • Gained 7.8 percent a year during the Eighties.

Property tax • $9.10 per $100 assessed valuation.

Unemployment rate (1989) • Five percent

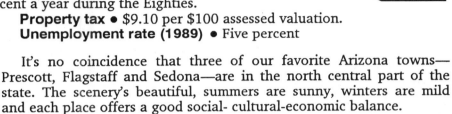

It's no coincidence that three of our favorite Arizona towns—Prescott, Flagstaff and Sedona—are in the north central part of the state. The scenery's beautiful, summers are sunny, winters are mild and each place offers a good social- cultural-economic balance.

Sedona is the most affluent of the three and it's certainly in a striking setting, surrounded by the redrock palisades of Oak Creek Canyon. In fact, this may be the most beautiful civic setting in the world. When Frank Lloyd Wright first saw the canyon, he said simply: "Nothing should ever be built here."

One of Arizona's preferred local retreats, Sedona lures natives by the thousands, seeking solace from the summer sun of Phoenix. They return in the fall to admire the saffron leaves of sycamore, aspen and cottonwood along Oak Creek. Sunlight and shadows play off red sandstone buttes, spires and fluted cliffs. We find it hard to believe that all who live here don't drop whatever they're doing each evening to admire the sunset.

Despite its tempting beauty, Oak Creek Canyon didn't attract settlers until the 1870s when farm families homesteaded land in the lower canyon. By 1902, the colony was large enough to be put on the map. Brothers Ellsworth and Carl Schnebly, the town's founders, petitioned for a post office. They operated it out of Carl's boarding house and named it for his wife, Sedona.

Early in this century, Hollywood movie makers were attracted by the area's handsome rock formations. Artists were drawn by the isolation and beauty. Then resort-builders arrived. That put an end to the isolation, but fortunately, most of the beauty remains.

Although it's nearly a century old, Sedona wasn't incorporated until 1988. It has grown considerably in recent years, more than doubling its population since 1976. While not a model of urban planning, the town still retains much of its early-day charm. There are no high-rises to block those orange-hued rocks and no neon to compete with the canyon's light-and-shadow shows.

The town is split between Coconino and Yavapai counties. The original site in Coconino county (which locals call "Uptown Sedona") hasn't changed much in the past 20 years. Much of the growth is on the Yavapai side, where developers have taken a cue from Uptown and avoided neon and high-rises. State Highway 89-A through "new" Sedona is lined with spur streets leading to planned residential areas with predictable names like Shadows Estates, Settlers Rest, the Palisades, Western Hills, Rolling Hills and Harmony Hills.

The town is blatantly tourist-oriented, but it's upscale tourism, for the most part. More than two dozen galleries display Western and other contemporary art. Performing arts thrive as well, with plays, musicales and outdoor concerts presented each summer. Some of Arizona's finest resorts are tucked beneath Oak Creek Canyon's redrock cliffs, and the town has a deserved reputation as a dining center.

Economy • Tourists and affluent retirees fuel Sedona's economic machinery.

Job prospects • More than half the jobs are in retail sales, tourism and other services. There isn't much available in the professions or skilled trades. Most people don't come here to earn money; they come here with money.

Real estate • Sedona is easy to love but difficult to afford. Average three-bedroom home prices are over $150,000 and those with any sort of view go much higher.

The media • Two local papers—the semi-weekly *Sedona/Red Rock News* and weekly *Tab*. Television feeds from Flagstaff, Prescott and Phoenix, plus cable.

Medical services • One in-patient and one out-patient clinic; hospitals are in Flagstaff and Cottonwood.

Industrial facilities • Tourism is the industry here.

Transportation • Nava-Hopi bus line. Scheduled air service by Air Sedona from Sedona Airport to Phoenix; 5,100-foot lighted runway.

Education • Extension courses provided by Yavapai Community College; several private schools plus public elementary schools. High school students go to Cottonwood or Flagstaff.

Local government • Incorporated in 1988; government services shared by Coconino and Yavapai counties.

Places to stay • Dozens of motels plus several world-class resorts. Three RV parks and several national forest campgrounds in Oak Creek Canyon.

Leisure facilities • A community center, art center, parks and picnic areas in Oak Creek Canyon, golf and tennis at area resorts.

Tourist lures • Sedona and its setting are the only lures tourists need. Jeep trips into redrock country, canyon hikes, music and art festivals, boutiques and galleries make this one of Arizona's most-visited communities.

Contacts • Sedona/Oak Creek Canyon Chamber of Commerce, P.O. Box 478 (Highway 89A and Forest Road), Sedona, AZ 86336; 282-7722.

City of Sedona, P.O. Box 30002, Sedona, AZ 86336; 282-3113.

VERDE VILLAGE

Elevation • 3,300 feet

Location • In Yavapai County, adjacent to Cottonwood in the Verde Valley.

Climate • Warm summers, mild to chilly winters. July average high 98.4, low 66; January average high 58.2, low 28.4. Rainfall 12.21 inches; snowfall five inches.

Population • 4,415

Population trend • Gained 17.4 percent a year during the Eighties.

Property tax • $13.15 per $100 assessed valuation.

Unemployment rate (1989) • 6.2 percent

Verde Village is a planned community established in 1970. It's populated primarily by retirees and summer weekenders from the Valley of the Sun. Three-fourths of its residents, in fact, are retired. During the 1980s, it was the fastest growing community in the Verde Valley and one of the fastest in Arizona.

Cottonwood and Yavapai County provide virtually all of Verde Village's services. See Cottonwood listing above for details.

Contact • Verde Valley Chamber of Commerce, 1010 S. Main St., Cottonwood, AZ 86326; 634-7593.

WILLIAMS

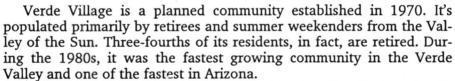

Elevation • 6,770 feet

Location • In Coconino County, 30 miles west of Flagstaff on I-40; 60 miles south of the Grand Canyon.

Climate • Temperate summers, mild to cold winters. July average high 83.1, low 54.8; January average high 44.3, low 21.3. Rainfall 21.21 inches; snowfall 75.8 inches.

Population • 2,500

Population trend • Gained 1.1 percent per year in the Eighties.

Property tax • $10.45 per $100 assessed valuation.

Think of Williams as a small, sleepy Flagstaff. Like its larger brother, it's rimmed by national forests, with four seasons and easy access to northwestern Arizona's natural attractions.

This is your place if you're the outdoor type seeking small-town living and a slow pace. You can golf in summer and hit the slopes at the Williams Ski Area in winter. This is not your place if you're job-hunting. Growth is very slow and unemployment is higher than the state average.

Williams is the closest town to the Grand Canyon's South Rim, and the chamber likes to boast about that. In fact, it calls itself the Williams-Grand Canyon Chamber of Commerce. A vintage steam train chugs visitors between the town and that grand gorge.

The small business district is caught in a pleasant 1930s time warp. Other than several new motels, it has changed little from the days when it was an important pause on the Santa Fe Railway and old Route 66. Cattle ranching began in the area in the late 1870s. The railroad arrived in the 1880s to haul logs for the local timber industry and the town began growing.

Economy ● The town's slow-paced economy is dependent primarily on tourism, with a bit of lumbering, agriculture and mining.

Job prospects ● They're very scarce; tourist jobs here are seasonal.

Real estate ● There's little in the way of new construction. Homes are in the $50,000 to $60,000 range.

The media ● One weekly, the *Williams News*. TV via relay from Flagstaff and Phoenix, plus cable.

Medical services ● One emergency center; nearest hospitals are in Flagstaff.

Industrial facilities ● One 40-acre industrial park.

Transportation ● Greyhound; Nava-Hopi bus lines; steam train to the Grand Canyon. Williams Municipal Airport has a 6,000-foot runway; charter service.

Education ● One elementary and one high school.

Local government ● Incorporated in 1901; mayor, six council members and a city manager.

Places to stay ● Twenty-three motels; five RV and trailer parks, plus campgrounds in the surrounding Kaibab National Forest.

Leisure facilities ● Community center, five parks, a golf course, tennis courts, bowling alley, Williams Ski Area and riding stables.

Tourist lures ● The Grand Canyon, obviously, is the biggest lure. The vintage steam train service, started in 1990, was doing well at last report. The surrounding national forest lures the outdoor set.

Contacts ● Williams-Grand Canyon Chamber of Commerce, 820 W. Bill Williams Ave., Williams, AZ 86046; 635-4061.

Economic Development Commission, City of Williams, 113 S. First St., Williams, AZ 86046; 635-4451.

Chapter Ten

THE METROPOLITAN MIDDLE ᚕᚕᚕᚕᚕ

PHOENIX AND THE VALLEY OF THE SUN

The Valley of the Sun, a great desert basin rimmed by ruggedly handsome peaks, is the social, political and economic heart of Arizona. Sixty percent of the state's population lives here. Most of its 20 communities have merged together like thin pancake batter, creating an urban megalopolis 30 miles across. It's beginning to resemble a desert version of Los Angeles.

Despite its urban sprawl, it still retains some of the flavor of frontier Arizona. It's a delightfully curious mix of Old West and New Wave. You can pull on your Levi's and eat cowboy steaks or wrap yourself in society's most sophisticated trappings.

THE WAY IT WAS ● In a state rich with Spanish, Mexican and cowboy lore, settlement in the valley was rather routine. Indians farmed the area for several centuries, diverting water from the Salt River. Judging from archaeological sites, their population may have reached 100,000. Then they mysteriously vanished around 1400 A.D., abandoning their irrigation canals.

Later Pima Indians noted the deserted ditches and called their builders "Hohokam," which means "gone away" or "used up."

This Sonoran Desert basin dozed in the sun until a fellow with the forgettable name of John Smith started a hay camp in 1864. Ex-Confederate soldier Jack Swilling arrived three years later and formed a company of unemployed miners to dig out the abandoned Hohokam canals. The group soon had a fine wheat and barley crop. One of the settlers, a sophisticated Englishman named Darrel Duppa, predicted that a great city would rise from the site of the former Indian camp, as the fabled Phoenix bird rises from its own ashes every 500 years.

This Phoenix didn't take that long.

The area grew quickly, particularly after the Roosevelt Dam was completed on the Salt River in 1911, encouraging agricultural expansion. Then Arizona got a share of Colorado River water and the Phoenix bird took off, like the roadrunner with Wile E. Coyote on its tail. It has never looked back.

World War II brought the military, looking for year-around weather for flight and combat training. At the war's end, all that sunshine tempted many GIs to return.

THE WAY IT IS • The valley has become a major urban center with attendant congestion and even an occasional tinge of smog. In less than 50 years, it has made the transition from cow ponies to helicopter traffic spotters. For a period during the Eighties, Phoenix was out-pacing every other major city in America in population gain.

However, most of the present growth is not in Phoenix, but in its suburbs. The city itself gained only 2.5 percent a year during the Eighties. By comparison, Gilbert picked up 20 percent annually, Peoria 16 and Chandler 13. Some valley towns have doubled or tripled their population. Chandler, on the eastern rim, was America's fastest growing city of any size in 1986. According to 1990 census figures, Mesa was the nation's second fastest-growing city over 100,000 population in the decade of the Eighties.

The area's growth slowed toward the end of the decade, but it didn't stop. Population experts predict that the valley will regain its full momentum by the mid-1990s.

Some of the cities we recommend below are outside the valley itself. A few are a short drive from Phoenix, and others are south, along the Interstate 10 corridor between Phoenix and Tucson. Actually, no one has precisely defined the boundaries of this "Valley of the Sun." The is an invention of local boosters, not cartographers.

PHOENIX

Elevation • 1,117 feet

Location • In Maricopa County, in the geographic and economic heart of the Valley of the Sun.

Climate • Warm to hot summers; balmy winters with some chilly evenings. July average high 104.4, low 78.3; January average high 64.6, low 38. Rainfall 6.74 inches; rare traces of snow.

Population • 984,275.

Population trend • Gained 2.5 percent a year during the Eighties.

Property tax • Varies with area; averages $12.05 per $100 assessed valuation (based on ten percent of real value).

Unemployment rate (1989) • 4.4 percent

It's wonderful that the Phoenix bird rose to build a new city over prehistoric Hohokam canals. But did the old bird have to get this big?

By every measure, Phoenix is the state's social, economic and manufacturing leader. From 1980 to 1987, it ranked first in population gain among major U.S. cities, swelling by 30 percent. It's now the ninth largest city in the country.

Phoenix is not only growing; it's rebuilding and improving. It has plunged into the largest municipal improvement project in America's history. In 1988, citizens voted a $1.1 billion bond issue for a total revamping of the downtown area. By the time construction dust settles in the mid-1990s, the town will have a new art museum, history museum, science and technology museum, theater for the performing arts, aquatic center and several new public parks.

Amazingly however, in the ninth largest city in America, in an urban core of high-rises and busy sidewalks, you can still find a place to park.

The Phoenix story began rather simply. Early settlers realized that the old Hohokam canals could still draw water from the nearby Salt River. A town was surveyed in 1870 and a few adobe houses went up. The railroad arrived in 1887, bringing people anxious to get a look at the Wild West. They began replacing those mud huts with Victorian houses and brick bungalows that gave the place a New England-in-the-desert look. Just 19 years after its founding, Phoenix snatched the state capitol from Prescott.

Then with an assured water supply from the Salt River Project, the town soon became Arizona's largest city.

Economy • It's versatile, vibrant and growing. Manufacturing produces most of the income. It employs more than 140,000 people and accounts for nearly one in five jobs. Phoenix is the nation's third largest producer of electronics. Retirees and tourists are a significant part of this economic base as well.

Job prospects • Obviously, they're varied. Tourism and other services employ the most people—28.1 percent. Next is manufacturing, with 18 percent, followed by retailing at 17.7 percent. Thousands of seasonal tourist jobs open up in winter. Since Phoenix is the state capital, government is a major employer. The city's unemployment rate declined nearly two percentage points during the last decade.

Real estate • Housing is likewise varied, with homes ranging from $60,000 to $80,000 in the older southwest Phoenix area up to $100,000 in the newer developing areas. When we talked with realtors from a Century 21 office in 1991, the real estate market was moderately active.

The city's overall housing cost is higher than most of the rest of Arizona, yet it's a bargain when compared with other major cities. For instance, home prices are about half what they are in Los Angeles and the San Francisco Bay Area.

The media • Two major dailies, the *Arizona Republic* and *Phoenix Gazette*, plus 50 or more smaller newspapers in the metropolitan area. Eight local TV stations and cable.

Medical services • Twenty hospitals, two psychiatric hospitals and many clinics and extended care facilities.

Industrial facilities • Numerous industrial parks; many with air and rail service.

Transportation • Served by Greyhound and Amtrak. Sky Harbor International Airport is the ninth largest in the world for operations. Twenty-two airlines offer more than 400 daily departures. Eleven other airports are in the area.

Education • Arizona State University is in nearby Tempe; Phoenix has 79 technical and business colleges, four religious colleges and five community colleges. Private elementary and high schools number 50.

Local government • Incorporated in 1881; became the state capitol in 1889. The city government is operated by a mayor, eight-member council and city manager.

Places to stay • More than 170 resorts, hotels and motels. Dozens of mobile home and RV parks.

Leisure facilities • The full range of spare time goodies: public pools, golf courses, tennis courts, art galleries, museums and 38 parks, including seven huge wilderness parks in the surrounding mountains.

Tourist lures • Only the Grand Canyon draws more visitors to Arizona. Tourist attractions include the excellent Heard Indian Museum, many other fine museums, Arizona State Capitol, Desert Botanical Garden, Heritage Square and the Phoenix Zoo. Of course, many visitors come just for the sun—to luxuriate in luxury resorts. The most famous, the Arizona Biltmore, is in Phoenix, while others are in the rocky foothills around Phoenix, Scottsdale and Paradise Valley.

Contacts • Public Information Office, City of Phoenix, 251 W. Washington St., Phoenix, AZ 85003; 262-7176.

Phoenix and Valley of the Sun Convention and Visitors Bureau, 505 N. Second St., Suite 300, Phoenix, AZ 85004; 254-6500.

Phoenix Economic Growth Group, 400 N. Fifth St., Room 1625, Phoenix, AZ 85004; (800) FOR-PHNX or 253-9747.

Phoenix Chamber of Commerce, 34 W. Monroe St., Suite 900, Phoenix, AZ 85003; 254-5521.

APACHE JUNCTION

Elevation ● 1,715 feet

Location ● In Pinal County along the foothills of the Superstition Mountains, at the junction of highways 60 and 89. About 30 miles east of Phoenix.

Climate ● Hot, dry summers; warm, mild winters with cool nights. July average high 104.3, low 74.2; January average high 64.9, low 35.6. Rainfall 7.52 inches; occasional traces of snow.

Population ● 16,730

Population trend ● Gained six percent a year during the Eighties.

Property tax ● $16.67 per $100 assessed valuation.

Unemployment rate (1989) ● 10.4 percent.

Apache Junction came of age in the last decade as a Snowbird and retirement retreat. It has nearly a hundred RV and mobile home parks and it's also a bedroom town for the Valley of the Sun.

Scattered over ruggedly scenic desert below the legendary Superstition Mountains, the town sits at the junction of the Apache Trail (State Highway 88) and U.S. 60. It's the gateway to the Salt River Canyon and Tonto National Forest.

The "Trail" was carved through the rough canyon early in this century as a construction road for the Theodore Roosevelt Dam. Completed in 1911, it's the cornerstone of the Salt River Project, providing water to the Valley of the Sun. In the 1920s, Highway 60 was cut through the Pinal Mountains to the south, linking Phoenix with the silver and copper mines of Globe.

Apache Junction was born in 1922 when entrepreneur George Cleveland Curtis put up a tent and started peddling sandwiches and water to travelers along the two routes.

Economy ● It's based almost entirely on the three R's of Arizona growth: recreation, retirement and real estate. Its popularity as a bedroom community to next-door Phoenix has led to a moderate boom in home construction.

Job prospects ● They aren't very good, but it's a nice place to live if you're willing to commute to work in Phoenix. Retail trades, services and public administration comprise half the work force.

Real estate ● Several planned communities, including senior villages, have been built in recent years. An average three-bedroom detached home ranges between $46,000 to $55,000.

The media ● One weekly, *The Apache Junction Independent*. TV provided by Phoenix, plus relays from Tucson and cable channels.

Medical services • One medical clinic, plus a hospital eight miles west.

Industrial facilities • No industrial parks, since the town is primarily residential and tourist-oriented.

Transportation • Served by Greyhound; nearest airports are in the Phoenix metro area.

Education • Apache Junction extension of Central Arizona College (two-year), plus four elementary, one junior high and one high school.

Local government • Incorporated in 1978; mayor, six council members and a city manager.

Places to stay • Five motels and 93 mobile home and RV parks.

Leisure facilities • Four parks and a public pool.

Tourist lures • The Superstition Mountains, home to the legendary Lost Dutchman Mine, are in Apache Junction's back yard. Lost Dutchman State Park offers camping, picnicking and hiking trails. Reservoirs of the Salt River Canyon and old Western-style towns such as Tortilla Flat and Gold Field also draw visitors.

Contacts • Apache Junction Chamber of Commerce, P.O. Box 1747, Apache Junction, AZ 85217; 982-3141.

Office of Economic Development, City of Apache Junction, 1001 N. Idaho Rd., Apache Junction, AZ 85217; 982-8002, extension 63.

ARIZONA CITY

Elevation • 1,505 feet

Location • In Pinal County along the I-10 "growth corridor" between Phoenix and Tucson, about 55 miles from each city. Eight miles from Casa Grande.

Climate • Warm to hot summers; warm winters with some cool evenings. July average high 105, low 75.1; January average high 67, low 35.7. Rainfall 8.45 inches; occasional trace of snow.

Population • 2,025

Population trend • Gained 10.5 percent per year in the Eighties.

Property tax • $15.48 per $100 assessed valuation.

Unemployment rate (1989) • 10.6 percent.

Arizona City was invented in 1960 as a planned community, with a lake, golf course and parks among its amenities. It sits amidst rich agricultural fields, halfway between Phoenix and Tucson.

Economy • It's based largely on light industry and retail, with some retirees.

Job prospects • Although the unemployment rate was rather high at this writing, the town is working to attract industry and prospects may have improved by now. Among its smokeless industries are Meyers Bakery, Davis Electronics and Parsons Textiles. Agriculture is still active in the area.

Real estate • Virtually all homes are in planned developments and other subdivisions, since this is a new city. Prices for a three-bedroom range from $50,000 to $80,000, according to the Casa Grande Board of Realtors.

The media • Daily *Dispatch* and weekly *Shopper*, both from Casa Grande. TV from Tucson and Phoenix.

Medical services • See Casa Grande listing below.

Industrial facilities • Two industrial parks.

Transportation • See Casa Grande listing below.

Education • Central Arizona College near Casa Grande; one elementary and one high school in Arizona City.

Local government • Unincorporated; government services provided by the Pinal County Board of Supervisors.

Places to stay • Six motels and two RV parks in the surrounding area.

Leisure facilities • Eighteen-hole golf course, 48-acre lake, public park, community center and tennis courts.

Tourist lures • Not many. Nearby Picacho Peak State Park, site of the westernmost Civil War battle, offers camping, picnicking and hiking.

Contact • Arizona City Chamber of Commerce, P.O. Box 5, Arizona City, AZ 85223; 466-5141.

AVONDALE

Elevation • Approximately 1,000 feet

Location • In Maricopa County, on the western edge of the Valley of the Sun, just off I-10, about 20 miles from downtown Phoenix.

Climate • Warm to hot summers; balmy winters with some cool evenings. July average high 106.8, low 75.3; January average high 66.9, low 35.8. Rainfall 7.56 inches; rare traces of snow.

Population • 12,545

Population trend • Gained 4.9 percent a year during the Eighties.

Property tax • $11.40 per $100 assessed valuation.

Unemployment rate (1989) • 6.6 percent

Avondale is the largest of several small communities on this western rim of the Phoenix basin. If you don't care for the fused together metro-glop of greater Phoenix, you might like to settle out here. One can still find open desert between the borders of Avondale, Goodyear, Buckeye and Litchfield Park. Go a short distance farther west, and you find only desert—all the way to the California border.

The demographics of these communities are rather similar. They're growing more slowly than the valley's ballooning suburbs, so they're still rather small and they offer a balanced economy of manufacturing, retailing and a bit of agriculture. (See listings for Buckeye, Goodyear and Litchfield Park below.)

Avondale was developed by the Goodyear Tire and Rubber Company, which came here initially to grow cotton for tire treads, then started an aviation facility. A post office was opened in 1911 and the town was incorporated in 1945.

Economy • Nearby Luke Air Force Base, farming, light industry and retailing provide a balanced economic base.

Job prospects • There's considerable employment diversity among these outer fringe towns. Avondale's economic development department is nurturing a mix of industry, commercial and retail jobs.

Real estate • Avondale's growth has spurred the local construction industry. You can find older three-bedroom homes for as little as $50,000, ranging up to $80,000 if there's a bit of land attached.

The media • The weekly *Westsider, Chronicle* and *West Valley News* cover the local scene; dailies come from Phoenix. TV viewing is from Phoenix as well, along with an area cable company.

Medical services • A 192-bed hospital is 12 miles away; Avondale has a 120-bed nursing center.

Industrial facilities • Several industrial parks are in the area.

Transportation • Served by Greyhound. The Phoenix-Goodyear Airport, operated by the city of Phoenix, is nearby, with an 8,500-foot lighted runway. Phoenix' Sky Harbor International Airport is about 20 miles east.

Education • Classes available through Maricopa Community College; Avondale has four elementary schools and one high school.

Local government • Incorporated in 1946; mayor, six-member council and city manager.

Places to stay • Four motels, one resort and several RV parks in the area.

Leisure facilities • Six parks, five golf courses, an auto race track, community center and senior center, plus tennis, racquetball and handball courts.

Tourist lures • It's a family town, not a tourist town. Locals like the solitude of the surrounding desert, not yet devoured by asphalt. It's a short drive to the cultural and tourist offerings of Phoenix.

Contacts • Avondale Industrial Development Authority, City of Avondale, 525 N. Central, Avondale, AZ 85323; 932-2400.

Tri City West Chamber of Commerce, 501 W. Van Buren, Suite K, Avondale, AZ 85323; 932-2260.

BUCKEYE

Elevation ● 890 feet

Location ● In Maricopa County, on the far western edge of the Valley of the Sun just below I-10, about 30 miles from Phoenix.

Climate ● Warm to hot summers; balmy winters with some chilly evenings. July average high 107.3, low 74.3; January average high 67.1; low 34.3. Rainfall 7.08 inches; occasional trace of snow.

Population ● 3,985

Population trend ● Gained 1.7 percent a year during the Eighties.

Property tax ● $11.86 per $100 assessed valuation.

Unemployment rate (1989) ● 4.4 percent

Buckeye began life as a farming town in 1888 and got its nice earthy name from the Buckeye Canal, one of the first modern irrigation ditches in the state.

This quiet little hamlet is one of the slowest-growing communities in the valley and still maintains a small-town atmosphere. It's not economically isolated however; jobs and shopping are available in surrounding Avondale, Goodyear and Litchfield Park.

Economy ● Buckeye offers a balance between agriculture and light manufacturing.

Job prospects ● The job base isn't large and the town isn't growing much, but there are possibilities with several small factories here. Sixteen percent of the jobs are in this sector, while 19 percent are in the services area and 14 percent in retailing. Farming still provides 11 percent of the local payroll.

Real estate ● A few modern subdivisions are a-building. Prices range from $40,000 for older homes to $80,000 for newer ones.

The media ● Three weeklies, the *Buckeye Valley News, Westsider* and *West Valley View*; dailies come from Phoenix, along with most TV channels. The area has a small cable TV company as well.

Medical services ● No local hospital; eight within 36 miles.

Industrial facilities ● Several small industrial parks are close to Interstate 10.

Transportation ● Served by Greyhound; Buckeye Municipal Airport has a 4,300-foot runway; Phoenix' Sky Harbor International is about 35 miles away.

Education ● One private elementary school, plus a public elementary and high school.

Local government • Incorporated in 1931; mayor, six-member council and town manager.

Places to stay • Six motels, seven mobile home parks and an RV park.

Leisure facilities • A town museum, three parks, community center and tennis, racquetball and handball courts.

Tourist lures • Like Avondale, it's not a tourist area. The many lures of the Valley of the Sun are a short drive away.

Contacts • Buckeye Valley Chamber of Commerce, P.O. Box 717 (904 Monroe St.), Buckeye, AZ 85326; 386-2727.

Town of Buckeye, P.O. Box 175 (508 Monroe St.), Buckeye, AZ 85326; 256-2488.

Western Gateway Team, 800 S. Litchfield Rd., Goodyear, AZ 85338; 932-9138.

CAREFREE and CAVE CREEK

Elevation • Carefree 2,500 feet; Cave Creek 2,200 feet

Location • In Maricopa County, 25 miles northeast of Phoenix.

Climate • Warm to hot summers; mild winters with some chilly evenings. July average high 102, low 75.4; January average high 62, low 38.8. Rainfall 12.35 inches; occasional trace of snow.

Population • Carefree 1,760; Cave Creek 3,415.

Population trend • Carefree gained 6.9 percent and Cave Creek increased 8 per cent per year during the Eighties.

Property tax • $8.08 per $100 assessed value.

Unemployment rate (1989) • 7.5 percent in Cave Creek; no figures available for Carefree.

Sitting on the far fringes of the Valley of the Sun, these hamlets are twins in location only. As the name suggests, Carefree is a modern planned community. It appeals primarily to retired folks and commuters to Phoenix. Cave Creek is on the rustic side, a Western-style town that began as a mining camp in the 1870s.

Both towns are in handsome, rocky desert surrounded by rockier hills. They rate high on our list of desirable Arizona communities, particularly for retired folks or Snowbirds. However, temporary winter facilities are rather limited. The area is a bit cooler than Phoenix, since it's a few hundred feet higher.

The two hamlets balance one another nicely. One can luxuriate in

El Pedrigal Marketplace is an architectural curiosity near Carefree.

luxury resorts such as the Boulders and shop in stylish boutiques in Carefree, then get a cowboy steak at a saloon restaurant in Cave Creek.

Interstate 17, ten miles west, offers a quick 25-minute trip to downtown Phoenix. For serious shopping and dining, upscale Scottsdale is just a few miles south of Carefree.

Economy • It's pretty much based on tourism and bedroom commuting. The towns want to keep their rural desert ambiance and aren't working actively to attract industry.

Job prospects • They're pretty limited, since the focus here is retirement and commuting to Phoenix.

Real estate • Housing is expensive in this highly desirable area, ranging from $150,000 to $200,000 for a newer three-bedroom detached home.

The media • One weekly, the *Foothills Sentinel* and a monthly, the *Carefree Enterprise*. Many Phoenix TV channels, plus cable.

Medical services • One 24-hour medical center; complete facilities in nearby Scottsdale and Phoenix.

Industrial facilities • None.

Transportation • Nearest commercial transit is in Scottsdale and Phoenix.

Education • Public schools only.

Local government • Cave Creek incorporated in 1986 and Carefree in 1984. Council-manager government in Cave Creek; mayor, six council members and town administrator in Carefree.

Places to stay • One motel, plus the luxury Boulders Resort.

Leisure facilities • Two community centers, an adult center, two parks and three golf courses.

Tourist lures • Folks come here mostly for desert scenery, boutiques of Carefree and the frontier ambiance of Cave Creek. The surrounding desert rises into the wilds of Tonto National Forest, with hiking trails, Indian ruins and ample solitude.

Contacts • Carefree/Cave Creek Chamber of Commerce, P.O. Box 734, Carefree, AZ 85377; 488-3381.

Town of Cave Creek, 37622 N. Cave Creek Rd., Cave Creek, AZ 85331; 488-1400.

Town of Carefree, P.O. Box 740 (11 Sundial Circle), Carefree, AZ 85377; 488-1471 and 254-6232.

CASA GRANDE

Elevation • 1,398 feet

Location • In Pinal County, off I-10 midway between Phoenix and Tucson.

Climate • Warm to hot summers; dry, balmy winters with cool evenings. July average high 106.2, low 76; January average high 66, low 35. Rainfall 8.12 inches; snowfall rare.

Population • 18,610

Population trend • Gained 2.4 percent per year during the Eighties.

Property tax • $14.99 per $100 assessed valuation.

Unemployment rate (1991) • 6.9 percent

Casa Grande is a thriving working class town named for a large Indian adobe about 20 miles away. It was established in 1879 as a way station on a railroad being built to link Phoenix and Tucson. Incorporated in 1915, it's the largest community in Pinal County.

The surrounding area is essentially irrigated desert. The countryside isn't particularly attractive, but the air is clean, the climate's nice and homes are affordable.

The town is becoming popular with retirees, offering two senior centers and several mobile home parks. A few Snowbirds alight here as well, drawn by the relatively inexpensive facilities.

Economy • Originally agricultural-based, it's shifting toward light industry and the services sector.

Job prospects • They're "average" according to the local Job Service office. The best possibilities are in retail sales, cashiering, tourist-related jobs and business skills such as word processing and public contact work.

Real Estate • There's a fair amount of new home construction in the area, plus some older homes on the market, with prices for a three-bedroom ranging from $50,000 to $80,000. The market is "average," says the local board of realtors.

The media • One daily, the *Casa Grande Dispatch*. TV relays from Phoenix, plus a 26-channel cable service.

Medical services • A 100-bed hospital and 128-bed long-term care facility.

Industrial facilities • Eight industrial parks, some with rail access.

Transportation • Served by Greyhound. Casa Grande Airport has two 5,200-foot runways; served by feeder and charter lines.

Education • Signal Peak campus of Central Arizona Community College east of Casa Grande; one private elementary school plus eight public elementary and one high school.

Local government • Incorporated in 1915; mayor, six council members and a city manager.

Places to stay • Since Casa Grande is on the heavily-traveled Phoenix-Tucson corridor, it has 14 motels and 15 RV parks.

Leisure facilities • Ten parks, four golf courses within ten miles, two senior centers, two public pools, plus the usual tennis courts, bowling alleys and such.

Tourist lures • This is a good base of operations for exploring north and south, since it's midway between Phoenix and Tucson. Casa Grande Ruins National Monument and the fine Gila River Indian Arts and Craft Centers are nearby.

Contacts • Greater Casa Grande Chamber of Commerce, 575 N. Marshall St., Casa Grande, AZ 85222; 836-2125.

City of Casa Grande, 300 E. Fourth St., Casa Grande, AZ 85222; 421-8600.

Greater Casa Grande Valley Economic Development Foundation, 520 N. Marshall St., Casa Grande, AZ 85222; 836-6868.

CHANDLER

Elevation • 1,210 feet

Location • In Maricopa County, in the southeast corner of the Valley of the Sun.

Climate • Warm to hot summers; balmy winters. July average high 103.8, low 76.4; January average high 65, low 37.3. Rainfall 8.42 inches; occasional trace of snow.

Population • 88,785

Population trend • Gained 13 percent a year during the Eighties.

Property tax • $11.54 per $100 assessed valuation.

Unemployment rate (1989) • 3.9 percent

Chandler is one of the valley's authentic boom towns, zooming from 29,673 in 1980 to nearly 90,000 in 1990. Its growth rate was more than triple that of the rest of Maricopa County. All this adds up to an abundance of new housing, good job prospects and a generally upscale economy.

It doesn't have the cultural and tourist offerings of other valley communities, but no matter. Everything is within a few minutes' drive. Tempe's Arizona State University, for instance, is just across the freeway.

The town began when veterinarian Alexander John Chandler staked out an 1,800-acre ranch in the early 1890s. A smart operator, he brought in irrigation water, he then subdivided and sold off parcels for small farms. There's not much agricultural land left today, however.

Economy • It's very diversified, with a mix of construction, high tech industries, retail trade and service jobs.

Job prospects • Space age firms like Intel Corporation, Microchip Technology and Space Data Corporation offer potential, along with construction and retailing. Also, it's a short commute to the larger Phoenix job market.

Real estate • Prices for three-bedroom detached homes range from $70,000 to $100,000.

The media • The daily *Chandler Tribune* and weekly *Chandler Independent*, plus several other dailies in the Valley of the Sun. TV from Phoenix stations and cable.

Medical services • A 120-bed hospital.

Industrial facilities • Fifteen industrial parks, many with rail and air service.

Transportation • Served by Greyhound. Two local airports with lighted runways; Phoenix Sky Harbor International is 15 miles away.

Education • Two private elementary schools, a private high school plus the usual public schools.

Local government • Incorporated in 1920; mayor, six council members and a city manager.

Places to stay • Three hotels and four motels.

Leisure facilities • Three golf courses, three public pools, various parks and playing fields, plus tennis courts, racquetball courts and such.

Tourist lures • Most are elsewhere, although Chandler has two museums.

Contacts • Chandler Chamber of Commerce, 218 E. Arizona Ave., Chandler, AZ 85224; 963-4571.

Planning Department, City of Chandler, 200 E. Commonwealth St., Chandler, AZ 85225; 786-2867.

FLORENCE

Elevation • 1,493 feet

Location • In Pinal County, midway between Phoenix and Tucson on U.S. Highway 89.

Climate • Warm to hot summers; balmy winters with cool evenings. July average high 106.1, low 74; January average high 66.8, low 36.1. Rainfall 9.50 inches; occasional trace of snow.

Population • 6,890

Population trend • Gained 2.9 percent per year in the Eighties.

Property tax • $13.79 per $100 assessed value.

Unemployment rate (1989) • 2.8 percent

Sitting off to one side of the Phoenix-Tucson corridor, Florence is a pleasant surprise. It's one of Arizona's oldest towns, dating from 1866 when one Levi Ruggles laid out a townsite near a ford in the Gila River.

It's a handsome old town, with many 19th century homes in the Florence Townsite National Historic District. More than 100 of these structures are listed on the National Register of Historic Places. Styles range from Sonoran to Victorian to Arizona territorial. The Western-flavor downtown, with false front stores and sidewalk overhangs, seems right out of a cowboy movie set. In fact, it's often used by Hollywood film makers.

Although it's smaller than Casa Grande, Florence is the seat of Pinal County. Its courthouse is the town's architectural gem—an 1891 yellow brick structure with gingerbread trim and a hexagonal clock tower. Florence also is home to Arizona State Prison, built in 1909 to replace the notorious Yuma Territorial Prison.

With a rather slow growth rate, the town is a better bet for retirees than for job-seekers.

Economy • It's heavily focused on public administration and services, which account for two-thirds of the local payroll. The town isn't getting much job growth. In fact, retail sales slipped slightly between 1988 and 1989.

Job prospects • Despite a low unemployment rate, job possibilities are only average. The prison and county offices employ a third of the town's work force.

Real estate • Three-bedroom home prices range from $50,000 to $80,000.

The media • One weekly, the *Florence Reminder*; daily news coverage is provided by the *Casa Grande Dispatch*. TV relays from Phoenix and Tucson, plus cable.

Medical services • One 91-bed hospital, a nursing home and a residential care service home.

Industrial facilities • No industrial parks.

Transportation • Nearest airport is Coolidge, ten miles west.

Education • One elementary, junior high and high school.

Local government • Seat of Pinal County since 1875. Incorporated in 1908; mayor, six council members and a town manager.

Places to stay • One motel and two RV parks.

Leisure facilities • Two nine-hole golf courses, two parks, recreation center, a public pool and tennis courts.

Tourist lures • The historic district draws visitors, along with the present courthouse and the former court building, now McFarland State Historic Park. Casa Grande Ruins National Monument is nearby.

Contacts • Florence Chamber of Commerce, P.O. Box 929 (291 Bailey St.), Florence, AZ 85232; 868-5837.

Pinal County Development Board, P.O. Box 967, Florence, AZ 85232; 868-4331.

Town of Florence, P.O. Box 490 (1207 Main St.), Florence, AZ 85232; 868-5889.

FOUNTAIN HILLS

Elevation • 1,520 to 3,000 feet

Location • In Maricopa County, 30 miles northeast of Phoenix, just above Scottsdale.

Climate • Warm to hot summers; balmy winters with some cool evenings. July average high 105.1, low 74.2; January average high 66.7, low 36.4. Rainfall 8.06 inches; occasional trace of snow.

Population • 11,000

Population trend • Gained 16.6 percent a year in the Eighties.

Property tax • $9.42 per $100 assessed valuation.

Unemployment rate (1989) • 3.6 percent

An upscale planned community started in 1970, Fountain Hills is carefully laid over a rugged desert panorama, with elevations ranging up to 3,000 feet. It was created by Lake Havasu City's McCulloch Properties and designed by Charles Wood Jr., who also fashioned Disneyland.

No, Fountain Hills doesn't look like Disneyland. It's an attractive town with nice homes, backyard pools and a stylish downtown area with a giant fountain as its focal point. In fact, it's the tallest man-made geyser in the world. The surrounding Fountain Park is a nice place to be on a hot day.

Although retired people are drawn here, it actually has a rather low median age of 37. Many residents are professionals who commute to work in the Valley of the Sun.

Economy • It's essentially an upper middle class bedroom town, with small businesses and services as its economic base.

Job prospects • The low unemployment rate can be misleading. Fountain Hills doesn't have a large job base. The local labor force comprises less than 20 percent of the population. Most workers commute elsewhere.

Real estate • Housing is predictably expensive in this upscale suburb. Three-bedroom detached homes start around $100,000 and top $150,000 for newer models.

The media • The weekly *Times of Fountain Hills* and monthly *Sentinel*. TV from Phoenix, plus cable.

Medical services • One family health center and a clinic; other facilities nearby in Scottsdale.

Transportation • Mesa and Scottsdale airports are 13 miles away; Phoenix Sky Harbor International is 30 miles.

Education • One private K-12 school and two public elementary schools.

Local government • Incorporated in 1989; governed by the Town of Fountain Hills City Council.

Places to stay • Nearest motels and RV parks are in Mesa and Scottsdale.

Leisure facilities • Fountain Park, 18-hole golf course, equestrian center, botanical garden, community center and tennis courts.

Tourist lures • Some come to see that tall fountain, while the surrounding desert draws hikers and seekers of solitude. McDowell Mountain Regional Park is just north. Saguaro Lake and Canyon Lake of the Salt River Project are northeast.

Contact • Fountain Hills Chamber of Commerce, P.O. Box 17598 (12635 N. Saguaro Blvd.) Fountain Hills, AZ 85268; 837-1654.

GILBERT

Elevation • 1,273 feet

Location • In Maricopa County's southeast corner, next door to Chandler and about 20 miles from downtown Phoenix.

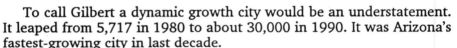

Climate • Warm to hot summers; balmy winters with cool evenings. July average high 104.3, low 74.1; January average high 64.9, low 35.6. Rainfall 7.52 inches; occasional trace of snow.

Population • 27,365

Population trend • Gained 19 percent a year.

Property tax • $12.55 per $100 assessed value.

Unemployment rate (1989) • 2.6 percent

To call Gilbert a dynamic growth city would be an understatement. It leaped from 5,717 in 1980 to about 30,000 in 1990. It was Arizona's fastest-growing city in last decade.

Obviously, Gilbert is more geared to employment and family-raising than it is to retirement. It has one of the lowest unemployment rates in the state. According to a 1990 estimate, 20,000 new homes will go up by century's end. There's nothing particularly scenic about the rather level desert terrain hereabouts. What Gilbert offers, obviously, is room to grow.

The town isn't all new. It dates back to an 1890s homestead filed by William A. Gilbert, and it was incorporated in 1920.

Economy • A pro-growth attitude, broad employment base and expanding shopping centers add fire to Gilbert's economic engine.

Job prospects • It offers one of Arizona's best markets, with a low unemployment rate and a constantly-expanding job base. The labor force increased by nearly 50 percent in the Eighties while joblessness dropped, even with the state's late-decade recession. Retail trade and services account for 40 percent of the local jobs while factories provide 17 percent. Not surprisingly, one out of eight jobs is in construction.

Real estate • Older three-bedroom homes start around $70,000 and new subdivisions range up to $100,000.

The media • One weekly, the *Gilbert Independent*; Phoenix provides the dailies. TV also comes from Phoenix and from a cable company.

Medical services • Two hospitals in Chandler and four in Mesa.

Industrial facilities • Twelve industrial parks with rail and air access.

Transportation • Served by Greyhound. Chandler and Mesa municipal airports are nearby; Phoenix Sky Harbor is 19 miles northwest.

Education • Mesa Community College is three miles northwest; Gilbert has the usual public schools.

Local government • Incorporated in 1920; mayor, six council members and a town manager.

Places to stay • Motels and mobile home parks in Chandler and Mesa.

Leisure facilities • Twenty-four golf courses within 15 minutes, public pool, recreation center, eleven parks plus racquetball and tennis courts.

Tourist lures • Gilbert is not far from the Superstition Mountains and Salt River Canyon.

Contacts • Gilbert Chamber of Commerce, P.O. Box 527 (1400 N. Gilbert Rd.), Gilbert, AZ 85234; 892-0056.

Economic Development Department, Town of Gilbert, P.O. Box 837 (119 N. Gilbert Rd.), Gilbert, AZ 85234; 892-0800.

GLENDALE

Elevation • 1,100 feet

Location • In Maricopa County, northwestern area of the Valley of the Sun.

Climate • Warm to hot summers; mild winters. July average high 104.4, low 78.3; January average high 64.6, low 38. Rainfall 6.74 inches; occasional trace of snow.

Population • 145,490

Population trend • Gained 4.6 percent a year during the Eighties.

Property tax • $12.68 per $100 assessed valuation.

Unemployment rate (1989) • 4.3 percent

Glendale is another of the mushroomburbs of the valley, a mix of bedroom community, shopping centers and manufacturing. Nearby Luke Air Force Base, the nation's largest fighter training facility, provides some civilian employment. Electronics, precision metal working and casting and aerospace activities also add to the job base.

Like Chandler and Gilbert, its main asset is growth space. began rather modestly, as a farming settlement by the Illinois Church of the Brethren in 1892.

Economy • It travels the spectrum from metal fabricating to light manufacturing to a growing retail market to military-civilian payrolls at Luke Air Force Base.

Job prospects • Glendale offers a broad selection of jobs, plus the possibility of civil service employment at the air base.

Real estate • A three-bedroom home in the Glendale area ranges from about $70,000 to $90,000.

The media • The biweekly *Glendale Star*, plus dailies from Phoenix, which also provides the community's TV.

Medical services • Three hospitals in Glendale and another three within a ten-minute drive; also six nursing homes.

Industrial facilities • Numerous industrial parks and factories.

Transportation • Served by Greyhound. Glendale Airport has a 5,350-foot lighted runway; Phoenix Sky Harbor is 30 minutes away.

Education • Glendale Community College, American Graduate School of International Management, plus three private elementary and one private high school, and the usual public schools.

Local government • Incorporated in 1910; mayor, six council members and a city manager.

Places to stay • Three motels and nine RV parks.

Leisure facilities • Many parks in Glendale and the surrounding area, six swimming pools, three golf courses, senior citizens' center, two roller rinks plus tennis and racquet ball courts and such.

Tourist lures • Glendale isn't a tourist town, but the Valley of the Sun's attractions are nearby.

Contacts • Glendale Chamber of Commerce, P.O. Box 249 (7105 N. 59th Ave.), Glendale, AZ 85311; 937-4754.

Economic Development Department, City of Glendale, 5850 W. Glendale Ave., Glendale, AZ 85301; 435-4169.

GOODYEAR

Elevation • Approximately 1,000 feet

Location • In Maricopa County, on the western fringe of the Valley of the Sun, 17 miles from Phoenix.

Climate • Warm to hot summers; mild winters with cool evenings. July average high 106.8, low 75.3; January average high 66.9, low 35.8. Rainfall 7.56 inches; occasional trace of snow.

Population • 5,230

Population trend • Gained 7.4 percent per year in the Eighties.

Property tax • $12.88 per $100 assessed valuation.

Unemployment rate (1989) • Four percent

If the name sounds familiar, it's because this little town was established by the Goodyear Tire and Rubber Company in 1916 to raise Egyptian cotton for tire cords. Originally, it was going to be called Egypt. Later, Goodyear located its aircraft division here.

This is another of those small communities on the western edge of

Valley of the Sun communities are the spokes; downtown Phoenix is the hub of Arizona's most dynamic growth area.

the valley, appealing to people who want to see some desert between the city borders. This isn't ruggedly handsome desert like that around Scottsdale and Fountain Hills, but at least it's open space.

Economy • Once focused on the nearby Litchfield Naval Air Facility and Goodyear Aircraft, the economic base is diversifying to include more light industry.

Job prospects • The unemployment rate is rather low, and such industries as Rubbermaid, a new McKesson plant and a large grocery distribution center provide job possibilities.

Real estate • A few subdivisions are being built, with three-bedroom prices between $60,000 and $80,000. Some older homes may be found for as little as $40,000 to $50,000.

The media • Two weeklies, the *Westsider Chronicle* and *West Valley View*. Daily news and TV programming comes from Phoenix; there's also TV cable service.

Medical services • A 192-bed hospital is 12 miles east.

Industrial facilities • Six industrial parks are nearby.

Transportation • Served by Greyhound. Phoenix-Goodyear Municipal Airport has an 8,500-foot lighted runway. Sky Harbor is about 20 miles east.

Education • Extension courses from Maricopa Community College, plus local public schools.

Local government • Incorporated in 1946; mayor, six-member council and city manager.

Places to stay • Four motels, one resort and one RV park.

Leisure facilities • A golf course, six parks, community center, public pool and tennis courts.

Tourist lures • Not much, other than the quiet of the surrounding desert. The lures of greater Phoenix are half an hour away.

Contacts • City of Goodyear, 119 N. Litchfield Rd., Goodyear, AZ 85338; 932-3494.

Tri City West Chamber of Commerce, 501 W. Van Buren, Suite K, Avondale, AZ 85323; 932-2260.

Western Gateway Team, 800 S. Litchfield Rd., Goodyear, AZ 85338; 932-9138.

LITCHFIELD PARK

Elevation • Approximately 1,000 feet

Location • In Maricopa County, just north of Goodyear on the western edge of the Valley of the Sun.

Climate • Hot summers; mild winters with cool evenings. July average high 106.8, low 75.3; January average high 66.9, low 35.8. Rainfall 7.56 inches; occasional trace of snow.

Population • 4,220

Population trend • Gained 1.6 percent per year in the Eighties.

Property tax • $8.88 per $100 assessed valuation.

Unemployment rate (1989) • 2.3 percent

Litchfield Park also was hatched by the Goodyear Tire and Rubber Company, and it was named for the firm's vice president, Paul W. Litchfield. It was started in 1926 as a planned, self-contained company town. Much of that careful planning is still evident in this prim little city.

Like its Goodyear neighbors, Litchfield Park is growing rather slowly, but expect that pace to increase in the Nineties as ever-expanding Phoenix creeps westward.

Economy, education and other community features • Similar to Goodyear's (see above).

Local government • Incorporated in 1987; mayor, six-member council and city manager.

Places to stay • One resort; motels and RV parks in surrounding communities.

Leisure facilities • Three golf courses, four parks and a public pool.

Tourist lures • See Goodyear above.

Contacts • City of Litchfield Park, 214 W. Indian School Road, Litchfield Park, AZ 85340; 935-5033.

Tri City West Chamber of Commerce, 501 W. Van Buren, Suite K, Avondale, AZ 85323; 932-2260.

Western Gateway Team, 800 S. Litchfield Rd., Goodyear, AZ 85338; 932-9138.

MESA

Elevation • 1,225 feet

Location • In Maricopa County, 14 miles east of Phoenix.

Climate • Warm to hot summers; balmy winters with some chilly evenings. July average high 104.3, low 74.1; January average high 64.9, low 35.6. Rainfall 7.52 inches; occasional trace of snow.

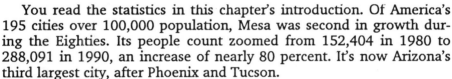

Population • 277,860

Population trend • Gained 6.9 percent a year during the Eighties.

Property tax • $9.67 per $100 assessed valuation.

Unemployment rate (1989) • Four percent

You read the statistics in this chapter's introduction. Of America's 195 cities over 100,000 population, Mesa was second in growth during the Eighties. Its people count zoomed from 152,404 in 1980 to 288,091 in 1990, an increase of nearly 80 percent. It's now Arizona's third largest city, after Phoenix and Tucson.

Mesa was settled by a group of Mormons, who set up camp on a bluff above the Salt River in 1877. They named their village after the Spanish word for plateau—mesa. Like the pioneers of neighboring Phoenix, they cleaned out old Hohokam canals and soon had a thriving farming town. They wouldn't recognized their creation today, of course.

Despite its sprawling growth, downtown Mesa is quite attractive, with Spanish colonnaded sidewalks, brick crosswalks and streets lined with palms and orange trees.

Economy • Mesa's economic base is broad and solid. Seven of Fortune magazine's top five hundred companies are located here. Manufactories range from propulsion equipment and helicopters to food processing and electronics.

Job prospects • With a thriving economy and low jobless rate, this is a good place to look for work. Among its major employers are McDonnell Douglas Helicopters, Rosarita Foods, General Motors Proving Grounds and Motorola, Inc.

Real estate • A variety of homes is available, from conventional subdivisions to planned communities to townhouses. Home prices for a three-bedroom start around $80,000 and range up to $100,000.

The media • One daily, the *Mesa Tribune* and a weekly, the *Independent*. Eight Phoenix TV channels plus cable.

Medical services • Four hospitals and 18 extended care and convalescent homes.

Industrial facilities • Eighteen industrial parks, plus several major manufacturing complexes.

Transportation • Served by Greyhound. Falcon Field has a lighted 4,300-foot runway; Phoenix Sky Harbor is 12 miles west.

Education • Mesa Community College, plus Arizona State University in next-door Tempe; numerous public schools.

Local government • Incorporated in 1883; mayor, six-member council and city manager.

Places to stay • Fifty-seven hotels and motels, plus numerous RV and mobile home parks with 27,000 total spaces.

Leisure facilities • Many parks in Mesa and surrounds, 21 golf courses in the area, ten pools, plus tennis, racquetball and handball courts.

Tourist lures • Mesa has five museums, including the excellent Mesa Southwest Museum and the Champlin Fighter Museum at Falcon Field, with several World War I and II planes on display.

Contacts • Mesa Convention and Visitors Bureau, 120 N. Center St., Mesa, AZ 85201; 969-1307.

Planning Department, City of Mesa, 55 N. Center St., Mesa, AZ 85201; 644-2181.

Mega Corporation, 100 N. Center St., Mesa, AZ 85201; 644-2398.

PARADISE VALLEY

Elevation • 1,421 feet

Location • In Maricopa County, north of the Phoenix Mountains, just above Scottsdale.

Climate • Warm to hot summers; balmy winters with cool evenings. July average high 104.1, low 80.9; January average high 64.5, low 42.6. Rainfall 8.40 inches; snowfall rare.

Population • 12,175

Population trend • Gained one percent a year during the Eighties.

Property tax • $11.27 per $100 assessed valuation.

Unemployment rate (1989) • Two percent

Paradise Valley, in a high desert basin north of Phoenix, is the Beverly Hills of the Valley of the Sun. It's a contented scatter of expensive homes, estates tucked into rough-hewn foothills and an occasional resort.

It was established in the late 1880s as a farming community by settlers who diverted water from the nearby Verde River. By the post-war years, most of the farms had been bought up as homesites by the more prosperous folks of growing Phoenix. Somewhat higher than the Valley of the Sun, it's a little cooler in summer.

Economy • Most residents commute to work elsewhere, although the town has its own small business and commercial district.

Job prospects • The unemployment rate is low because people don't try to find work here; it's an upscale bedroom community.

Real estate • Homes are expensive, ranging from $100,000 and well beyond. Some are walled estates and mini-ranches; if you have to ask the price, you can't afford them.

The media • Two weeklies, the *Paradise Valley Voice* and *Paradise Valley Independent*. The area is served by the *Scottsdale Daily Progress* and Phoenix newspapers. TV service via cable and from Phoenix.

Medical services • Three hospitals in the area, two emergency centers and five extended care facilities.

Industrial facilities • There aren't any; that's what the rest of the greater Phoenix area is for.

Transportation • Mostly BMWs and Mercedes. Greyhound service from Phoenix; scheduled air service from Scottsdale Municipal Airport and Sky Harbor International.

Education • A mix of private and public schools in the area; several colleges nearby.

Local government • The Town of Paradise Valley (which does not encompass all of the valley) was incorporated in 1961; mayor, six-member council and town manager.

Places to stay • Six resorts and motels; dozens more in nearby Scottsdale and Phoenix.

Leisure facilities • Eight golf courses, two pools, plus various tennis and racquetball courts, soccer fields and such in surrounding areas.

Tourist lures • Paradise Valley is between upscale Scottsdale and the desert villages of Carefree and Cave Creek. Nearby North Mountain Park and Squaw Peak offer picnicking and hiking.

Contact • Greater Paradise Valley Chamber of Commerce, 16042 N. 32nd St., Suite C-2, Phoenix, AZ 85032; 482-3344.

PEORIA

Elevation • Approximately 1,100 feet

Location • In Maricopa County, about 20 miles northwest of Phoenix.

Climate • Warm to hot summers; balmy winters with some chilly evenings. July average high 106.3, low 74.7; January average high 66.5; low 35. Rainfall 7.65 inches; occasional trace of snow.

Population • 46,570

Population trend • Gained 15.9 percent per year in the Eighties.

Property tax • $11.89 per $100 assessed valuation.

Unemployment rate (1989) • 5.3 percent

Once a quiet desert farming town, Peoria is now part of the greater Phoenix growth explosion. Its population leaped from 12,307 in 1980 to nearly 50,000 in 1990.

The town was established in 1886; settlers named it for their hometown of Peoria, Ill. Despite rapid growth, it retains some of its small town characteristics. Farms and open desert still surround much of the community. Most of the industrial areas are focused along a roadway that loops around the town from the adjacent U.S. 60 freeway.

Economy • City officials are very pro-growth. The Peoria Economic Development Group is working to draw both business and industry.

Job prospects • With its industrial, medical and retail growth, Peoria offers above average employment opportunities. Construction and manufacturing comprise about 23 percent of the work force. The services industry is largest at 28 percent, followed by retailing, 19 percent.

Real estate • A good selection of homes is available and more are being built. Prices for a three-bedroom in this area range from $70,000 to $90,000.

The media • Two weeklies, the *Peoria Times* and the *Westsider*. TV from Phoenix and a local cable company.

Medical services • Five hospitals and five extended care facilities within a five-mile radius.

Industrial facilities • Two industrial parks with rail access.

Transportation • Served by Greyhound. Glendale Municipal Airport is adjacent; Phoenix Sky Harbor is about 25 miles away.

Education • Rio Salado Community College offers adult classes; plus the usual public schools.

Local government • Incorporated in 1954; mayor, six-member council and city manager.

Places to stay • One motel and two RV parks.

Leisure facilities • Ten parks, a community center, two golf courses, a public pool and 17 tennis courts.

Tourist lures • As evidenced by its single motel, tourists don't flock here. Lake Pleasant Regional Park is 15 miles north, providing fishing, boating and swimming.

Contacts • Peoria Chamber of Commerce, P.O. Box 70 (8322 W. Washington St.), Peoria, AZ 85380; 979-3601.

City of Peoria, P.O. Box 38 (8355 W. Peoria Ave.), Peoria, AZ 85380; 979-7325.

Peoria Economic Development Corp., Inc., 8815 W. Peoria Ave., Suite 2, Peoria, AZ 85380; 486-2011.

SCOTTSDALE

Elevation • 1,260 feet

Location • In Maricopa County, just northeast of Phoenix.

Climate • Warm to hot summers; balmy winters with some chilly evenings. July average high 104.8, low 77.5; January average high 64.8, low 37.6. Rainfall 7.05 inches; rare traces of snow.

Population • 132,605

Population trend • Gained 4.6 percent a year during the Eighties.

Property tax • $9.42 per $100 assessed valuation.

Unemployment rate (1989) • 3.1 percent

When we first visited this area 20 years ago, Scottsdale was a quiet, upscale Western-style hamlet. Today, unfortunately, this picturesque town has contracted the valley's growth fever.

We say it's unfortunate because Scottsdale wasn't just another patch of desert waiting to be developed, like Chandler or Glendale. It was a neat little town in an attractively craggy setting. It still has its boutiques, art galleries and Western shops, but they're surrounded by suburbia.

Has Scottsdale lost its charm? We'll leave that to the eye of the beholder. It's certainly an attractive community, with lots of red tile roofs and white stucco walls. Some of the valley's most opulent resorts are located here. Craggy Camelback Mountain, so named because it resembles a kneeling camel, offers a dramatic backdrop. Most of the posh resorts are tucked into these foothills. Others share cactus country with luxurious Southwestern-style homes in rock-rimmed Paradise

Valley to the north.

Scottsdale was born in 1894 when Rhode Island Banker Albert G. Utley arrived here, subdivided 40 acres of desert and sold off lots. Utleydale or Utleyburg didn't sound right. So he named his new town for former Army chaplain Winfield Scott, an early resident who did much to encourage settlement.

Through the years, it became famous for its rustic cowboy charm. Horses had the right-of-way and hitchin' rails stood before false-front stores. Today, with its fashionable shopping centers and expensive desert homes, it more resembles Palm Springs with a Stetson, which isn't necessarily bad. Despite the surrounding suburbia, it's still one of the most desirable residential areas in the valley.

Economy • It's a mix of tourism, upscale shopping and financial services. Some of the valley's finest retail malls and boutiques are here.

Job prospects • Other than the tourist industry, most of Scottsdale's employment base is clerical and white collar. About 65 percent of the jobs are in retailing, finances and services.

Real estate • Scottsdale embraces some of the valley's most expensive homes. Expect prices for a three bedroom to range between $90,000 and $120,000. Several fashionable planned subdivisions are tucked into the Camelback foothills.

The media • One local daily, the *Scottsdale Progress*. TV from Phoenix, plus cable.

Medical services • Four hospitals, two clinics, three emergency medical centers and a psychiatric hospital.

Industrial facilities • Several complexes are available for light industry.

Transportation • Served by Greyhound via connections in Phoenix. Scottsdale Municipal Airport, with an 8,250-foot runway, has commuter hops to Sky Harbor, which is ten miles away. And yes, it does seem odd to have a ten-mile air link. Presumably, they don't serve in-flight meals.

Education • Scottsdale Community College, plus several public and private elementary and high schools.

Local government • Founded in 1888; mayor, six-member council and city manager.

Places to stay • More than 40 resorts, hotels and motels.

Leisure facilities • About 30 golf courses in the area, plus numerous parks, three public pools, 110 art galleries and the usual bowling alleys, tennis, racquetball and handball courts.

Tourist lures • The drive from Scottsdale through Paradise Valley to Carefree/Cave Creek provides some of Arizona's finest desert vistas. Mountain parks in the area offer picnicking and hiking.

Contacts • Scottsdale Chamber of Commerce, P.O. Box 130 (7333

Scottsdale Mall), Scottsdale, AZ 85252; 945-8481.

City of Scottsdale, 3939 Civic Center Rd., Scottsdale, AZ 85251; 994-2414.

SUN CITY and SUN CITY WEST

Elevation • About 1,000 feet

Location • In Maricopa County, about 20 miles northwest of Phoenix.

Climate • Warm to hot summers; balmy winters with some chilly evenings. July average high 106.3, low 65.2; January average high 66.5, low 35. Rainfall 7.65 inches; rare traces of snow.

Population • Sun City, 42,350; Sun City West, 19,000

Population trend • Sun City gained half a percent a year during the Eighties. Most new growth is in Sun City West.

Property tax • $6.40 per $100 assessed valuation in Sun City; $6.53 in Sun City West.

Unemployment rate (1989) • 4.6 percent in Sun City, 8.9 percent in Sun City West.

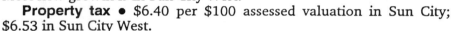

The world's largest senior community, Sun City covers a large patch of low, landscaped desert. It was founded by the Del E. Webb company in 1960, reached its planned capacity in the 1980s and has grown very little since then. Newer Sun City West, however, has gone from zero to nearly 20,000 since it was created in 1978.

Sun City residents enjoy a comfortable, self-contained lifestyle, with their many golf courses, swimming pools, tennis courts and more than 300 social and service clubs. Sun City West is home to the Sundome Center for the Performing Arts, the country's largest single-level auditorium. It draws regional and international entertainers.

Economy • It's based primarily on retirement income, services and retailing.

Job prospects • People come here to avoid work, not to find it. Eighty percent of the jobs are in retailing, financial services and the service industry. Most are filled by people living elsewhere.

Real estate • All homes are in planned developments, with prices starting around $70,000 and ranging up to $190,000 for detached homes. Duplexes and cluster homes also are available. To live here, at least one member of the family must be 55 or older.

The media • One daily, the *News Sun* and three weeklies, the *Sun City Independent, Westsider* and *Sun City Western News*. TV from Phoenix, plus cable service.

Medical services • One hospital in Sun City and three others nearby; several extended care facilities in the area.

Industrial facilities • None, since these are planned senior communities.

Transportation • Served by Greyhound. Glendale and Phoenix-Goodyear airports are nearby; Sky Harbor is 30 minutes southeast.

Education • Rio Salado Community College offers adult education classes here. Public elementary and high schools are in nearby towns.

Local government • Both are unincorporated; administrative services are provided by the Maricopa County Board of Supervisors.

Places to stay • Four motels and three RV parks within a five-mile radius.

Leisure facilities • Seven recreation centers in Sun City and three in Sun City West, eight area golf courses, Sundome Center for the Performing Arts, plus other senior-oriented recreational facilities.

Tourist lures • An attractive desert peak with the mundane name of Tank Mountain provides hiking and picnicking, ten miles west. Lake Pleasant Regional Park is 15 miles west, with boating, hiking, swimming, riding and picnic facilities.

Contact • Northwest Valley Chamber of Commerce, 12211 W. Bell Rd., Suite 204, Surprise, AZ 85374; 583-0692.

TEMPE

Elevation • 1,105 feet

Location • In Maricopa County, just southeast of Phoenix.

Climate • Warm to hot summers; balmy winters with some chilly evenings. July average high 104.3, low 73.4; January average high 65.5, low 35.4. Rainfall 7.63 inches; rare traces of snow.

Population • 147,015

Population trend • Gained 3.6 percent a year during the Eighties.

Property tax • $11.07 per $100 assessed value.

Unemployment rate (1989) • 3.6 percent

Arizona State University dominates both the cultural and economic life of this fast-growing city. More than 70 percent of Tempe's residents are college-educated, and the large ASU campus functions as the area's cultural center.

The town began life in 1872 when Charles Trumbull Hayden opened a general store and flour mill on the banks of the Salt River. He called the place Hayden's Ferry. In 1878, Darrel Duppa, who is credited with naming Phoenix, commented that the area resembled the Vale of Tempe in Thessaly, Greece. The name stuck.

Many of the town's early buildings, including Hayden's home, have been preserved in the Old Town section near the ASU campus. Tempe's downtown is a pleasant mix of contemporary and Western rustic, with palm-lined streets and shaded sidewalks.

Economy • Manufacturing forms Tempe's broad economic base, with retailing, services and, obviously, the huge campus of Arizona State University making major contributions.

Job prospects • Factories account for 18.6 percent of local employment. Most jobs, 33 percent, are in the services sector, followed by the retail trades at 20 percent.

Real estate • Figure on a $80,000 to $100,000 range for three-bedroom detached homes in the Tempe-Mesa area.

The media • One daily, the *Tempe News Tribune* and a weekly, the *New Times*. TV from Phoenix, plus cable.

Medical services • Two hospitals and two extended care units.

Industrial facilities • They're extensive; Tempe has 46 industrial parks, offering facilities for heavy and light industry and warehousing.

Transportation • Served by Greyhound. Sky Harbor International Airport is next door, actually closer to Tempe than any other Valley of the Sun city.

Education • ASU is obviously the focal point. Tempe also has three Christian religious schools; plus eight private elementary and high schools. Several campuses of Maricopa Community College District are nearby.

Local government • Incorporated in 1894; mayor, six-member council and city manager.

Places to stay • Twenty-one hotels and motels, plus several mobile home and RV parks.

Leisure facilities • Forty parks in the area, four public pools, five golf courses, plus tennis and racquetball courts and a community center.

Tourist lures • Arizona State University Campus is attractive and worth a visit, and the city has three museums.

Contacts • Tempe Chamber of Commerce, 60 E. Fifth St., Suite 3, Tempe, AZ 85281; 967-7891.

City of Tempe, 31 E. Fifth St., Tempe, AZ 85282; 968-8221.

WICKENBURG

Elevation ● 2,100 feet

Location ● In Maricopa County, 58 miles northwest of Phoenix on U.S. 89.

Climate ● Warm to hot summers; mild winters with some frosty nights. July average high 103.6, low 69.7; January average high 63.3, low 30. Rainfall 10.77 inches; traces of snow.

Population ● 4,250

Population trend ● Gained 2.1 percent per year in the Eighties.

Property tax ● $8.60 per $100 assessed value.

Unemployment rate (1989) ● 2.2 percent

Wickenburg may be the cutest little cow town in America. Sitting contentedly in the middle of a scenic desert, safe from the Valley of the Sun's scatter, it looks like a John Wayne movie set. However, it's authentic, the descendant of a once-rambunctious mining and ranching town.

Folks here want to preserve this old west image, while catering to tenderfeet and rhinestone cowboys. False-front stores offer Western clothing, Indian crafts and curios. Art galleries sell paintings, sculptures and ceramics; most have Western themes. Rimmed by five cowboy resorts, Wickenburg is the dude ranching capital of America.

Despite its ranching reputation, it was gold, not beef, that put the town on the map. In 1862, an Austrian named Henry Wickenburg hitched his hopes to an ornery burro and began prospecting in the nearby hills. He struck it rich with the Vulture Mine. Some say he picked up a rock to throw at a vulture, or at his stubborn mule when it was spooked by a vulture, and the stone was veined with gold.

Either version of the story sounds like campfire talk. But one truth is undeniable: Gold mines in the area yielded $30 million between 1862 and 1900. Miners needed water to wash their diggin's, so they settled along the Hassayampa River and Wickenburg was born.

As the mines played out, cattlemen began running their herds in the brushy desert. Easterners, reading newspaper reports and dime novels about the Wild West, came out to see what all the excitement was about. Dude ranching, born in Montana, quickly spread to Arizona. Wickenburg and Tucson were early dude ranch centers, and they still are. Nowadays, of course, folks call them guest ranches.

Economy ● Tourism has replaced gold and cattle as the town's reason for being. Indeed, 80 percent of Wickenburg's jobs are directly tied to visitor services. The town attracts a few retirees and Snowbirds and a little gold still trickles in from the hills.

Job prospects • Despite a low unemployment rate, Wickenburg's job potential is only average. Growth, which generates jobs, is rather slow and the locals seem to like it that way.

Real estate • A few modern subdivisions are a-building and the average three-bedroom detached home starts around $80,000.

The media • One weekly, the *Wickenburg Sun*; Phoenix provides the dailies. TV comes from Phoenix and a local cable company.

Medical services • One hospital and two extended care facilities.

Industrial facilities • A small industrial park.

Transportation • Served by Greyhound and Reno-Las Vegas Bus Line. Lighted, 5,000-foot runway at Wickenburg Municipal Airport; charter air service.

Education • Two private schools and a public elementary, junior high and high school.

Local government • Incorporated in 1909; mayor, six-member council and town manager.

Places to stay • Eight motels, five guest ranches, 11 mobile home parks and two RV parks.

Leisure facilities • Community center, youth center, five parks, two golf courses, a public pool and several tennis courts.

Tourist lures • Wickenburg has several historic buildings downtown and one of the finest small archives in the west—the Desert Caballeros Western Museum. Several ghost towns sleep in the nearby hills, while saguaro cactus and Joshua trees thrive in the surrounding desert.

Contacts • Wickenburg Chamber of Commerce, P.O. Drawer CC, Wickenburg, AZ 85358; 684-5479.

Town of Wickenburg, P.O. Box 1269, Wickenburg, AZ 85358; 684-5451.

YOUNGTOWN

Elevation • Approximately 1,000 feet

Location • In Maricopa County, 15 miles northwest of Phoenix.

Climate • Warm to hot summers; mild winters with some chilly evenings. July average high 106.3, low 74.7; January average high 66.5, low 35. Rainfall 7.65 inches

Population • 2,635

Population trend • Gained 1.8 percent a year during the Eighties.

Property tax • $3.42 per $100 assessed valuation.

Unemployment rate (1989) • 5.7 percent

The grandaddy of senior villages, Youngtown was started in 1954 by the Youngtown Land and Development Company. Although it's the world's first retirement town, it has remained small and compact while next-door Sun City and Sun City West have mushroomed.

It's an attractive, neatly groomed town with an active retail core and typical senior amenities such as a clubhouse, lake, golf courses and tennis courts.

Economy • It's retirement-based, with its income derived from pensions, savings and investments.

Job prospects • Mostly, the residents work at retirement. More than half the town's few jobs are in the service, financial and retail sectors.

Real estate • Home prices start around $80,000 to $90,000 for a three-bedroom unit.

The media • Served by the weekly *Sun City Independent* and dailies from Phoenix, which also provides local TV service. A 31-channel cable system is available, as well.

Medical services • One hospital; extend care facilities are in surrounding communities.

Industrial facilities • None.

Transportation • Served by Greyhound. Glendale and Phoenix-Goodyear airports are nearby; Sky Harbor is 28 miles away.

Education • Rio Salado Community College offers adult education classes in Sun City. Public elementary and high schools are in nearby towns.

Local government • Incorporated in 1960; mayor and six-member council.

Places to stay • One hotel and two motels.

Leisure facilities • Clubhouse, lake, four parks, six golf courses and a cactus botanical garden.

Tourist lures • Lake Pleasant Regional Park is 15 miles west, with boating, hiking, swimming, riding and picnic facilities.

Contact • Northwest Valley Chamber of Commerce, 12211 W. Bell Rd., Suite 204, Surprise, AZ 85374; 583-0692.

Town of Youngtown, 12030 Clubhouse Square, Youngtown, AZ 85363; 933-8286.

Chapter Eleven

TUCSON AND BEYOND

THE SOUTHEAST AND FAR EAST

We begin our final community chapter with a quick lesson in what's left of Arizona's geography. The lesson includes our reasons for recommending only a few places in the eastern third of state as your possible future home.

Heading southeast from the Valley of the Sun, the land slopes gradually upward. If you follow I-10 from Phoenix, you'll gain more than a thousand feet by the time you reach Tucson, although you're still in desert terrain. If you continue east from Tucson, you'll encounter scattered mountain clusters, floating like alpine islands on a high prairie.

Swerving north along the state's eastern edge, you'll hit more mountains. The area takes on the look of the Pacific Northwest. This rumpled eastern third of Arizona offers much to the wanderer, hiker, hunter and fisherperson. But its potential for new settlement or retirement is limited.

We like many of the towns in this region, sturdy, no-nonsense places like Willcox, Clifton, Safford, Hollbrook and Globe. They're cast in pleasant time warps with turn-of-the-century neighborhoods and brick business areas. However, most offer little for growing families since they aren't growing much themselves. And their cold winters discourage year-around retirees or Snowbirds.

Much of this area is taken up by large Indian nations. The Navajo, Hopi, White Mountain Apache and San Carlos Apache reservations occupy half of Arizona's eastern third. (We hope that makes sense mathematically.)

THE WAY IT WAS • The state's history is rooted in the southeast. The first Spanish incursions into present-day Arizona occurred here. Franciscan Father Marcos de Niza entered this region in 1539, seeking the Seven Cities of Cibola. Francisco Vasquez de Coronado followed a

165

Tucson blends yesterday and today nicely; the Moorish domed Pima County Courthouse offers contrast to a modern office building.

year later, probably traveling up the San Pedro River Valley just east of Sierra Vista.

In 1700, Father Eusebio Kino established Mission San Xavier del Bac, near today's Tucson. The military garrison of Tubac was founded in 1752 to put down a Pima rebellion, and the Tucson presidio followed in 1775.

Americans began settling here after the 1848 Treaty of Guadalupe Hidalgo ceded much of Arizona to the United States. Indians, Apaches this time, continued exhibiting their resentment toward the intruders.

Cochise and Geronimo gained international fame for their stubborn resistance—a fame somewhat distorted by later novelists and movie producers. Not until Geronimo's final surrender in 1886 was Arizona considered safe for settlement.

THE WAY IT IS • Southeastern and far eastern Arizona offer interesting contrasts. While Tucson is the state's second largest urban center, the southeast corner is thinly settled. The only community of any size is Sierra Vista. And the far eastern mountains are among the leastpopulated areas of the state.

The southeast, particularly Cochise County, has emerged in recent years as an important tourist destination. Many newcomers have chosen to stay, attracted by the benign climate and inexpensive housing of places like Sierra Vista, Bisbee, Pearce and Sunsites. In the far eastern mountains, retirees are discovering such hamlets as Pinetop, Lakeside, Show Low, Springerville and Eagar.

We begin our community profiles with Tucson, one of our favorite cities. Although it's a major urban center, it's quite different than Phoenix to the northwest. Tucson is history, old money and tradition. Phoenix is new-wave, fast-paced, new money and very pro-growth. Although Tucson is growing as well, life is a bit slower there. It's more focused on the past and present than on some glossy future.

The two are quite similar geographically; both occupy desert basins surrounded by rugged mountains. Tucson is 1,300 feet higher, so it's a bit cooler despite its more southern location. The biggest difference is—well—bigness itself. Phoenix is nearly twice as large, and its husky suburban cities make it even larger. By Contrast, Tucson is an urban island with few communities on its periphery.

TUCSON

Elevation • 2,390 feet

Location • In Pima County, 90 miles north of Mexico.

Climate • Warm to hot summers; cool winters with some chilly evenings. July average high 100.1, low 73.3; January average high 66, low 36.7. Rainfall 10.73 inches; traces of snowfall.

Population • 402,506

Population trend • Gained 2.2 percent a year during the Eighties.

Property tax • $14.95 per $100 assessed valuation (based on ten percent of real value).

Unemployment rate (1991) • 4.3 percent

Occupying the northeastern rim of the Sonoran Desert, Tucson sits in a virtual cactus garden, surrounded by five mountain ranges. In winter, you can work on your suntan at pool side, then drive to the Mount Lemmon ski area in an hour and strap on the sticks.

If it weren't for the Gadsden Purchase, we might need a Mexican tourist card to visit here. When the American-Mexican border was set by the Treaty of Guadalupe Hidalgo, much of this region was on the Mexican side. Then in 1854, the 30,000-square-mile Gadsden Purchase was negotiated and the town many call the Old Pueblo became part of America.

Tucson itself goes well beyond the 1850s. When mission-builder Eusebio Kino visited the area in 1687, he found Tohono O'odham Indians living in a village they called *Stjukshon* (Stook-shon). It means "blue water at the base of a black mountain." It referred to springs in the now-dry Santa Cruz River and a dark promontory called Sentinel Peak. The Spanish altered it to *Tucson*, which they pronounced "TUK-son."

Father Kino returned in 1700 to build a mission in the Indian village of Bac. Tucson was established next door in 1775 by a wandering Irishman scouting for the Spanish crown. When more outsiders began settling in the area, the original inhabitants naturally objected. They went on the warpath and a walled presidio was built to protect the intruders.

After the Gadsden Purchase put Tucson on our side of the border, it continued growing as a ranching and provisioning center. A Butterfield Stage stop was opened in 1857 and Tucson's cantinas became notorious hangouts for drifters, outlaws and lonesome cowpokes. Folks said the outpost was so primitive that stage passengers who spent the night had to sleep in a "Tucson bed"—using their stomach for a mattress and their back for a blanket.

The Old Pueblo suffered the indignity of capture by Rebel troops during the Civil War. Union forces sent them scattering in the Battle of Picacho Pass in 1862. Tucson lured the territorial capital from Prescott in 1867, only to have it taken away ten years later.

By the turn of the century, this was a busy if still rather remote town of 10,000. World War II brought thousands of servicemen to Davis-Monthan Army Air Corps Base. Many of them liked the idea of January suntans and returned.

Although it's much smaller than Phoenix, Tucson isn't exactly a hamlet. Viewed from surrounding hills, it spreads as a vast carpet of commerce over the high desert. Indeed, greater Tucson covers 500 square miles.

However, wide thoroughfares get you quickly from one end of town to the other. Interstate 10 cuts a northwest-southeast diagonal, providing quick access to the region's opposite corners. I-19 whisks you down south. Surprisingly, Tucson suffers little commuter congestion. Traffic-watchers get excited over a ten-minute delay on I-10.

Today's Tucson wears its Spanish heritage handsomely. Tile-roofed and flat-roofed pueblo architecture predominates. The town has more good Mexican restaurants than you can shake a tortilla at. Mexican arts and crafts add color to curio shops. Many signs are bilingual, since 26 percent of Pima County's citizens are Hispanic.

Tucson's growth during the Eighties was slower than Phoenix, 2.2 percent a year compared with 2.5. However, it hasn't been sitting still; most of its acceleration came a decade earlier. In the 1970s, metropolitan Tucson was the 15th fastest growing area in the country, with a 51.2 percent population gain.

Look for the city to take off again during the mid-Nineties. A U.S. Supreme Court ruling giving Arizona a larger share of Colorado River water goes into effect then, and Tucson will get much of that.

Economy • Manufacturing, tourism, the federal government (Davis-Monthan Air Force Base) and high tech industries provide the bricks for its economic foundation. The largest single employer is the University of Arizona.

Job prospects • The biggest employment areas are in tourism and other services, accounting for a fourth of the jobs. Retail sales and transportation offer possibilities, as well. Specific skills needed, according to a local Job Service office, are in the machine trades, aircraft maintenance and customer service reps in the communications and aircraft industries.

Real estate • Tucson's housing is varied, ranging from older homes downtown to elegant gated communities in the foothills. Much of the architecture, both old and new, is Spanish and pueblo style. Houses are 20 to 30 percent less expensive than in Phoenix, with prices for a three-bedroom home ranging from $60,000 to well beyond $100,000. Fixer-uppers in older neighborhoods can go for $40,000 to $50,000.

The media • Two dailies, the *Tucson Star* and *Tucson Citizen*, plus some suburban weeklies.

Medical services • Fifteen hospitals including facilities at the extensive University of Arizona Medical School, plus several clinics and extended care places.

Industrial facilities • They range from heavy fabricating plants to space age electronics. Several industrial parks are available, offering complete services, including rail and air.

Transportation • Reached by Greyhound and Amtrak. Tucson International Airport is served by more than a dozen airlines.

Education • The University of Arizona is the community's education focal point and a source of many cultural offerings. Others schools include Tucson branches of the University of Phoenix, Pima Community College, ten business and vocational schools, 103 private and 27 parochial schools and the usual public schools.

Local government • The seat of Pima County, incorporated in 1877; mayor, six-member council and city manager.

Places to stay • A hundred and fifty-six hotels, resorts and motels, plus several dude ranches in the area and dozens of RV and mobile home parks.

Leisure facilities • Thirty-five golf courses, 128 city and county parks, 18 museums and galleries, 23 municipal pools, plus many tennis, racquetball and handball courts and sports fields.

Tourist lures • Mission San Xavier, the much-heralded Arizona-Sonora Desert Museum, Old Tucson Western movie town, Mount Lemmon ski area, regional mountain parks and numerous other attractions.

Contacts • Tucson Economic Development Corporation, 456 W. St. Mary's Rd., Suite 200, Tucson, AZ 85702; 623-3673.

Tucson Metropolitan Chamber of Commerce, P.O. Box 991 (465

W. St. Mary's Road), Tucson, AZ 85702; 792-2250.

City of Tucson, 250 W. Alameda, Tucson, AZ 85726; 791-4204.

Metropolitan Tucson Convention & Visitors Bureau, 130 S. Scott Ave., Tucson, AZ 85701; 624-1817.

BISBEE

Elevation ● 5,490 feet

Location ● In Cochise County, just above the Mexican border.

Climate ● Warm summers, cool to chilly winters; July average high 89.3, low 64.5; January average high 56.9, low 33.7. Rainfall 16.21 inches; snowfall 4.54 inches.

Population ● 8,080

Population trend ● Gained 1.4 percent a year in the Eighties.

Property tax ● $13.15 per $100 assessed valuation.

Unemployment rate (1991) ● 5.2 percent

Bisbee is a durable old mining town cantilevered into the steep flanks of Mule Pass Gulch. Like Jerome, it's the sort of place where your upper neighbor can look down your chimney. The post office department complains that it's too steep for mail delivery.

Headframes and tailing dumps mark the slopes; corrugated buildings shelter smelters and stamp mills. Hillsides have been ripped away to expose orange, rust and gray-green wounds. You *know* this is mining country. Driving east beyond the Victorian business district, you encounter something even more dramatic—the great terraced cavity of the Lavender Pit Mine. It's so close it appears ready to swallow the town.

Why do we recommend Bisbee as a place to settle? It's rich in history, it has a classic 19th century downtown area, handsome old homes and a temperate year-around climate. And it's a short hop to Mexico or urban Tucson. The surrounding terrain is varied, since Bisbee is on a topographic bridge between the Sonoran Desert and eastern high country. The town has one minus, however: The job market is weak.

Although it emerged as a mining center, Bisbee didn't blossom overnight. It grew steadily and sturdily as big corporations gouged deep into the earth for copper, gold, silver, lead and zinc. Army Scout Jack Dunn filed a claim in the area in 1877, and mining began in earnest. In, around and under Bisbee, more than $2 billion worth of ore was pulled from miles of shafts and deep open pits.

Reveling in this wealth, it grew like a vertical San Francisco, with plush Victorian homes, fine restaurants and—of course—bordellos. Brewery Gulch was Bisbee's version of San Francisco's Barbary Coast, with more than 50 drinking, gambling and whoring establishments.

At its peak, it was the world's largest copper-mining town, with a population of 20,000. Operations continued at the underground Queen Mine and Lavender Pit until 1975, when shrinking returns and falling copper prices forced their closure.

Logic says the town should have withered and died, but retirees and tourists began arriving, drawn by the mild climate and yesterday charm. Boutiques, galleries and antique shops were opened in the red brick and tufa buildings. The large Queen Mine, unable to process copper profitably, is processing visitors through underground tours.

The town even attracts a few movie companies, since the hillside buildings can become, with a little creative camera work, a bit of Old Spain, Greece or Mexico.

Economy ● Tourism and light manufacturing have stabilized the town since the big mines shut down.

Job prospects ● They aren't strong, although the area is enjoying modest growth. Best prospects are in retail and wholesale trades, tourist and other service jobs. The local Job Service office rated employment prospects as "below average."

Real estate ● Three-bedroom detached home prices range from $50,000 upwards. Restorable Victorians go for much more.

The media ● One daily, the *Bisbee Review* and two weeklies, the *Bisbee Observer* and *Bisbee Gazette*. TV service from Tucson, plus a 23-channel cable company.

Medical services ● A hospital with combined acute care and long-term care capabilities.

Industrial facilities ● Several parks are available, including one at the airport. Nearby Naco has a "twin plant" industrial park operating both sides of the border.

Transportation ● Bridgeport Transport to Tucson. Bisbee Municipal Airport has a 5,990 foot lighted runway.

Education ● Cochise Community College is 17 miles east; the town has one elementary, junior high and high school.

Local government ● Incorporated in 1905; mayor, six council members and city manager.

Places to stay ● Several hotels and motels (including two historic hotels) and nine bed and breakfast inns; four campgrounds and RV parks.

Leisure facilities ● Seven parks, a golf course, nine art galleries, tennis courts and a ball park.

Tourist lures ● Three museums and many historic buildings; public tours at the Queen Mine; viewing areas at the Lavender open pit mine.

Contacts • Bisbee Chamber of Commerce, P.O. Drawer BA (Seven Naco Rd.), Bisbee, AZ 85603; 432-2141.

City of Bisbee, 118 Arizona St., Bisbee, AZ 85603; 432-5446.

CATALINA

Elevation • 3,100 feet

Location • In Pima County, 20 miles north of Tucson on U.S. Highway 89.

Climate • Warm summers, cool winters with some chilly nights. July average high 93.2, low 67.3, January average high 57.7, low 34.3

Population • 4,500

Population trend • Gained 5.8 percent a year in the Eighties.

Property tax • $16.74 per $100 assessed valuation.

Unemployment rate (1989) • 7.1 percent

Catalina is a pleasant if somewhat ordinary-looking community in an impressive setting—tucked into the foothills of the Santa Catalina Mountains. It's primarily a retirement area; the planned senior villages of SaddleBrooke and Sun City Vistoso are four miles away.

The town was established in the 1950s by two land developers. It has experienced considerable growth in the past two decades, more than doubling its 1970 population.

Economy • There isn't much of a base; it's mostly retirement-oriented, with a few small businesses.

Job prospects • Not very good. Its unemployment rate is much higher than the state average. Most working folks commute to nearby Tucson.

Real estate • Housing is cheaper than in Tucson, and this is one of the area's draws. Prices for detached homes begin around $60,000 in Catalina; in the retirement communities, they range from $70,000 to $100,000.

The media • The semi-monthly *Catalina Oracle*. TV relays from both Tucson and Phoenix, plus a local cable company.

Medical services • One county clinic; nearest major facilities are in Tucson.

Transportation • No commercial transport or airport. Tucson International is about 25 miles south.

Education • A public elementary and middle school; high school is nine miles away.

Local government • Village council with nine elected representatives.

Places to stay • Three resorts within a ten-mile radius.

Leisure facilities • A public swimming pool.

Tourist lures • Nearby Catalina State Park offers hiking, camping, picnicking and such. Hiking trails extend into the Santa Catalina Mountains of Coronado National Forest.

Contact • Greater Catalina/Golder Ranch Village Council, P.O. Box 8674-CRB, Tucson, AZ 85738; 791-2265.

GREEN VALLEY

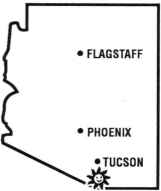

Elevation • 2,900 feet

Location • In Pima County, 30 miles south of Tucson on I-19.

Climate • Warm to hot summers; mild winters with some chilly evenings. July average high 101.3, low 68.4; January average high 67.1, low 31. Rainfall 10.86 inches; snowfall rare.

Population • 15,600

Population trend • Gained four percent a year in the Eighties.

Property tax • $10.59 per $100 assessed valuation.

Unemployment rate (1989) • 9.4 percent

A semi-arid no-man's land between Tucson and Nogales has emerged as a carefully planned community of contented senior souls. Located in the high desert of the Santa Cruz River Valley, Green Valley was established in 1964. It has become one of Arizona's largest senior complexes.

More than just a retirement town, it now offers shopping centers and other amenities that make air-conditioned desert living quite pleasant. Its location is attractive, as well, near both Tucson and Nogales, which offers the best shopping of Arizona's Mexican border towns.

Economy • Most of it is based on retirement income, since 85 percent of its residents are pensioned. A number of employed folks commute north to Tucson.

Job prospects • Since it's a senior village, it doesn't offer more than a few service and clerical jobs. The Green Valley Chamber of Commerce describes employment prospects as "below average."

Real estate • Most homes are set into attractive park-like complexes, rimmed by common areas and golf courses. Prices for a three-bedroom home start around $72,500. Sales activity is "average," with older homes, new subdivisions, condos and townhouses on the market, according to the Green Valley Board of Realtors.

The media • The twice-weekly *Green Valley News & Sun*. Seven Tucson TV channels and a local cable company.

Medical services • A 24-hour emergency clinic, two extended care homes and a mental health clinic.

Industrial facilities ● None.

Transportation ● Buses of Citizen Auto Stage run between Tucson and Nogales. Tucson International Airport is 23 miles north.

Education ● One elementary school; high school students go to Sahuarita, three miles north.

Local government ● Unincorporated. Governmental services provided by the Pima County Board of Supervisors.

Places to stay ● Two motels.

Leisure facilities ● Typical senior village amenities—four golf courses, 23 swimming pools, tennis, shuffleboard, putting green and driving range.

Tourist lures ● The Titan Missile Museum is next door, and historic Tubac and Tumacacori National Monument are 30 miles south. Madera Canyon, offering picnicking, hiking camping and birdwatching, is 12 miles southeast.

Contact ● Green Valley Chamber of Commerce, P.O. Box 566 (108 W. Continental, Room 187), Green Valley, AZ 85622; 625-7575.

ORO VALLEY

Elevation ● 2,450 feet

Location ● In Pima County, six miles from the northern edge of Tucson.

Climate ● Warm to hot summers; mild winters with cool nights. July average high 100.3, low 70.6; January average high 66.6, lows 32.4. Rainfall 15.68 inches; half an inch of snowfall.

Population ● 5,520

Population trend ● Increased 15.7 percent a year in the Eighties.

Property tax ● $14.34 per $100 assessed valuation.

Unemployment rate (1989) ● 3.4 percent

Cradled by handsome peaks, Oro Valley is the fastest-growing community in southeastern Arizona. It more than tripled its size during the last decade. The town offers an attractive mix of modern subdivisions, golf courses and the cactus gardens of the surrounding Sonoran Desert. And it's all within half an hour of downtown Tucson.

Oro Valley was settled as a farming area about 30 years ago, then it was incorporated in 1974.

Economy ● It's pretty much based on service and retail trades.

Job prospects ● They're limited in Oro Valley itself, but Tucson is an easy drive.

Real estate ● Most homes are in modern subdivisions; average price of a three-bedroom detached home is $110,000.

The media • One weekly, the *Oro Valley Territorial.*

Medical services • No hospitals in Oro Valley; they're plentiful in Tucson.

Education • The usual public schools; no private schools or colleges

Local government • Incorporated in 1974; mayor, four-member council and town manager.

Places to stay • None locally.

Leisure facilities • Community golf courses, parks, tennis and racquetball courts and a public swimming pool.

Tourist lures • The Santa Catalina Mountains offer hiking, picnicking and other outdoor things. Catalina State Park is just east.

Contact • Town of Oro Valley, 10900 N. Stallard Place, Suite 100, Oro Valley, AZ 85737; 297-2591.

PINETOP/LAKESIDE

Elevation • 7,200 feet

Location • In Navajo County; east central Arizona in the White Mountains.

Climate • Warm summers; cool to cold winters. July average high 85.8, low 55.5; January average high 44.2, low 17.7. Rainfall 22.31 inches; snowfall 38.2 inches.

Population • 2,725

Population trend • Gained 1.8 percent a year in the Eighties.

Property tax • $11.11 in Pinetop; $11.15 in Lakeside

Unemployment rate (1989) • 16.5 percent

We recommend these two towns only as retirement places, primarily because of their attractive forested settings. They're both perched rather dramatically on the edge of the Mogollon Rim, just above the forested White Mountain Apache Indian Reservation.

It gets cold here in the winter. But you won't suffer Minnesota-style blizzards, and you probably will get white Christmases. With their high unemployment rates, these aren't good places for job-hunters.

The two communities were founded by Mormons in the early 1880s. Several lakes are nearby, giving Lakeside its name. While there's no shortage of pine trees hereabouts, Pinetop actually was named for a saloon keeper who served the soldiers at Fort Apache. Pinetop and Lakeside incorporated as a single town in 1984.

Economy • It's mostly tourist and recreation oriented.

Job prospects • In a word—"scarce"—says the Pinetop/Lakeside Chamber of Commerce. Come here to get away from work, not to find it.

Real estate • Woodsy, chalet-style homes are typical of the area, and they're not expensive. An average three-bedroom detached home goes for about $75,000.

The media • Two biweeklies, the *White Mountain Independent* and *Apache Scout.*

Medical services • A 57-bed hospital in Show Low, ten miles northwest.

Industrial facilities • One 90-acre industrial park.

Transportation • White Mountain Passenger Lines (bus). Nearest airport is in Show Low, which offers feeder and charter service (see below).

Education • Northland Pioneer Community College has a campus in Show Low; public schools in Pinetop/Lakside.

Local government • Incorporated in 1984; mayor, six-member council and town manager.

Places to stay • Numerous motels and rustic cabins, plus the Sunrise summer/winter resort on the adjacent Apache reservation.

Leisure facilities • Three golf courses, a health center, two pools, 70-acre recreation area and tennis and racquetball courts.

Tourist lures • Thousands come to escape the desert heat and sniff the pine-scented air of surrounding Apache-Sitgreaves National Forest. Adjacent White Mountain Apache Reservation offers hunting, fishing, camping and hiking. The Apaches' Sunrise resort is one of Arizona's major ski facilities; it's also open in summer.

Contacts • Pinetop/Lakeside Chamber of Commerce, P.O. Box 266, Pinetop, AZ 85935; 367-4920.

Economic Development Coordinator, Town of Pinetop/Lakeside, Box 10 (1360 Niels Hansen Lane), Lakeside, AZ 85929; 368-8696.

White Mountain Apache Tribe, P.O. Box 700, Whiteriver, AZ 85941; 338-4346.

SHOW LOW

Elevation • 6,300 feet

Location • In Navajo County, east central Arizona in the White Mountain foothills.

Climate • Warm summers, cool to cold winters. July average high 85.8, low 55.5; January average high 44.2, low 17.7.

Population • 5,600

Population trend • Gained three percent a year during the Eighties.

Property tax • $9.02 per $100.

• FLAGSTAFF

• PHOENIX

• TUCSON

Unemployment rate (1989) • 4.9 percent

Show Low is where the Pinetop/Lakeside folks come to shop. It's the commercial center of this high mountain region. Somewhat lower than Pinetop/Lakeside, it's a bit milder here in winter. Although the town itself has a pleasant alpine look, it sits just above eastern Arizona's high grasslands and has a cowboy past.

In fact, it was a cowpokes' card game that gave the town its silly name. C.E. Cooley and Marion Clark had built up a 100,000- acre cattle spread in the 1870s. Deciding to end their partnership, they drew cards to see who would "show low"; the one drawing the lowest card would win. Cooley drew the deuce of clubs, so Clark moved on. The town's main street has an equally silly name—Deuce of Clubs.

Economy • It's a bit more diverse than Pinetop/Lakeside, offering a mix of tourism, logging and forest products manufacturing.

Job prospects • Limited; not much beyond lumbering and the service sector.

Real estate • It's a mix of older downtown homes, a few new subdivisions on the fringes and chalet-style homes among the trees. Prices start around $75,000 for a three-bedroom.

The media • The biweekly *White Mountain Independent*.

Medical services • A 57-bed hospital, plus several clinics.

Industrial facilities • A 70-acre industrial park with airport access.

Transportation • White Mountain Passenger Lines (bus service). Show Low Airport has a 6,000-foot lighted runway, with a daily commuter flight to Phoenix.

Education • Show Low Campus of Northland Pioneer Community College; four elementary, one junior high and one high school.

Local government • Incorporated in 1953; mayor, six-member council and city manager.

Places to stay • Fourteen motels, nine campgrounds and five RV parks.

Leisure facilities • One golf course, soccer fields, tennis and racquetball courts.

Tourist lures • A repeat of Pinetop/Lakeside: people are drawn by the piney woods, plus the recreational lures of the White Mountain Apache Reservation.

Contacts • Show Low Chamber of Commerce, P.O. Box 1083, Show Low, AZ 85901; 537-2326.

White Mountain Certified Development Company, 200 W. Cooley, Show Low, AZ 85901; 537-7469.

City of Show Low, 200 W. Cooley Rd., Show Low, AZ 85901; 537-5724.

SIERRA VISTA

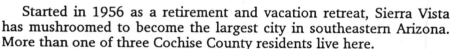

Elevation ● 4,623 feet

Location ● In Cochise County, 70 miles southeast of Tucson.

Climate ● Warm summers, cool winters with some chilly evenings. July average high 88.6, low 66.4; January average high 58.4, low 34.2. Rainfall 14.64 inches; snowfall seven inches.

Population ● 34,300

Population trend ● Gained 3.6 percent a year in the Eighties.

Property tax ● $12.87 per $100 assessed valuation.

Unemployment rate (1991) ● 8.2 percent

Started in 1956 as a retirement and vacation retreat, Sierra Vista has mushroomed to become the largest city in southeastern Arizona. More than one of three Cochise County residents live here.

Its popularity is not surprising. Surrounding mountains provide an impressive backdrop and national climate experts rate this area as one of the most temperate in the nation. With an average maximum high of 75 and low of 50, it's practically a room temperature community. Housing is relatively inexpensive, with detached homes available for as little as $50,000. The area is decidedly pro-growth, and it has considerable retirement facilities. If you want to get above the desert heat, Sierra Vista is a good bet.

Rivaling neighboring Tucson in land area, it looks more like a well-planned suburb than a town. It's an expansive spread of shopping centers, subdivisions, service stations and stoplights.

Economy ● Once retirement- oriented, it's diversifying into light manufacturing, services and retail trade.

Job prospects ● At this writing, job prospects were "below average," according to the local Job Services office. It may improve as the community grows, however. Best possibilities are in retail sales and public administration. The largest employer is next-door Fort Huachuca, with more than 11,700 military and civilians drawing government paychecks.

Real estate ● Three bedroom home prices begin around $50,000 for a used one and range well beyond $100,000. The market is "moderately active," according to the Sierra Vista Association of Realtors, with a mix of older homes, new subdivisions, townhouses and condos available.

The media ● One daily, the *Sierra Vista Herald,* plus the weekly *Huachuca Scout.* TV feeds from Tucson, Nogales and Phoenix, plus cable service.

Medical services • Three hospitals and two extended care facilities.

Industrial facilities • Two industrial parks; Sierra Vista is a "Foreign Trade Zone Grantee."

Transportation • Served by Bridgewater Transport with connections to Greyhound. Municipal Airport has three runways, with feeder service by two regional carriers.

Education • Cochise Community College; five public elementary, one junior high and one high school.

Local government • Incorporated in 1956; mayor, six-member council and city manager.

Places to stay • Ten motels. Several RV and mobile home parks in the area, mostly in next-door Huachuca City.

Leisure facilities • A community center, nine parks, four pools, two golf courses, plus tennis and racquetball courts.

Tourist lures • Sierra Vista is near several southeast Arizona attractions, including historic Fort Huachuca (with an excellent Army museum), Coronado National Monument, Ramsey Canyon Nature Preserve and historic Tombstone.

Contacts • Sierra Vista Chamber of Commerce, 77 Calle Portal, Room A-140, Sierra Vista, AZ 85635; 458-6940.

Sierra Vista Economic Development Foundation, P.O. Box 2380, Sierra Vista, AZ 85635; 458-6948.

City of Sierra Vista, 2400 E. Tacoma St., Sierra Vista, AZ 85635; 458-3315.

SPRINGERVILLE/EAGAR

Elevation • 6,965 feet

Location • Apache County, on U.S. Highway 60 in east-central Arizona near the New Mexico border.

Climate • warm summers; cool winters with cold nights. July average high 83.3, low 51.6; January average high 46.7, low 14.6.

Population • 2,125

Population trend • Springerville gained 4.3 percent and Eagar six percent a year during the Eighties.

Property tax • $5.20 per $100 assessed valuation

Unemployment rate (1989) • Springerville 8.8 percent and Eagar 14.9 percent.

Although Springerville next-door Eagar have rather cold winters, we recommend them because they offer inexpensive housing, extensive recreation possibilities and low property tax. Employment is lim-

The bad guys bite the dust in this reenactment of the Shoot-out at the O.K. Corral in Tombstone, performed periodically for tourists.

ited, but it's a fine retirement retreat for folks who don't mind a January chill.

The two hamlets are in Round Valley, a grassy basin on the northeastern edge of the White Mountains. They were established in the late 1870s on the banks of the Little Colorado River—Springerville as a trading post and Eagar as a homestead.

It's a short drive to Sunrise Ski Area and other summer-winter offerings of the White Mountain Apache Reservation and Apache-Sitgreaves National Forest. Several good fishing lakes are in the area.

Economy • It's a mix of tourism, lumbering and agriculture.

Job prospects • Springerville and Eagar offer very few jobs, and their unemployment rate is much higher than the state average.

Real estate • Most homes are used, although a moderately high growth rate has spurred some new construction. Prices for a three-bedroom range from $35,000 for a fixer-upper to $68,000 for a newer one. Some attractive homes on wooded acreage go up to $135,000.

The media • The biweekly *White Mountain Independent*; daily news comes from Phoenix or Albuquerque. TV relay brings in Phoenix, Tucson and several cable channels.

Medical services • One 25-bed hospital, a 44-bed convalescent hospital and 10-unit "assisted living" apartment.

Industrial facilities • Some small industrial areas are being developed.

Transportation • Springerville Babbit Field has two lighted runways with full facilities. Charter service available.

Education • Community college extension, plus one public elementary, middle and high school.

Local government • Both incorporated in 1948; mayor, city council and town manager in each.

Places to stay • Six motels in Springerville and nine RV parks in the area; several campgrounds in the nearby forests.

Leisure facilities • Public pool, art museum, tennis and racquetball courts and two parks.

Tourist lures • The White Mountains offer fishing, hiking, camping, hunting, cross-country and downhill skiing.

Contacts • Springerville/Eagar Chamber of Commerce, P.O. Box 181, Springerville, AZ 85938; 333-2123.

Economic Development Director, Town of Springerville, P.O. Box 390, Springerville, AZ 85938; 333-2656.

Town of Eagar, P.O. Box 1300 (174 S. Main St.), Eagar, AZ 85925; 333-4128.

TOMBSTONE

Elevation • 4,540 feet

Location • In Cochise County, 17 miles northeast of Sierra Vista.

Climate • Warm summers; mild winters with cool evenings. July average high 93.7, low 65.4; January average high 61.4, low 33.6. Rainfall 12.77 inches; snowfall seven inches.

Population • 1,865

Population trend • Gained 1.5 percent a year in the Eighties.

Property tax • $11.59 per $100 assessed valuation.

Unemployment rate (1989) • 4.5 percent

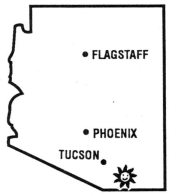

If you'd like to rub shoulders with history and you're attracted by inexpensive housing, this may be your place. Don't expect fancy subdivisions and golf courses; Tombstone is as funky as it sounds. Hollywood didn't make the town famous, but it didn't hurt its reputation, either. The shoot-out at the O.K. Corral really did happen, and local townsfolk reenact it for tourists most weekends.

The town earned its funereal name in 1877 when prospector Ed Schieffelin decided to check out an area where Chiricahua Apaches were still on the warpath. "All you'll find out there is your tombstone," a friend warned.

Ed found a big silver strike instead. Word spread and other argonauts poured in. A town was staked out two years later, in Goose Flat, two miles from Schieffelin's hillside mine. Soon, it was one of the largest, wildest and wickedest mining camps in the Southwest. It attracted such characters as Doc Holliday, Johnny Ringo, Bat Masterson and, of course, the Earp brothers.

By 1881, Tombstone boasted about 10,000 citizens, and it became the seat of Cochise County. In that same year, the Earps shot it out with the Clantons and McLaurys near the O.K. Corral. Actually, it was more of a blood feud than a police action. The Earps had accused the Clantons and McLaurys of cattle thievery and sheltering stage robbers at their ranches. The cowboys boasted openly that they would kill the Earps for besmirching their reputations.

"They tried to pick a fuss out of me," Wyatt testified at the hearing following the shoot-out.

After the excitement of the West's most publicized gun battle faded, Tombstone began fading as well. Most of the town burned in 1882, then water began seeping into its mines. Falling silver prices and labor problems closed the last of the mines early in this century. The county seat was moved to Bisbee in 1931. The "town too tough to die" was about to do it. The population dropped to 150.

Then tourists began trickling in, lured by stories of the Earp brothers and the shoot-out. The town's old Western look, unchanged because nobody could afford to modernize, became an asset.

Today, downtown Tombstone is a National Historic Landmark. Visitors clunk along boardwalks shaded by overhangs from false front stores. They catch rides in horse-drawn surreys and browse through boutiques with names like "Madame Mustache, Purveyor of Pleasure." The town is a mix of history and harmless hokum, with shops, museums and quasi-museums in century-old buildings. A few retired people live here, drawn by the town's hospitality and inexpensive housing.

Economy • It's tourism, pure and simple.

Job prospects • There aren't any to speak of. Even the O.K. Corral shoot-out participants are unpaid amateurs. The employment centers of Sierra Vista and Bisbee are a short drive away.

Real estate • Home prices are a bargain—from $40,000 to $50,000 for a three-bedroom, according to the Tombstone Chamber of Commerce. The selection is limited, however.

The media • *The Tombstone Epitaph* is still published, although it's a tourist paper; the news is 100 years old. There is a modern weekly, with the predictable name of *Tombstone Tumbleweed*.

Medical services • The nearest facilities are in Sierra Vista, 17 miles away.

Industrial facilities • None.

Transportation • Tombstone has an unpaved airport; nearest scheduled air service is in Sierra Vista.

Education • Three public schools (K-12); community college in Sierra Vista.

Local government • Incorporated in 1881; mayor, four-member council and city clerk.

Places to stay • Seven motels, two bed and breakfast inns and three RV parks.

Leisure facilities • Three parks, a pool and two tennis courts.

Tourist lures • Tombstone's funky appearance and reputation are the only lures that tourists need. It has five historic museums, many 18th century buildings and a more-or-less bonafide Western atmosphere.

Contacts • Tombstone Tourism Association, P.O. Box 917, Tombstone, AZ 85638; 457-3548.

City of Tombstone, P.O. Box 339, Tombstone, AZ 85638; 457-3562.

TUBAC

Elevation • Approximately 3,000 feet

Location • In Santa Cruz County, 40 miles south of Tucson on I-19.

Climate • Warm to hot summers; balmy winters with cool nights. July average high 97.1, low 65.5; January average high 65.9, low 31.2

Population • 902

Population trend • Gained 16.4 percent a year in the Eighties.

Property tax • $12.49 per $100 assessed valuation.

Unemployment rate (1989) • 12 percent.

Most historians say this is where Arizona was born. It's the state's oldest non-Indian settlement, started as a Spanish presidio in 1752. The year before, Pima Chief Oacpicagigua had led a revolt against missionaries and settlers, who had gained virtual control over the Indians' land—and their lives. The army was called to quell the uprising, then the troops stayed around to build a fort.

Tubac commander Juan Bautista de Anza left here in 1776 on his historic overland trek to establish the pueblos of San Francisco and San Jose in California. The Gadsden Purchase brought the community under American rule and it was Arizona's largest town by 1860. Then its protective troops were withdrawn to fight in the Civil War, and hostile Apaches forced its abandonment. A few settlers filtered back after the Indians' final defeat, but it never regained its former stature.

Tubac today is a pleasantly scruffy art colony, with more than 50 galleries housed in a mix of old and new adobe and brick buildings. This is where "art and history meet," proclaims a sign at the edge of town. It offers little in the way of job prospects, but you may consider retirement here if you're historically and artistically inclined.

Statistically, Tubac is growing rapidly—gaining more than 16 percent a year in the Eighties. But it had only 230 citizens in 1980, so it's hardly a metropolis today. Two-thirds of its new residents are retired.

Economy • It's based mostly on tourism and retirement.

Job prospects • They're very limited, with a high unemployment rate to prove it. Nearby areas offer limited employment as well.

Real estate • The few homes available start at around $50,000 to $60,000.

The media • Nearest newspaper is the *Green Valley News*, published 20 miles north. Five TV channels from Tucson.

Medical services • One clinic; full medical services available in Nogales, 23 miles south.

Industrial facilities • None.

Transportation • Served by Greyhound and Citizens Bus Lines; no airport.

Education • Two elementary schools and a junior high. Upper grades are bussed elsewhere.

Local government • Unincorporated; services provided by the Santa Cruz County Board of Supervisors.

Places to stay • One country club with 32 rooms and cabanas; a larger resort in Rio Rico, ten miles south.

Leisure facilities • Tubac Center of the Arts and several art galleries and a community center.

Tourist lures • Visitors come for the galleries and boutiques, and to prowl about Tubac Presidio State Historic Park, and Tumacacori National Monument a few miles south.

Contact • Tubac Chamber of Commerce, Kino Park, Tubac, AZ 85621; 398-2704.

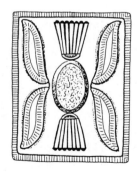

PART THREE

THE ATTRACTIONS

Once you've settled in your special corner of Arizona, you'll want to explore the rest of the state. But where to begin? You already know that it's an amazingly diverse place, with snow-clad pinnacles as well as cactus gardens.

Since you may be spending the rest of your days here, or at least the rest of the winter, why not see it all? Take it one chapter at a time, as we have done on the pages that follow.

Much of the material in this section is distilled from our earlier book, **The Best of Arizona**. If you'd like more information than we list in these chapters, you might pick up a copy at a book store. Or it can be ordered directly from the publisher; details are on the last page of this book. We also recommend other books on Arizona's attractions, history and Indian nations in Chapter 19.

Chapter Twelve

THE NORTHWESTERN CORNER🏔️🏔️🏔️

GRAND CANYON AND VICINITY

We begin our Arizona exploration with the state's most famous attraction—that magnificent 227-mile chasm across its northwest corner. Grand Canyon National Park is Arizona's most-visited landmark, drawing four million people a year.

This high-country corner of Arizona contains other lures as well. Find time to explore the remote and intriguing Arizona Strip on the north side of the Canyon and the Glen Canyon National Recreation area above Page. South of the Canyon, you can hike to the isolated Indian village of Supai, reached only by foot or horseback, deep in a beautiful canyon. Or you can catch a vintage steam train from the woodsy town of Williams to Grand Canyon.

Grand Canyon National Park ● One of the world's most famous natural attractions, the Grand Canyon is not a single ravine but a vast network of hundreds of chasms carved deep into the Kaibab Plateau. Most people visit the South Rim, which has extensive facilities including several lodges, restaurants, museums, gift shops, campgrounds and even an airport. The less-visited but equally spectacular North Rim is our favorite. It's wonderfully uncrowded, drawing only a tenth as many folks as the opposite side. And it offers complete visitor facilities.

The best way to experience the canyon is to hike into its wild depths, or run the roller-coaster rapids of the Colorado River. You can book overnight accommodations at Phantom Ranch or reserve spots at several campgrounds. This must be done well in advance. Phantom Ranch lodgings should be booked a year or more ahead. Several outfits run whitewater trips through the canyon. Our favorite is Grand Canyon Dories, the only operator to use nimble hardboats instead of large inflatable rafts.

The South Rim remains open the year around, but the North

Rim—which is much higher—closes after the first snow flies, usually in late October.

For information • Superintendent, Grand Canyon National Park, P.O. Box 129, Grand Canyon, AZ 86023. Call 638-7888 or 638-7770 for South Rim information and 638-7864 for North Rim information.

Backcountry Reservations Office, P.O. Box 129, Grand Canyon, AZ 86023. (Backcountry camping and hiking reservations can be made only by mail or in person.)

Grand Canyon National Park Lodges (for South Rim and Phantom Ranch reservations), P.O. Box 699, Grand Canyon, AZ 86023; 638-2401 or 638-2631.

TW Recreational Services, Inc. (for North Rim reservations), P.O. Box 400, Cedar City, UT 84720; (801) 586-7686.

Grand Canyon Dories, P.O. Box 216, Altaville, CA 95221; (209) 736-0805.

For a list of other river-runners: River Sub-district, Grand Canyon National Park, P.O. Box 129, Grand Canyon, AZ 86023; 638-7843.

Below the South Rim, the Coconino Plateau slopes southwesterly through Kaibab National Forest, turning into a high prairie of Joshua trees and bunchgrass. If you follow U.S. Highway 180, then State Route 64 south, you'll climb into more forest, then hit the little town of **Williams** at Interstate 40. This woodsy community is home to a recently inaugurated steam train ride to the Grand Canyon.

For area information • Williams-Grand Canyon Chamber of Commerce, P.O. Box 235 (820 Bill Williams Ave.), Williams, AZ 86046; 635-2041.

Grand Canyon Railway • *518 E. Bill Williams Ave., Williams, AZ 86046; (800) THE-TRAIN or (602) 635-4000. Adult round-trip $47, kids 12 and under $23; plus $2 park admission.* Using vintage steam train equipment, this firm has resumed the historic run from Williams to the South Rim that began in 1901. It operates from March through December.

Northeast of Williams, much of the Grand Canyon is rimmed by the Hualapai and Havasupai Indian reservations. An eight-mile hike (or horseback ride) through pretty Havasu Canyon will take you to one of America's most remote villages.

Havasu Canyon and the Village of Supai • For camping permits or overnight lodging and horseback trips, contact: Havasupai Tourist Enterprise, Supai, AZ 86435; 448-2121. To reach the starting point, follow old Highway 66 west from Williams, then go north on Indian Route 18 through the Hualapai reservation to Hualapai Hilltop. From there, you can hike or ride down to Supai, a small Indian village that's reached only by trail. Below are several camping areas and two beautiful waterfalls.

THE ARIZONA STRIP AND GLEN CANYON

Approaching the Grand Canyon's North Rim, you'll pass through the Arizona Strip. Isolated from the rest of the state by the great chasm, this high plateau covering 12,000 square miles is home to only a handful of people. Many are descendants of early Mormon pioneers who came down from Utah in the mid-1800s. Some towns in the area, notably **Colorado City** and **Fredonia**, are still predominately Mormon. Following State Route 389 southeast from Colorado City, you'll come upon one of Arizona's many national monuments.

Pipe Springs National Monument • *HC-65, Box 5, Fredonia, AZ 86022; 643-7105. Daily 8 to 4:30; admission $1.* This small preserve, 17 miles southeast of Colorado City, contains the great fortified ranch headquarters of an early Mormon cattle spread. You can tour furnished rooms in the fortress-like ranch house and climb a low, steep bluff for a nice panorama of the Arizona Strip's grasslands.

From here, the highway continues on into Fredonia, where it merges with U.S. 89-A and swings southward. You can follow it and State Route 67 through Kaibab National Forest to the Grand Canyon's North Rim. Or continue east on 89-A to **Marble Canyon**, a steepwalled ravine where the Colorado River begins slicing into this high plateau. Most river-runners put in at **Lee's Ferry**, just northeast of the hamlet of Marble Canyon.

If you follow 89-A east, then U.S. 89 north, you'll enter **Page** and a large national recreation area that contains a mighty dam and a flooded canyon behind it.

For area information • Page-Lake Powell Visitor & Convention Bureau, Inn at Lake Powell, P.O. Box 727 (716 Rim View Dr.), Page, AZ 86040; 645-2741.

Glen Canyon National Recreation Area • *P.O. Box 1507, Page, AZ 86040; 645-2511.* Within this national recreation area are Glen Canyon Dam, Lake Powell and a million acres of eroded desert sandstone. Glen Canyon, whose serpentine side ravines and fantastic formations rivaled those of the Grand Canyon, was flooded by the dam. You can see the tops of this geological wonderland by taking boat cruises in and out the finger-like fjords of Lake Powell. It begins in Arizona and lies mostly in Utah. **Rainbow Bridge** is one of the attractions here, reached by tour boat from the Wahweap Marina in Page. While you're in the neighborhood, take the self-guiding tour of Glen Canyon Dam and stop at the Carl Hayden Visitor Center and museum; it's open daily from 8 to 5.

FLAGSTAFF AND SURROUNDS

During this northwestern Arizona exploration, you've been in one huge county—Coconino, which covers 18,629 square miles. If you head east on I-40, you'll encounter the county seat. More importantly, it's the gateway to some of Arizona's most varied attractions.

Flagstaff is a good base of operations for playing tourist in these parts. Within a short drive are seven national parks and monuments (including some of America's finest Indian ruins), a ski area, Arizona's highest peak and the redrock beauty of Oak Creek Canyon.

For area information • Flagstaff Chamber of Commerce, 101 Santa Fe, Flagstaff, AZ 86001; (800) 842-7293 or (602) 774-9541.

Winslow Chamber of Commerce, 300 W. North Road (P.O. Box 460), Winslow, AZ 86047; (602) 289-2434.

You'll find these attractions in and around Flagstaff:

Fairfield Snowbowl and Humphreys Peak • *P.O. Box 2430, Flagstaff, AZ 86002; 779-1951.* Although primarily a ski area, the Snowbowl also is popular with summer visitors. You can take a sky ride to the dizzying heights of the San Francisco Peaks and hike into the Kachina Wilderness Area. A trail leads from the Snowbowl to the top of Humphreys Peak, the tallest in Arizona, at 12,633. It's not a technical climb, but it is a long, hard trudge.

Lowell Observatory • *1400 West Mars Hill Road, Flagstaff, AZ 86001; 774-2096. Adults $1, families $3. Tuesday-Saturday 9:30 to 4:30, June through August; shorter hours the rest of the year.* Privately-endowed Lowell Observatory sits atop a pine-covered mesa, less than a mile from downtown. Visitors can view celestial exhibits and join hour-and-a-half lecture tours or wander about the grounds on their own. Call for information about telescope-viewing nights.

Museum of Northern Arizona • *Fort Valley Road (U.S. 180, three miles north); Route 4, Box 720, Flagstaff, AZ 86001; 774-5211. Adults $3, ages 5 to 21, $1.50. Daily 9 to 5.* Housed in a handsome fieldstone and timber complex, the museum is "dedicated to the anthropology, biology, geology and fine arts of the Colorado Plateau." It is, in short, one of Arizona's finest exhibit centers.

Riordan State Historic Park • *Riordan Ranch Road, P.O. Box 217, Flagstaff, AZ 86002; 779-4395. Adults $2, kids 18 and under free. Daily 8 to 5 in summer, 12:30 to 5 the rest of the year.* The park consists of the pioneer Riordan brothers' elaborate and unusual fieldstone double-home, joined in the middle by a gaming room. Admire turn-of-the-century furnishings, and learn about Flagstaff's early days in a museum in the old carriage house.

Sunset Crater National Monument • *Twelve miles north on U.S. 89, then east. Mailing address: 2717 N. Steves Blvd., Suite 3, Flagstaff, AZ 86004; 527-7042. Visitor center open daily 8 to 5; $3 per car (includes admission to Wupatki).* The focal point of this park is an almost perfect volcanic cindercone with a burnt orange cast, particularly at sunset. (Thus, the name). It's surrounded by the wild geological turmoil of eruptions that date back about 700 years.

Wupatki National Monument • *Fourteen miles north of Sunset Crater; same address but different phone: 527-7040. Visitor center open daily 8 to 5; $3 per car (includes admission to Sunset Crater).* Wupatki is home to several Indian ruins scattered about a high volcanic prairie. The largest and most elaborate is Wupatki Pueblo, a short walk from the visitor center. It's a four-story, 100-room village built of sandstone blocks instead of the usual adobe. A Mayan-style "ball court" is nearby.

Driving west from Flagstaff on I-40 toward Winslow, you'll discover two other attractions. One comes from the mysterious past; the other from outer space. Just north of Winslow, you'll see one of the most dramatic slices of desert badlands in Arizona. And it comes in a nice, manageable size.

Walnut Canyon National Monument • *Walnut Canyon Road (seven miles east, then three miles south), Flagstaff, AZ 86004; 526-3367. Daily 8 to 5; trail to ruins closes at 4; $1 per person or $3 per family.* Steep-walled Walnut Canyon shelters an elaborate Sinagua cliff dwelling built about 800 years ago. Recessed in overhangs between the rim and canyon floor, the ruins can be reached by a 251-step trail from the visitor center. Save some energy for the return trip.

Meteor Crater • *Forty miles east of Flagstaff to Meteor Crater exit, then six miles south. Mailing address: Meteor Crater Enterprises, 603 N. Beaver St., Suite C, Flagstaff, AZ 86001; 774-8350. Daily 6 a.m. to 6 p.m. in summer, shorter hours the rest of the year. Adults $6, seniors $5, kids 12 to 17, $2.50; 5 to 11, $1.* Imagine this: a monster chunk of nickel and iron weighing millions of tons streaks earthward at 43,000 miles an hour. It slams into the ground with a force that buries fragments hundreds of feet deep. What you'll see is the hole it left, plus an excellent museum about the crater with displays concerning meteorites, the universe and America's space program.

Little Painted Desert County Park • *Just off State Route 87, 13 miles north of Winslow; gates open 8 a.m. to 9 p.m. Flush potties and picnic ramada.* This is a surprising jewel of a park—a mini-badlands of softly contoured, pastel-hued sandstone. From a parking area, you can drive or walk along rim roads in either direction for varied vistas of this fluted amphitheater of erosion. A trail from the north rim road takes you into this sensuously rounded landscape.

SEDONA AND THE VERDE VALLEY

If you head south of Flagstaff on U.S. 89-A, you'll enter a mosaic of natural beauty, upscale tourism and pre-history. You'll discover the red ramparts of **Oak Creek Canyon**; the galleries, boutiques and elegant resorts of **Sedona**; the ancient Indian ruins of the Verde Valley and a rustic copper mining town.

For area information • Sedona-Oak Creek Canyon Chamber of Commerce, P.O. Box 487 (89-A and Forest Road), Sedona, AZ 86336; 282-7722.

Camp Verde Chamber of Commerce, P.O. Box 1665 (Main and Turner streets), Camp Verde, AZ 86322; 567-3341.

Jerome Chamber of Commerce, P.O. Box 788 (426 Hull Ave.), Jerome, AZ 86331; 634-9425 or 634-5716.

Verde Valley Chamber of Commerce, 1010 S. Main St., Cottonwood, AZ 86326; 864-7593.

The road into Oak Creek Canyon is one of the prettiest drives in America. It twists down through thick pondersosa forests to the valley floor, then follows sparkling Oak Creek. At the canyon's lower end, it emerges into a stunning panorama of redrock pinnacles, buttes and fairy castles above Sedona.

We've already established that Sedona is an art and tourist colony, cradled in one of the prettiest settings anywhere. Take time to explore is upscale shops and galleries, particularly in **Tlaquepaque,** a Spanish colonial style complex just south of town on State Route 179.

Inquire at the chamber or the **Coconino National Forest** office at 225 Brewer Road about scenic drives and hikes in the area. Several operators offer jeep trips into the redrock formations and balloon flights above them.

Also, stop to admire the **Chapel of the Holy Cross,** on Chapel Road off Highway 179, two miles south of town. Rising from the red rocks with a huge cross forming its facade, it rivals the rocks themselves as Sedona's best-known landmark.

Continuing south of Sedona into the Verde Valley, you'll find four more intriguing attractions. Two are remnants of the dim past and two are of more recent vintage.

Tuzigoot National Monument • *Between Cottonwood and Clarkdale on Tuzigoot Road; P.O. Box 68, Clarkdale, AZ 86324; 634-5564. Adults $1, families $3. Daily 8 to 5 (to 7 p.m. in summer).* These extensive Sinagua ruins crown a low ridge north of Clarkdale. They were built around the 13th century, then abandoned—probably because of drought. The pueblo was restored and an excellent museum was created as a WPA project during the Depression.

Montezuma's Castle National Monument • *P.O. Box 219, Camp Verde, AZ 86322; 567-3322. Daily 8 to 5 (to 7 p.m. in summer). Adults $1, families $3, kids 17 and under free.* It's not a castle and it was never visited by the Aztec chief Montezuma. It's a small but dramatic ruin perched high in a cliff face. Nearby and equally interesting (also equally misnamed) is **Montezuma Well,** a limestone sinkhole rimmed by several pueblo ruins.

Also worthy of a visit in the area is the **Yavapai-Apache Visitor Center** at the Montezuma Castle exit from I-17. This impressive facility, jointly operated by the national park service and Verde Valley Yavapai-Apache tribe, is a museum of Indian culture, with exhibits concerning attractions of the Verde Valley.

Fort Verde State Historic Park ● *In Camp Verde, just south of Montezuma's Castle; P.O. Box 397, Camp Verde, AZ 86322; 567-3275. Daily 8 to 5; adults $1, kids 17 and under free.* The park preserves remnants of a frontier army post built in the 1870s to protect settlers from Indians. A museum spotlights the Indian and white history of the Verde Valley.

If you follow 89-A southwest through the Verde Valley, you'll climb into the flanks of Mingus Mountain and enter the scruffy remnants of one of Arizona's most interesting old mining towns. **Jerome** isn't a ghost town, but a lively tourist village with dusty museums, 19th century homes, art galleries, curio shops and antique stores. From the late 1870s to the 1950s, billions of dollars in copper, gold and silver were gouged from Mingus Mountain's steep slopes. Two attractions here are worth stops:

Jerome State Historic Park ● *P.O. Box D, Jerome, AZ 86331; 634-5381. Daily 8 to 5; $1 for adults, kids free.* The park embraces the estate of James S. Douglas, one of Jerome's mining barons. The mansion offers a mix of period furnishings, historic videos and mining exhibits.

Gold King Mine Museum ● *P.O. Box 125, Jerome, AZ 86331. Adults $2, kids 6 to 17, $1. Daily 9 to 5:30.* This scruffy clutter of early-day mining equipment and 19th century memorabilia walks a fine line between a museum and a junkyard. And therein lies its character.

PRESCOTT TO WICKENBURG

Continuing southeast on Highway 89-A, you'll leave Mingus Mountain's slopes, drive through a grassy valley and begin climbing again—this time into the woods of Prescott National Forest. Cradled among these trees is **Prescott,** one of our favorite Arizona towns.

For area information ● Prescott Chamber of Commerce, P.O. Box 1147 (117 W. Goodwin St.), Prescott, AZ 86302; 445-2000.

Wickenburg Chamber of Commerce, P.O. Drawer CC, Wickenburg, AZ 85358; 684-5479.

Prescott certainly is a nice place to live, with its handsome tree-lined neighborhoods, three colleges, cultural offerings and brick-front downtown. It's a nice place to visit, too. Several museums, galleries, boutiques and antique shops lure tens of thousands of tourists each year. Among the reasons for coming here:

Prescott's Phippen Museum of Western Art ● *4701 N. Highway 89; Prescott, AZ 86302; 778-1385. Adults $2, kids $1. Various hours.* Located seven miles from town, the museum houses paintings, bronzes, sculptures and ceramics of past and present Western artists.

Sharlot Hall Museum ● *415 W. Gurley St., Prescott, AZ 86302; 445-3122. Tuesday-Saturday 10 to 5, Sunday 1 to 5; shorter hours No-*

vember through March. Free; donations appreciated. Covering more than a city block, the Sharlot Hall complex contains a dozen historic buildings, either original or reconstructed. The centerpiece is the governor's "mansion." This oversized log cabin served as the official residence when Prescott was the territorial capital in the late 1800s.

Smoki Museum • *100 N. Arizona St., Prescott, AZ 86302; 445-1230. Adults $1, kids under 12 free.* Pronounced "Smoke-Eye," this museum has a fine collection of stone tools, baskets, pottery and other artifacts excavated from Southwest Indian ruins.

Yavapai County Courthouse and Plaza • *Gurley and Montezuma streets.* The Greco-Roman style courthouse and surrounding tree-shaded lawn give Prescott a typical New England look. However, the town itself is definitely Western, with cowboy galleries and shops.

Across from the courthouse along Montezuma Street is "Whiskey Row," once the town's bawdy district and now a solid rank of oldstyle storefronts. Many house Western saloons. Check out the unusual **Bead Museum** with tens of thousands of beads and beadwork, at 140 S. Montezuma. It's open Monday through Saturday 9:30 to 4:30.

If you drive southeast from Prescott on State Highway 69, you'll drop quickly from pines to cactus. At the I-40 and Cordes Junction interchange, you'll encounter a most curious complex.

Arcosanti • *c/o Mayer, AZ 86333; 632-735. Tours on the hour from 10 to 4; four people minimum, $4 per person.* Arcosanti is the creation of Italian architect and visionary Paolo Soleri. Seeking to solve many world problems in one architectural swoop, he is trying—with eager young helpers—to build an idyllic, energy-efficient, space-saving community. However, its geometric precast concrete shapes have begun to weather in the 22 years since the project was started. It looks more like a scruffy space station that crash-landed in the desert, or perhaps a low-budget EPCOT center.

If you take U.S. 89 southwest from Prescott, you'll discover a completely different concept in a community. **Wickenburg** works to preserve its cowboy past, instead of fretting about an Orwellian future. It calls itself the "Dude Ranch capital of the world," a title well-earned, since five guest ranches function in the attractive surrounding desert.

We've already touched on its colored history. Wickenburg was first a gold rush boomtown, then an important ranching center. Today, it still looks like yesterday, with false front stores and boardwalks. And it proudly hosts one of the finest small museums in Arizona.

Desert Caballeros Western Museum • *20 N. Frontier St. (At Wickenburg Way), Wickenburg, AZ 85358; 684-2272. Monday-Saturday 10 to 5; Sunday 1 to 4. Adults $2, kids free.* The focal point of this museum is a full-scale turn-of-the-century Western street scene. Excellent dioramas and artifacts recall the area's development from the Paleozoic to the present. An adjoining gallery displays Western art by such notables as Russell, Remington and Catlin.

Chapter Thirteen

RIO COLORADO & THE SOUTHWEST ▓▓

THE COLORADO RIVER CORRIDOR

We've discussed this aquatic playground in Chapter 8. A series of reservoirs are formed as the Colorado River bumps into dam after dam, trying to flow from the Grand Canyon to the Sea of Cortez. The area's aquatic playgrounds and warm winters lure tens of thousands of Snowbirds.

If you live elsewhere in the state and want to visit this area, we'd suggest coming in the spring or fall. Summers sizzle, with daytime averages above 105 degrees. Winter nights, while pleasantly balmy, can get a bit cool for moonlight swims. But in the spring and fall, temperatures are close to idyllic.

For instance, in Lake Havasu City, the average April daytime high is 87 and the low is 53.6. In October, the ranges are 91.4 and 57.8. Some Snowbirds, we suspect, may fly home too soon.

If you visit these corridor communities, bear in mind that they aren't bastions of culture or architectural gems. Many, like Bullhead City, look hastily assembled. Few have significant tourist attractions, other than their next-door reservoirs.

From a tourist standpoint, we'll suggest a driving tour down the corridor, traveling from north to south.

For area information ● Bullhead Area Chamber of Commerce, P.O. Box 66, Bullhead City, AZ 86430; 754-4121.

Kingman Area Chamber of Commerce, P.O. Box 1150 Kingman, AZ 86402; 753-6106.

Lake Havasu City Chamber of Commerce, 1930 Mesquite Ave., Suite 3, Lake Havasu City, AZ 86403; 855-4115.

Parker Area Chamber of Commerce, P.O. Box 627, Parker, AZ 85334; 669-2174.

Hoover Dam and Lake Mead National Recreation Area ● *601 Nevada Highway, Boulder City, NV 89005-2426; (702) 293-8907. Also, Boulder City Chamber of Commerce, 1497 Nevada Highway, Boulder*

City, NV 89005; (702) 754-4121. When Hoover Dam was completed in 1935, it was the world's highest, holding back the world's largest man-made lake. Tours are conducted several times daily through this incredible concrete wedge; hours are 9 a.m. to 4:15 p.m. Also interesting is the **Alan Bible Visitor Center** on the Nevada side, three miles from the dam on U.S. Highway 93. It has films on Hoover Dam construction, wildlife exhibits, a botanical garden, gift shop and bookstore. Nine Marinas rim the national recreation area's two reservoirs— Lake Mead upstream and Lake Mohave downstream.

Boulder City, Nevada, is worth a visit as well. Built to house the dam's construction workers, it's an attractive hamlet sitting on a landscaped knoll, adding a splash of green to this tawny desert. Its arcaded Arizona Street is a fine example of Art Deco middle America. The **Boulder City/Hoover Dam Museum** has dam construction exhibits and films and a gift shop.

Driving south on U.S. Highway 93, you'll swing inland through **Kingman**, where you might want to pause at the **Mohave Museum of History and Arts** at 400 W. Beale St. (753-3195). It's open Monday through Friday from 10 to 5 and weekends 1 to 5. Exhibits trace the area's history and geology, and a special display focuses on Kingman's hometown hero, the late gravel-voiced actor Andy Devine. Should you want to learn more about the area, the **Chamber of Commerce** is next door.

From Kingman, return to Rio Colorado by following State Route 68 west. For a more interesting and roundabout approach, take an unnamed highway southwest to the funky old semi-ghost town of **Oatman**. Continue to State Route 95, then go north to **Bullhead City.**

Bullhead is interesting only for its winter climate and recreation on Lake Mohave. If you feel like pulling a few slot machine handles, you can drive or take a free shuttle boat over to the glossy casinos of **Laughlin, Nevada**.

From Bullhead, you'll stay rather close to the river until you bump into I-40. Drive eastward briefly, then head south on Highway 95 to **Lake Havasu City.** As we've already discussed, the attraction here is the transplanted **London Bridge**. Promoters call it the second most-visited attraction in Arizona, after the Grand Canyon. It is interesting, sitting there in the desert, looking like a left-over Roman ruin in North Africa.

From Havasu, you'll drive to **Parker**, an unassuming little town on the Colorado River Indian Reservation. **Parker Dam** offers self-guided tours that are moderately interesting. The town itself, rather ordinary-looking, is noted for the greatest concentration of RV and mobile home parks along the river. Prices are modest, so the area is popular with budget-minded Snowbirds.

South from Parker, you swing away from the river and hit I-10 at

Quartzsite, which we've already branded as the ugliest town in Arizona. You can stop by the simple little **Quartzsite Museum**, which keeps somewhat irregular hours. Before leaving town, visit a curious pyramidal monument to **Haiji Ali**. He was a Syrian who came over as part of a late 19th century experiment to use camels for Southwestern desert transport. The experiment flopped, but "Hi Jolly" hung around Quartzsite and become a local character.

YUMA TO ORGAN PIPE AND KITT PEAK

Highway 95 continues skirting away from Rio Colorado until it reaches the only town of substance in this corridor, **Yuma**. With a population topping 50,000, it offers a fine historic park and a rather nice city museum. You might swing west on I-8 into California, where you'll see sand dunes that look right out of a Lawrence of Arabia movie.

For area information • Yuma County Chamber of Commerce, P.O. Box 6468 (377 S. Main St.), Yuma, AZ 85366; 344-3800.

Yuma Territorial Prison State Historic Park • *Prison Hill Road (P.O. Box 10792), Yuma, AZ 85366-8792; 783-4771. Daily 8 to 5; adults $2, kids under 17 free.* Hollywood made the old prison more notorious than it really was. Ironically, it was designed to be a model lockup with a library, schooling and even crafts classes. But it had no air conditioning and summers were beastly, even if the guards weren't. It's now a museum, with exhibits of those late 19th century days when the bad guys wore black and white stripes.

Century House Museum • *240 Madison Ave., Yuma, AZ 85364; 782-1841. Tuesday-Saturday 10 to 4. Free; donations encouraged.* Exhibits in this 1870 adobe mansion focus on early pioneer families and Indian cultures of the area. The adjacent **Adobe Annex** houses boutiques and a pleasant patio restaurant.

Yuma Crossing Park • *Along the riverfront, extending from the old Yuma Quartermaster Depot to the prison; 329-0471.* Grand plans are afoot to turn this early California gateway into a major living history center. It may or may not have been accomplished by the time you arrive.

There's not much south of Yuma, except for the pleasantly dusty Mexican border town of **San Luis.** If you head east on I-8 to **Gila Bend,** then swing south onto State Route 85, you'll eventually reach one of our favorite patches of desert.

Organ Pipe Cactus National Monument • *Route 1, Box 100, Ajo, AZ 85321; 387-6849. Gates always open; visitor center open daily 8 to 5; $3 per vehicle.* Arizona's largest national monument preserves a striking section of the great Sonoran Desert that covers much of southern Arizona and northern Mexico. Twenty-nine species of cactus grow here. The park becomes a dazzling garden of lupine, poppies and cactus blooms during early spring.

Continuing east from here on State Route 86, you'll travel through the barren desert of the huge **Tohono O'odham Indian Reservation.** As you leave southwestern Arizona and approach Tucson, take time to drive up to the world's largest astronomical facility.

Kit Peak National Observatory • *P.O. Box 26732, Tucson, AZ 85726-6732; 620-5350. Daily 10 to 4. Call for film and lecture schedules.* Kitt Peak scatters its gleaming white domes over the rocky ramparts of the Quinlan Mountains. Self-guiding tours take you to the 500-foot long McMath solar telescope and several other sky-searchers. A small visitor center features astronomical exhibits and crafts of the Tohono O'Odham Indians.

Chapter Fourteen

PHOENIX AND SURROUNDS 🔺🔺🔺🔺

VALLEY OF THE SUN ATTRACTIONS

It will come as no surprise that Phoenix is a major destination for tourists as well as for job-seekers, retirees and Snowbirds.

Most of the lures here are man-made—fine museums, huge air-conditioned malls and elegant resorts. Phoenix was rated second in the nation for visitor services, accommodations and dining by the New York-based Zagat Guide survey in 1988. It has more Mobil Travel Guide five-star resorts than any other city in the country, and four AAA five-diamond resorts.

With all this, it's still a remarkably inexpensive city in which to play tourist. A recent survey revealed that a visitor spends less than $100 a day for lodging and meals, the third lowest of any major city in the country. Los Angeles costs twice as much and New York is triple that figure.

For area information • Phoenix and Valley of the Sun Convention and Visitors Bureau, 505 N. Second St., Suite 300, Phoenix, AZ 85004-3998; 254-6500. Visitor information hotline—252-5588. Visitor centers are located on the northwest corner of Adams and Second streets in the downtown Hyatt Regency Hotel block and in Terminals 2 and 3 at Sky Harbor International Airport.

Toll-free reservations number: (800) 528-0483 outside Arizona. In the state, call collect (602) 257-4111. You can reserve hotels, motels, apartments, condos, car rentals and ground and air tours.

Phoenix attractions

The Heard Museum • *22 E. Monte Vista (off Central Avenue), Phoenix, AZ 85004; 252-8840. Monday-Saturday 10 to 5, Sunday 1 to 5. Adults $3, seniors $2.50, students $1.* The Heard is Arizona's finest museum and probably the best treasury of Indian culture in the world. Excellent exhibits, living history demonstrations, videos, movies and art displays convey the story of the Native Americans—yesterday and today.

Arizona Historical Society Museum • *1242 N. Central Ave. (Culver Street), Phoenix, AZ 85004; 255-4470. Tuesday-Saturday 10 to 4; free.* The state's Spanish, Mexican and American history is portrayed in artifacts, photos and dioramas. A new historical society museum was scheduled to open in Papago Park in the spring of 1992.

Arizona Mineral Museum • *McDowell Road and 19th Avenue at the state fairgrounds, Phoenix, AZ 85009; 255-3791. Weekdays 8 to 5, Saturday 1 to 5; free.* The museum focuses on the state's geology, minerals and mining history, with specimens, core samples, mining tools and mine models.

Arizona Museum of Science and Technology • *80 N. Second St. (Adams), Phoenix, AZ 85004; 256-9388. Monday-Saturday 9 to 5, Sunday noon to 5. Adults $3.50, kids 4 to 12 and seniors $2.50.* At this writing, the museum was in rather limited quarters on Second Street. By the time you read this, however, a new state-of-the-art facility may be completed as part of the $1.1 billion downtown renewal program.

Arizona State Capitol Museum • *1700 W. Washington (17th Avenue), Phoenix, AZ 85007; 255-4675. Weekdays 8 to 5; tours at 10 and 2; free.* Arizona's government has outgrown its copper-domed, tufa and granite state capitol, and moved into modern quarters. Much of the original structure, built in 1900 as the territorial capitol, is now a museum of the state's history.

Desert Botanical Garden • *1201 N. Galvin Parkway (in Papago Park), Phoenix, AZ 85008; 941-1225. September-May, 9 a.m. to sunset, June-August, 8 a.m. to sunset. Adults $3.50, seniors $3 and kids 5 to 12, $1.* It's Arizona's finest botanical garden, featuring desert flora from around the world. March to May is the peak blooming season.

Hall of Flame Firefighting Museum • *6101 E. Van Buren St. (in Papago Park), Phoenix, AZ 85008; 275-3473. Monday-Saturday 9 to 5. Adults $3, seniors $2 and kids 6-17, $1.* This is the world's largest museum of firefighting equipment. Exhibits include hand-drawn pumpers, early hook-and-ladder rigs and the earliest motorized fire trucks.

Heritage Square • *Sixth and Monroe streets; 262-5071.* The square contains eight historic Phoenix homes from the late 19th and early 20th centuries. Some have museum-quality period furnishings; others house shops and restaurants.

Phoenix Art Museum • *1625 N. Central Ave. (McDowell Road), Phoenix, AZ 85004; 257-1222. Tuesday-Saturday 10 to 5 (to 9 p.m. Wednesdays), Sunday 1 to 5. Adults $3, seniors $2.50 and students $1.40.* The museum's eclectic collection includes paintings, sculptures and other art objects of the American West, Europe and Asia.

Phoenix Zoo • *5180 E. Van Buren (in Papago Park), Phoenix, AZ 85072; 273-1341. Daily 9 to 5. Adults $6, kids 4 to 12, $3.* It's both a zoo and a botanical garden. Critter enclosures are framed in a setting of desert flora, eucalyptus trees, trickling streams and shady patios.

Pioneer Arizona Living History Museum • *c/o Black Canyon State (Pioneer Road exit 225 from I-17), Phoenix, AZ 85027; 993-0212. Wednesday-Friday 9 to 3, weekends 9 to 4; shorter hours in summer. Adults $4.50, seniors and students 16 and older, $4; kids 4 to 12, $3.* Homes and businesses of early-day Arizona have been assembled on a chunk of desert 30 miles north of Phoenix. They range from adobe to Victorian to brick.

Pueblo Grande Museum • *4617 E. Washington St., (44th Street), Phoenix, AZ 85034; 275-1897. Monday-Saturday 9 to 4:45, Sunday 1 to 4:45; fifty cents.* Now surrounded by the expanding city, this site preserves a large Hohokam pueblo. Although there's little left of the original village, an excellent museum captures the lifestyles of the first Phoenix inhabitants.

SCOTTSDALE, CAREFREE & CAVE CREEK

For area information • Carefree/Cave Creek Chamber of Commerce, P.O. Box 734, Carefree, AZ 85377; 488-3381.

Scottsdale Chamber of Commerce, 7333 Scottsdale Mall, Scottsdale, AZ 85251-4498; 945-8481.

Taliesin West • *108th Street (East Shea Boulevard), Scottsdale, AZ 85261; 860-2700; call for reservations. Tours daily, on the hour 10 to 4 (at 9, 10 and 11 in summer). Adults $6, kids 5 to 12, $2.50.* The former winter home and studio of Frank Lloyd Wright has become a world-acclaimed architectural school. Tours are conducted through this fascinating—mostly triangular—sandstone complex that embodies Wright's concept of "organic architecture."

Cosanti • *6433 Doubletree Ranch Road (Invergorden), Scottsdale, AZ 85253; 948-6145. Daily 9 to 5; $1 donation.* This is the home and studio of Paolo Soleri, whose disciples are building Arcosanti, southeast of Prescott (Chapter 12). You can tour his studio, which has a precast extra-terrestrial look, and buy his artistically-interesting bronze and ceramic bells and wind chimes.

Rawhide • *23023 N. Scottsdale Rd. (Pinnacle Peak Road), Scottsdale, AZ 85261; 563-5600. October-May—5 to 10 p.m. weekdays and noon to 10 weekends; June-September—5 to 10 daily. Free; museum admission $1.* Rawhide is a pretend cowboy town with false-front stores housing boutiques, restaurants, saloons and other things Western. It's kinda cute. You can have a friend arrested for $3, and hung for another $2. If this works up an appetite, dine on hickory-broiled steak while listening to live country music.

Carefree and Cave Creek • These two hamlets on the fringe of the Valley of the Sun are worth a visit. The planned desert community of Carefree offers two lures, the **world's largest sundial** and **El Pedrigal Festival Marketplace**, a shopping center that looks like a cross between Frank Lloyd Wright architecture and Tune Town.

In rustic Cave Creek, you can dine on cowboy steaks at one of several Western saloon-restaurants. The **Cave Creek Museum** displays relics of the community's mining past. It's at Basin and Skyline; open Thursday-Sunday from 1:30 to 4:30 (closed in summer).

TEMPE-MESA

For area information • Mesa Convention and Visitors Bureau, 120 N. Center St., Mesa, AZ 85201; 969-1307.

Tempe Chamber of Commerce, 60 E. Fifth St., Tempe, AZ 85281; 894-8158.

Arizona State University Campus • *Apache Boulevard in Tempe; 965-5728 (events phone).* Green lawns and palms create a parklike setting for ASU's gathering of brick buildings. The centerpiece is Frank Lloyd Wright's Gammage Center for the Performing Arts, a curious sandstone pink edifice of circles within circles. The effect is a bit like a masonry circus tent.

Champlin Fighter Museum • *4636 Fighter Aces Dr. (at Falcon Field, off McKellips Road), Mesa, AZ 85205; 830-4540. Daily 10 to 5. Adults $5, kids 14 and under, $2.50.* Twenty-eight World War I and II fighter planes, either restored or faithful replicas, are on display. The collection includes a rare Fokker triplane and a Sopwith Camel. Snoopy would love this place.

Mesa Southwest Museum • *53 N. MacDonald St. (First Street), Mesa, AZ 85201; 644-2230 or 644-2169. Tuesday-Saturday 10 to 5, Sunday 1 to 5. Adults $2.50, kids under 13, $1.* Mesa's fine city museum chronicles the area's history, from the vanished Hohokam Indians to the legend of the Lost Dutchman Mine. It's housed in an attractive Spanish-style building surrounded by desert gardens.

PHOENIX-TUCSON CORRIDOR

Interstate 10 that runs diagonally between Phoenix and Tucson is Arizona's busiest corridor. Highway 89, just to the northeast, is a much more genteel route. Several tourist lures can be encountered along each.

For area information • Apache Junction Chamber of Commerce, P.O. Box 1747, Apache Junction, AZ 85217; 982-3141.

Florence Chamber of Commerce, P.O. Box 929, Florence, AZ 85232; 868-5889.

Greater Casa Grande Chamber of Commerce, 575 N. Marshall St., Casa Grande, AZ 85222; 836-2125.

U.S. 89-60 Freeway running east from Phoenix will take you to **Apache Junction.** It's a growing community in an attractive desert below the grimly fascinating ramparts of the **Superstition Mountains**. You've probably heard the tale of the Lost Dutchman Mine. A German prospector named Jacob Waltz supposedly found a rich gold cache in the Superstitions in the 1860s, but he died without revealing its whereabouts.

You can explore the foothills of these rough-hewn mountains and indulge in a bit of water sports by following State Route 88 northeast from Apache Junction. Known locally as the Apache Trail, it takes you to **Lost Dutchman State Park,** with camping, picnicking and hiking trails, then into rugged **Salt River Canyon,** where dams of the Salt River project have created several reservoirs.

If you continue south from Apache Junction on Highway 89, you'll encounter the attractive western-style town of **Florence.** Check out the **Florence Townsite National Historic District** and the gingerbread-Victorian **Pinal County Courthouse.** Save an hour or so for an interesting historical museum:

McFarland State Historic Park • *Main and Ruggles streets, Florence, AZ 85631; 868-5216. Thursday-Monday 8 to 5. Adults $2, kids under 17 free.* This adobe served variously as Pinal County's courthouse, jail, sheriff's office and hospital. Displays depict each era. It's named for Ernest W. McFarland, a local boy who went on to author the G.I. Bill of Rights as a U.S. Senator, then became chief justice of the Arizona Supreme Court.

As you continue south toward Tucson, Highway 89 becomes the **Pinal Pioneer Parkway,** passing through attractive desert gardens. Signs identify the roadside flora. Think of it as a 55-miles-an-hour nature trail. Interstate 10 is a faster but less interesting route between Arizona's two metropolitan centers. It also offers a couple of tourist lures:

Gila River Arts and Crafts Center • *Casa Blanca Road (I-10 exit 175, then half a mile west), P.O. Box 457, Sacaton, AZ 85247; 963-3981. Daily 9 to 5 (shorter hours in summer); free.* More than 30 different tribes and 2,000 years of Native American history are represented in this modern cultural center. It's located on Gila River Indian Reservation.

Casa Grande Ruins National Monument • *P.O. Box 518 (off Highway 287), Coolidge, AZ 85228; 723-3172. Daily 7 to 6; $3 per family, $1 per person; kids 17 and under, free.* This four-story adobe is the tallest free-standing Hohokam structure in Arizona. Although it was the centerpiece of an ancient village, historians don't know why it was built. It may have been a ceremonial building or an observatory.

Picacho Peak State Park • *P.O. Box 275, Picacho, AZ 85241; 466-3183; $3 per car.* Stop for a picnic or hike to the 1,400-foot summit of this monolith, which is shaped like a giant tiger's fang. The westernmost battle of the Civil War was fought near here on April 15, 1862. A group of California volunteers routed a troupe of Texans trying to rope Arizona into the Confederacy.

Chapter Fifteen

TUCSON AND SURROUNDS ▚▚▚▚

TUCSON ATTRACTIONS

Arizona's second largest city rivals its big brother in both the quality and quantity of its tourist attractions. It offers a fine mix of indoor culture and outdoor recreation. Five mountain ranges rim Tucson's high desert basin and a huge slice of this arid terrain has been preserved in Tucson Mountain Park.

One of Arizona's oldest cities, Tucson is a tempting blend of the cosmopolitan, the old pueblo and the great outdoors.

All of this—and it claims to have more days of sunshine than any other American city.

For area information • Metropolitan Tucson Convention & Visitor's Bureau, 130 S. Scott Ave., Tucson, AZ 85701; 624-1889. City Arts line (for cultural activities), 942-0595.

Arizona-Sonora Desert Museum • *2021 N. Kinney Rd. (in Tucson Mountain Park), Tucson, AZ 85743; 883-2702. Daily 7:30 to 6 in summer, 8:30 to 5 the rest of the year. Adults $6, kids 6 to 12, $1.* One of America's finest outdoor museums, it's devoted to preserving, exhibiting and studying the Sonoran Desert's flora, fauna, geology, climatology and culture. Winding paths take visitors to beaver and otter ponds, a bird aviary, open animal habitats, cactus gardens and a new underground earth sciences center.

Arizona Historical Society Museum • *949 E. Second St. (Park Avenue), Tucson, AZ 85719; 628-5774. Monday-Saturday 10 to 4, Sunday noon to 4; free.* Located just outside the University of Arizona campus, it covers the state's history from the beginning of white settlement. Cattle brands, Bull Durham pouches, high-wheel bicycles and cowboy regalia help tell the story.

Arizona State Museum • *University Avenue at Park Avenue, c/o University of Arizona, Tucson, AZ 85721; 621-6302. Monday-Saturday 9 to 5, Sunday 2 to 5; free.* Occupying two buildings just inside UA's main gate, the museum focuses on prehistoric and modern Indian cultures of the Southwest. Displays include a look at past and present Apache society and "cave archaeology", showing how both prehistoric and modern societies have used earth recesses for shelter.

De Grazia Gallery in the Sun • *6300 N. Swan Rd. (Skyline Drive), Tucson, AZ 85718; 299-9191. Daily 10 to 4; free.* The late Ted De Grazia, who specialized in color-splashed paintings of Indians, Mexicans and other Southwestern subjects, built this adobe studio complex to display his works. It's now a combined gallery and gift shop, with the artist's images on sale in every medium from serigraphs to refrigerator magnets.

El Presidio Historic District • *Bounded by Pennington, Church, Washington and Main streets downtown.* This is the original site of the Presidio of Tucson, although little remains from that era. Several adobe and wood frame 19th century houses contain boutiques, galleries and restaurants.

Fort Lowell Museum • *Craycroft and Fort Lowell, Tucson, AZ 85719; 885-3832. Wednesday-Saturday 10 to 4; free.* Part of a large city park and recreation area, Fort Lowell Museum is a reconstruction of a military camp established in 1873.

Grace H. Flandrau Planetarium • *University of Arizona campus at University and Cherry; 621-STAR. Museum and astronomy store open Monday 1 to 4, Tuesday-Thursday 10 to 4 and weekends 1 to 5; free. Call for hours of planetarium shows and telescope viewings.* It's a science center as well as a planetarium. Push buttons and pull levers to learn about lasers, radio waves and holography.

International Wildlife Museum • *4800 W. Gates Pass Rd. (Camino de Oeste), Tucson, AZ 85745; 629-0100. Open Wednesday-Sunday: Labor Day to Memorial Day 9 to 5:30, the rest of the year 8:30 to 6. Adults $4, seniors, students and military $3.50, kids 6 to 12, $1.50.* Housed in a structure resembling a North African desert fort, this facility displays more than 300 varieties of stuffed animals. It appears to be a contradiction in themes: some displays talk about conservation while others extol the virtues of big-game hunting.

Mission San Xavier del Bac • *San Xavier Road (nine miles south, off I-19); 294-2624. Church, museum and gift shop open daily 9 to 5:30. Free; contributions appreciated.* Affectionately called the "White Dove of the Desert," San Xavier is one of the most beautiful missions in North America. Constructed around 1778, its elaborate facade and whitewashed twin domes offer a near perfect example of Spanish colonial architecture. On weekends, members of the Tohono O'odham tribe set up a market to sell their crafts and tasty Indian fry bread.

Mount Lemmon • *Reached via the Catalina Highway from northeast Tucson.* This scenic highway spirals quickly from saguaro forests to the piney forests of Mount Lemmon. Castle-like eroded rock formations line the route. In winter, you can hit the mountain's ski slopes.

Old Pueblo Museum • *In Foothills Shopping Mall (La Cholla Boulevard, just north of Ina Road); 742-2355. Monday-Friday 10 to 9, Saturday 10 to 6 and Sunday noon to 5; free.* This strikingly-modern shopping mall museum features changing exhibits of the flora, fauna, culture and artwork of the Southwest.

Old Tucson • *201 S. Kinney Rd. (in Tucson Mountain Park), Tucson, AZ 85746; 883-6457. Daily 9 to 9. Adults $8.95, kids 4 to 11, $4.95.* This is a Hollywood version of a Western frontier town, and we mean that literally. Built for a 1939 epic called Arizona, it's now a combined working movie set and cowboy entertainment park. Placards around the grounds describe the more than 150 horse operas filmed here.

Pima Air Museum • *6000 E. Valencia Rd. (Wilmot), Tucson, AZ 85706; 574-0462. Daily 9 to 5. Adults $4, seniors and military $3, kids 10 to 17, $2.* The museum traces the history of American aviation, with exhibits indoors and out. You'll see a replica of the Wright brothers plane and more than 150 military aircraft from several wars. A large gift shop brims with aviation memorabilia.

Sabino Canyon • *Sabino Canyon Road; 749-8700. Open daily; various hours for tram rides and the visitor center.* Steep-walled Sabino Canyon cuts into the foothills of the Santa Catalina Mountains. A pretty creek runs winds along its floor and stands of saguaro march up its steep flanks. You can catch a tram into the heart of the canyon or hike it.

Saguaro National Monument • *Rincon Mountain section off Old Spanish Trail east of Tucson; 296-8576; 7 a.m. to 6 p.m.; $3 per vehicle, $1 per hiker or biker. Tucson Mountain section off Sandario Road in Tucson Mountain Park; 883-6366. Open 24 hours; visitor center daily 8 to 5; free.* The two sections of this national monument serve the same function—to preserve and interpret the giant saguaro cactus and other desert flora, along with fauna and geology of the Sonoran Desert. Both have interpretive centers and self-guiding drives and hikes.

Tohono Chul Park • *7366 N. Paseo del Norte (northwest corner of Ina and Oracle), Tucson, AZ 85704; 742-6455. Daily 7 to sunset; exhibit hall, gift gallery and Tea Room open Monday-Saturday 8 to 5 and Sunday 11 to 5; free.* Arizona's finest privately-endowed park, Tohono Chul offers nature trails, patios, shade ramadas, two gift shops and an exhibit center. And it's all right in the middle of Tucson.

Tucson Mountain Park • *Eight miles west (Take Speedway west from downtown or Kinney Road northwest from State Highway 86); 883-4200. Day use hours: 7 a.m. to 10 p.m.* This huge Pima County park sprawls over 17,000 acres of rough-hewn Tucson Mountain foothills. Facilities include picnic areas, hiking and riding trails and a campground. Several attractions listed above are within the park.

Tucson Museum of Art • *140 N. Main Ave., (Alameda, next to El*

Presidio Historic District), Tucson, AZ 85701; 624-2333. Sunday noon to 4 and Tuesday-Saturday 10 to 4. Adults $2, seniors $1, kids free. Galleries are positioned along downward spiraling ramps in this modern exhibit center. Museum collections focus on Western and pre-Columbian art and contemporary sculpture.

University of Arizona campus ● *Campus Visitor Center open Monday-Friday 8 to 5 and Saturday 9 to 2; 621-5130.* This large campus in the heart of Tucson is a major cultural source as well as an important learning center. Eight museums and galleries occupy its sturdy red-brick buildings.

SOUTH TO NOGALES

Interstate 19 provides a fast link between Tucson and the twin border towns of **Nogales**, Arizona, and Nogales, Sonora. The first substantial habitat you'll encounter, other than dusty little Sahuarita, is the planned community of **Green Valley**. Nearby is a grimly fascinating reminder of the Cold War.

Titan Missile Museum ● *Green Valley Road (Exit 69, then west), Green Valley, AZ 85614; 625-7736. Wednesday-Sunday 9 to 5 (last tour at 4). Adults $4, seniors and military $3, kids 10 to 17, $2.* De-commissioned by disarmament talks, this missile complex has become a fascinating underground museum. Tours take visitors deep into the "hardened" command center, where a Titan II, now defused, perches on its launch pad. It's an intriguing reminder of those hair-trigger Cold War days.

Twenty miles south of Green Valley is dusty little **Tubac**. Arizona's oldest Spanish community, it's now a haven for artists, individualists and a few retirees. Slices of Arizona's history are preserved in a state park here, and in a national monument a few miles south.

Tubac Presidio State Historic Park ● *P.O. Box 1296, Tubac, AZ 85646; 398-2252. Daily 8 to 5; adults $1, kids free.* Little remains of the presidio, set up in 1752 to protect Spanish settlers from angry Indians. However, an interpretive center effectively illustrates its history. Exhibits trace Tubac's days as an early Indian village through its Spanish, Mexican and American periods.

Tumacacori National Monument ● *P.O. Box 67, Tumacacori, AZ 85640; 398-2341. Daily 8 to 5; $3 per family or $1 per person.* Founded in 1691 by Father Eusebio Kino, Tumacacori today is a noble ruin. The once impressive church is little more than a shell. An excellent museum contains artifacts of the period, a diorama of the mission in its heyday and other exhibits.

Chapter Sixteen

SOUTHEASTERN ARIZONA

THE COWBOY CORNER

What we've chosen to call the Cowboy Corner is Cochise County, a 90-mile by 70-mile history-laden rectangle on Arizona's southeastern edge. It could as well be called the Cochise Corner in honor of the Chiricahua Apache warrior, or the Copper Corner, for the great copper mines around Bisbee.

Some of America's most dramatic historical pageants were played out here. Francisco Vasquez de Coronado passed through in 1540 on his quest for the Seven Cities of Cibola. Cochise made a futile stand against intruding whites from 1858 until 1869, then Geronimo took up the lance of resistance. On October 26, 1881, in a dusty alley in Tombstone, three men died in the most celebrated gun battle in Western history.

These events are recorded in a variety of historic sites and monuments. In *The Best of Arizona*, we outlined a drive that hits the highlights of this corner. We offer an abbreviated version here.

For area information • Greater Bisbee Chamber of Commerce, P.O. Box BA, Bisbee, AZ 85603; 432-2141.

Sierra Vista Chamber of Commerce, 77 Calle Portal, Suite A-140, Sierra Vista, AZ 85635; 458-6940.

City of Tombstone Tourist Information Office, P.O. Box 339, Tombstone, AZ 85638; 457-2202.

Willcox Chamber of Commerce and Agriculture, 1500 N. Circle I Rd., Willcox, AZ 85643; 384-2272.

To approach our Cowboy Corner, drive east from Tucson on I-10, then turn south on U.S. 80 and follow it to **Tombstone**, the "town too tough to die." Tombstone couldn't die even if it wanted to; Hollywood would never let it.

The town itself is the main attraction, with a mix of museums, boutiques, restaurants and saloons in 19th century buildings. They stand alongside boardwalks where the boots of Wyatt Earp, Doc Holliday,

Johnny Ringo and Bat Masterson once clunked. Of the assorted lures, these two are the most interesting:

O.K. Corral and Camillus Fly Photo Studio • *Allen Street between Third and Fourth; 457-3456. Daily 8:30 to 5. Admission $1, shoot-out reenactment $2.* The recreated corral now includes the studio of frontier photographer Camillus S. Fly, several 19th century rigs and poorly-done statues of the gun battle's participants. Fly's studio has some fine examples of frontier photography, including pictures of Geronimo's surrender. The O.K. Corral fight is reenacted on the first and third Sundays of each month at 2 p.m.

Tombstone Courthouse State Historic Park • *219 E. Toughnut St. (Third Street), Tombstone, AZ 85638; 457-3311. Daily 8 to 5; adults $1, kids free.* This imposing brick structure with a witch's hat tower is now a museum of Cochise County yesterdays. Exhibits include Wyatt Earp memorabilia, mining paraphernalia, a mock-up saloon and—of course—assorted pictures of participants of the O.K. Corral gunplay.

From Tombstone, follow an numberless highway south to **Sierra Vista**, pick up Fry Boulevard (State Route 90) and take it west to **Fort Huachuca**. It's a still-active U.S. Army base dating back to 1877. A fine museum sits inside; pick up a visitor pass and directions at the gate.

Fort Huachuca Museum • *c/o U.S. Army Garrison, Fort Huachuca, AZ 85613-6000; 533-2714. Weekdays 9 to 6, weekends 1 to 6; free.* The museum comes in two parts. A former chapel and officers' club has exhibits tracing the fort's history from Apache uprisings through World War II. The Annex features a life-sized Western desert tableaux, with cowboys around their campfire.

From Fort Huachuca, return east on Fry Boulevard, then head south on Highway 92 along the foothills of the Huachuca Mountains. Follow signs to a memorial honoring old Frank Coronado, that great—and brutal—Spanish *conquistadore.*

Coronado National Memorial • *Route 2, Box 126, Herford, AZ 85615; 366-5515. Visitor center open daily; free.* This preserve in the wooded flanks of the Huachuca Mountains was established to mark Coronado's passage through Arizona. The visitor center focuses on the 30-year-old explorer's trek and other Spanish ventures into the Southwest. The surrounding woods offer hiking trails and picnic areas.

Next, follow Highway 92 east to **Bisbee**. It's a yesteryear mining town marked with headframes, tailing dumps and a sturdy, handsome downtown of 19th century architecture.

Bisbee Mining and Historical Museum • *Five Copper Queen Plaza (near Brewery Gulch), P.O. Box 14, Bisbee, AZ 85603; 432-7071. Monday-Saturday 10 to 4 and Sunday 1 to 4. Adults $2, kids free.* This imposing red brick structure was the posh headquarters of the Phelps Dodge Mining Company. It now preserves Bisbee's glory days as the world's largest copper mining town. Exhibits include mock-up mine shafts, mining equipment and early-day photos.

Queen Mine Tour and Lavender Pit Mine Tour • *Opposite downtown Bisbee; 432-2071. Queen Mine tours depart daily at 10:30, noon and 3:30; $5. Lavender Pit tour at noon daily, $4.* The Queen Mine tour is fun! A rattling old shuttle called a miner's mule takes you deep into a horizontal shaft. A guide, often a former miner, describes those days when men sweated underground to extract ore for the company millionaires. The Lavender Pit, a huge terraced hole in the ground, is just east of the Queen Mine. You can sign up for a tour at the Queen, or just drive over and park at the viewpoint.

Continue east from Bisbee, pick up U.S. 666 north and follow signs to a national monument with a geological and a human story to tell.

Chiricahua National Monument • *Dos Cabezas Route, Box 6500, Willcox, AZ 85643; 824-3560. Visitor center open daily 8 to 5. Families, $3, individuals $1.* This steep mountainside park preserves some incredibly eroded rock formations and covers five climate zones. These twisted volcanic rhyolite shapes offered shelter for Chiricahua Apaches during their clashes with intruding whites. Visitor center exhibits cover both the geology and recent history of this place.

North of Chiricahua National Monument, you'll drive into the pleasant old cowtown of **Willcox**. It has retained its 19th century look in the downtown historic district, and preserved its memories in two museums.

Museum of the Southwest • *1500 N. Circle I Rd., Willcox, AZ 85643; 384-2272. Monday-Saturday 9 to 5, Sunday 1 to 5; free.* Small and nicely done, this museum covers both the early Indian cultures and the cowboy life in this corner of Cochise County. A special display focuses on Cochise and Geronimo and their 25-year war with the U.S. Army and white settlers.

Rex Allen Cowboy Hall of Fame • *Railroad Avenue at Malley Street (P.O. Box 995), Willcox, AZ 85644; 384-4583. Monday-Saturday 10 to 4; adults $3, families $5.* Born on a homestead near here, Rex Allen went on to become a noted movie, TV and rodeo star. He's contributed hundreds of items—movie posters, his gaudy cowboy clothes, sheet music and other memorabilia—to this small storefront museum.

THE EASTERN MOUNTAINS

We now leave our Cowboy Corner and travel the far reaches of Eastern Arizona. If you drive north from Willcox on Highway 666, you'll leave the high prairie and climb into the foothills and forests of the White Mountains. At **Safford**, you can choose from two routes.

U.S. Highway 70 will take you northwest to **Globe**, another early day mining town. Just north is the large **White River Apache Res-**

ervation. Taking Highway 666 east will land you in the mountain mining town of **Morenci**. This area's main lures are the timberlands of Greenlee National Forest, offering fishing, camping, hiking, hunting and the like. The **Coronado Trail** (Highway 666) is a twisting route through some of Arizona's prettiest alpine scenery. It links **Clifton/Morenci** with **Springerville/Eagar**, sitting contentedly in a remote mountain valley.

If you choose the Globe route, stop at that town's excellent prehistoric Indian museum.

Besh-Ba-Gowah Archaeological Park • *Near Globe Community Center, southwest of town off Jesse Hayes Road; 425-0320. Daily 9 to 5; adults $1, kids 12 and under free.* Archaeologists and craftsmen have reconstructed Arizona's most realistic ancient Indian pueblos here. An adjacent museum offers fine graphics and implements of the Salado, an advanced hunting and gathering band that roamed these parts between from 1100 to 1400 A.D.

From Globe, State Route 88 takes you northwest to the forest-rimmed town of **Payson**, which offers a pair of interesting stops.

Tonto Natural Bridge • *Ten miles north of Payson on Highway 87 (P.O. Box 1600), Pine, AZ 85544; 476-3440. Daily 9 to 6 April to September and 9 to 5 the rest of the year. Bridge admission $3.50.* Privately owned, this is one of the world's largest travertine arches, spanning a 150-foot canyon.

North of here is the oldstyle town of **Holbrook**, sitting by itself in the high prairie. It forms the apex of a triangle between Payson and Springerville. Just to the east is a great forest that hit the ground and turned to stone.

Petrified Forest National Park • *P.O. Box 217, Petrified Forest, AZ 86028; 524-6228. Park gates open daily 7 a.m. to 8 p.m. in summer, 8 to 5 the rest of the year. Fees are $5 per car or $2 per hiker or biker.* Thousands of petrified trees are scattered, like broken columns of fallen temples, over 93,533 acres of grassland. A self-guiding drive will take you past some of the more interesting formations. Also within the preserve are some impressive vistas of the **Painted Desert**, just to the north. The park has two entrances, with an interpretive center near each—at U.S. Highway 180 southeast of Holbrook and off I-40 to the northeast.

Chapter Seventeen

FOUR CORNERS COUNTRY ▨▨▨▨▨

THE NAVAJO-HOPI RESERVATION

The Navajo and Hopi nations of Arizona's Four Corners region deserve their own chapter in this book. They encompass some of the state's most interesting terrain, from starkly beautiful canyons to netherworld sandstone spires.

The combined reservations cover about 29,000 square miles, occupying the northeastern corner of Arizona and spilling over into Utah and New Mexico. That's nearly as big as New Hampshire, Vermont, Massachusetts and Connecticut combined!

The Navajo Nation, spread over 25,000 square miles, is the largest Indian reservation in America. The Hopi reserve is much smaller, about 4,000 square miles, and it's surrounded by Navajo lands.

When you visit a reservation, you technically leave Arizona and enter a sovereign nation. You don't need a passport, of course, and both tribes welcome visitors. But they are self-governing and some of their laws differ from those outside. Alcohol is prohibited; you cannot buy a drink or a can of beer anywhere here. Safety belt use is required and the Navajo police use radar to enforce the 55 mph speed limit, although they don't appear to be fanatics about it. As on most other reservations, permits are required for hunting and fishing.

Many guidebooks are too preoccupied with what you should or shouldn't do on Indian lands. The prospective traveler becomes a bit intimidated. In our wanderings through this corner of the state, we were greeted with everything from open friendliness to stoic indifference. We never experienced a shred of resentment. Arizona's Native Americans generally observe a live-and-let-live attitude as far as visitors are concerned.

So we suggest a simple rule of conduct: Just be nice. You know the difference between showing an interest in someone's way of life and regarding them as a tourist curiosity.

Hopefully, you'll come away as we did—with a warm feeling of respect, not sympathy—for these people whose culture we nearly destroyed, who are still seeking their niche in this sometimes over-whelming society that engulfed them.

Here's a point of minor confusion: Arizona does not switch to day-light saving time, and neither does the Hopi Nation, but the Navajo Nation does.

Shopping

Bring your shopping appetite when you visit these Indian lands. Navajos have long been noted for their artistry in turquoise and silver jewelry and wool hand-woven blankets. The Hopi produce fine bas-ketry, pottery, silver and brightly colored *kachinas* (or *katsinas*), doll-like figures regarded as spiritual messengers.

Scores of roadside stands offer a bewildering variety of crafts, par-ticularly Navajo jewelry. Prices generally are lower than those in the shops, although there's a small chance that you might get something less than authentic. However, tribal councils oversee the handiwork of their craftsmen, so it isn't a major problem. If you're in doubt, you may want to shop at established gift centers. Expect to pay a bit more for your treasures.

For area information • Office of Public Relations, the Hopi Tribe, P.O. Box 123, Kykotsmovi, AZ 86039; 734-2331, ext. 360.

Navajo Tribe Office of Tourism, P.O. Box 663, Window Rock, AZ 86515; 871-6659 or 871-6436.

Navajo-Hopi Drive

Natural and historic lures of Navajo-Hopi land are widespread, so we've again devised a driving route.

Our starting point is **Page**, on the far northwestern tip of the Navajo Nation. Drive south on U.S. Highway 89, then turn east onto U.S. 160. Look for a small sign indicating **dinosaur tracks**, which are imprinted in hardpan on a side road just north of the highway. Several locals usually are there to point out the tracks and tell you a bit about them. A small gratuity will be appreciated.

You soon enter **Tuba City**, the largest town on the reservation. Mormons settled here in 1877, then sold to the government when they realized they were on Indian land. It was the reservation's admin-istrative center until offices were moved to Window Rock in the 1930s. The town offers an interesting architectural mix—cut sand-stone government buildings, ordinary bungalows, mobile homes and typical octagonal Navajo hogans. You'll see hogans throughout the reservation, either constructed of rough lumber or modern prefab sec-tions.

Follow Highway 264 south from Tuba City toward the **Hopi Na-tion.** You'll note a striking difference between Hopi and Navajo set-tlements. While most Navajo towns are rather conventional looking, many Hopi villages are centuries-old pueblos of stone and adobe.

Most of these pueblos occupy three mesas, simply called First, Second and Third. Some are true cliff dwellings, perched on shelves and niches high above the valley floor.

Among the more interesting pueblos are **Old Oraibi** *(Oh-RYE-bee)*, **Kykotsmovi** *(Kee-KOTS-mo-vee)*, **Shungopovi** *(Shung-O-PO-vee)*, **Shipaulovi** *(Shih-PAW-lo-vee)* and **Mishongnovi** *(Mih-SHONG-no-vee)*. Did you get those pronunciations?

To learn about the people and their ancient pueblos, visit the fine cultural complex on Second Mesa, in the heart of the Hopi Nation.

Hopi Cultural Center and Museum ● *On Highway 264, just beyond the Hopi Arts and Silvercraft Center, P.O. Box 7, Second Mesa, AZ 86043; 734-6650. Museum open Monday-Saturday 9 to 4; $3. Gift shops generally open daily 9 to 5.* This attractive sandstone pueblo-style complex features a museum, several gift shops, restaurant and the Hopi Cultural Center Motel (734-2401). The museum has examples of modern and ancient pottery, murals and dioramas of traditional villages and other things Hopi.

Try some of the special foods in the **Tunosvongya Restaurant,** such as chil-il ou gya va, a spicy blend of pinto beans, beef and chilies, or nok qui, stew with lamb, baked green chilies and Indian fry bread.

The Hopi still perform centuries-old ceremonial dances in traditional dress. Some are private, but others may be witnessed by visitors, and these are usually are held on weekends. Although schedules aren't posted in advance, you can check with the cultural center to see if a dance is planned in the area. Photography is forbidden at the dances, or in any of the Hopi villages.

Leaving Hopi land, follow Highway 264 east until you approach **Ganado,** and watch for signs to an interesting historic complex.

Hubbell Trading Post National Historic Site ● *P.O. Box 150, Ganado, AZ 86505; 755-3475. Daily 8 to 6 in summer and 8 to 5 the rest of the year; free.* Hubbell is both an historic landmark and a still-active Indian trading post. Such posts provided important social, cultural and economic ties between Native Americans and white settlers. They provided outlets for native crafts, and gave the Indians access to modern tools and canned goods.

The highway next takes you to **Window Rock,** the capital of the Navajo Nation. It looks like a typical American community, but the culture is definitely Navajo, as you'll learn at the museum and crafts center.

Navajo Tribal Museum and Arts and Crafts Center ● *27002 Highway 264 (P.O. Box 308), Window Rock, AZ 86515; 871-6673.* The museum displays examples of ancient and modern Navajo arts and crafts, and traces the development of Navajo silver work. At the adjacent arts and crafts center, you can buy a variety of native specialties, including silver, turquoise, blankets, sand paintings and such.

The town's namesake, **Window Rock**, is a natural arch sculpted through Kayenta sandstone. To find it, go half a mile north of the main junction to a traffic signal, then half a mile east past tribal administration buildings to **Window Rock Tribal Park.**

To reach your next Navajo Nation stop, back-track to Ganado and drive north on U.S. 191. Near the town of **Chinle**, you'll find one of Arizona's most spectacular canyons.

Canyon de Chelly National Monument ● *P.O. Box 588, Chinle, AZ 86503; 674-5436. Visitor center open daily 8 to 6 from May to September and 8 to 5 the rest of the year; free.* Canyon de Chelly (pronounced *shay*) and adjoining Canyon del Muerto are dramatic steep-walled ravines, dropping a thousand feet to neat patchwork farms on the valley floor. Cliff dwellings are tucked into hidden recesses and incredible sandstone shapes thrust skyward. It's one of Arizona's great visual treats. Roads take you to a series of viewpoints along both canyons.

Continue north from Chinle, following the highway past several free-standing redrock mesas. Then take Highway 160 east and north to the **Four Corners Monument.** It's interesting only for what it represents—the merger of Arizona, New Mexico, Utah and Colorado. The monument itself is a simple concrete slab with the four state seals embedded.

Now, head west on Highway 160 to **Kayenta** and drive north on U.S. 163 to the Navajo Nation's most famous attraction. It begins in Arizona and spills over into Utah.

Monument Valley Tribal Park ● *P.O. Box 93, Monument Valley, UT 84536; (801) 727-3287. Daily 7 a.m. to 8 p.m. mid-March through September, 8 to 5 the rest of the year. Adults $1, seniors 50 cents, kids under 12 free.* You've seen these awesome columns, buttes and fluted ridges in a hundred TV commercials and films. They're as dramatic as they appear in pictures, although the valley is actually quite small. It's a rather isolated basin, reached by an exceedingly bumpy road.

Continuing west on U.S. 160, you'll encounter the last major attraction of Navajo-Hopi land.

Navajo National Monument ● *HC 71, Box 3, Tonalea, AZ 86044; 672-2366. Visitor center open daily 8 to 4:30; lookout trail open during daylight hours.* This preserve contains three of the most complete Anasazi ruins and one of the finest small museums in the state. You must make reservations to visit two of the ruins, which are a considerable hike from the visitor center. The third can be seen from a nearby viewpoint. The visitor center museum features stone tools, pottery and other artifacts found at the three ruins. You can crawl inside a reconstructed living unit that's so realistic the occupants appear to have just stepped out for a bit.

THE OTHER INDIAN NATIONS

If you'd like to learn about Native Americans, Arizona is the ideal place to do so. The Navajo and Hopi nations offer a good preview of Indian life. But these are only two of 20 reservations in Arizona, and each tribe has its own characteristics, arts and crafts.

Indian lands occupy 27 percent of Arizona—more than any other state in the Union. Further, the state has America's largest native population—around 200,000. It's one of the few places where Native Americans have the land and resources to maintain their own identity as members of viable communities. They are a major force in the state, both culturally and politically.

Some reservations encompass lands that have been with the same tribes for centuries. Several Hopi villages, for instance, are among the oldest continually occupied settlements in America.

About three-fourths of Arizona's native people live on their tribal lands. Reservation land is communally owned and those who occupy it do not pay property taxes. As American citizens, they pay all other state and federal taxes, however. Surprisingly, America's original inhabitants weren't granted citizenship until 1924, and they weren't given the right to vote until 1948.

Most reservations welcome visitors and many shelter some of Arizona's finest natural attractions, hunting and fishing areas. To learn more about visiting the various Indian nations, contact the **Native American Tourist Center,** 4130 N. Goldwater Blvd., Suite 114, Scottsdale, AZ 85281; phone 945-0771.

Chapter Eighteen

SOUTH OF THE BORDER

DOWN MEXICO WAY

Arizona shares a long border and many ethnic ties with Mexico. Indeed, Southwestern cooking, architecture and even cowboying are heavily influenced by our friendly neighbors to the south. One out of six Arizonans trace their roots to Mexico.

Visiting the Mexican state of Sonora through any of the six border crossings is a simple matter. At most points, you can merely walk across the international boundary to nearby shopping areas, restaurants and cantinas. If your visit is less than 72 hours and you don't go beyond the border town, no formalities are required.

Bear in mind that these aren't typical Mexican cities, any more than Arizona border towns are typically American. Each is influenced by the presence of the other. Mexican border towns cater heavily to tourists, with an inordinate number of curio shops and restaurants.

While you won't experience a typical slice of Mexico, you'll enjoy meeting its friendly people and browsing through bordertown shops. They offer bewildering selections of leather goods, ceramics, costume jewelry, turquoise and silver, onyx and wood carvings, embroidered clothing and glassware. Incidentally, it's best to avoid weekend visits, because border crossings are much busier then.

Since most towns have shopping areas right next to the border, we recommend parking and walking across. U.S. Customs officials are more picky than their Mexican counterparts, and you might get stuck in a long line of cars, trying to get back into Arizona. Also, U.S. automobile insurance policies aren't recognized in Mexico.

Entry formalities

If you're an American or Canadian citizen and you aren't going beyond a border town, you need only to declare your citizenship for visits of 72 hours or less. If you plan to stay longer and/or go deeper, you'll need a Mexican Tourist Card and an automobile permit. These can be obtained quickly at the border, or from the Mexico Tourist Office at 2744 E. Broadway in Tucson. You'll need proof of citizenship such as a birth certificate, passport, voter's registration certificate or military ID. A driver's license won't work. For a vehicle permit, you'll need proof of ownership.

If you're a Mexican-American, take some evidence of U.S. residency for reentry. If you aren't an American citizen, check with Mexican border officials about documents you'll need before entering the country.

Auto insurance

Don't drive anywhere in Mexico without Mexican auto insurance. Although insurance isn't mandated by law, your vehicle might be impounded if you're involved in an accident. Few American insurance policies extend coverage to Mexico and even if they do, Mexican officials won't recognize them. If you have a rental car, make sure your rental agreement permits driving into Mexico, and get the proper insurance coverage.

Mexican auto insurance is available on both sides of the border. Rates are similar to those in the U.S. For instance, if your car is worth $10,000, the premium would be about $34 for five days or $725 a year. Don't bother shopping around; rates are set by the government.

We recommend **Sandborn's**, an American-owned company that specializes in Mexican insurance. In addition to insurance coverage, the firm provides a question-and-answer leaflet, Mexican milepost guides, camping directories and other helpful stuff. The firm has offices in Ajo, Douglas, Nogales and Yuma, or contact: Sandborn's, P.O. Box 310, McAllen, TX 78502. Members of **Good Sam** (a rec vehicle organization) can get insurance through their club.

Shopping

American money is widely accepted in border towns, so don't bother with currency exchanges. Expect to haggle over prices in curio shops. The rule of thumb is to offer a third what they ask, then meet somewhere in the middle. Don't embarrass the poor shopkeeper and take all the fun out of bargaining by paying full price.

You'll find good buys in a variety of items. Booze is cheap because of the lack of tax, and Mexican-made liquor such as tequila and brandy are less than half the price that they are in the States. But there are limits on what you can bring back; see below.

Se habla Ingles? • You won't have to resort to your high school Spanish in the border towns. English is spoken at virtually every shop, motel and restaurant.

Health measures

We've traveled extensively in Mexico without catching anything worse that diarrhea. But that's awfully unpleasant, so take precautions. Even in the finest restaurants, we routinely avoid drinking unbottled water or eating fresh vegetables that may have been washed in tap water. Those nasty little bugs that commit Montezuma's revenge can be killed by heat, so the best precaution is to eat hot food while it's still hot.

These health precautions aren't intended as an insult to the Mexican people. But it's a simple fact that through the decades, their digestive systems have developed an immunity to critters that raise havoc with ours. Conversely, Mexicans visiting the U.S. often experience digestive discomfort.

There's a simple solution to avoiding contaminated water where these nasty little critters lurk. When in doubt, remember that our Mexican friends make great beer!

Driving in the interior

It's as safe as driving across Arizona, but there's a major difference. Once you get away from the border, service facilities are scarce and car parts even scarcer. For an extended trip into Mexico, take spare parts such as fan belts, water pumps and such—things that might likely conk out. And don't forget plenty of bottled water in case you're stranded for a while. Remember, this is a desert.

Paved Mexican roads are generally good, although they're often narrower than ours. Watch out for potholes, tractors and cows who seem oblivious to the risk of colliding with a car. Because of open ranges in the state of Sonora and elsewhere, we make it a rule never to drive after dark.

Unleaded gasoline is plentiful in border towns, less so as you travel south. You may want to filter your gasoline through a fine sieve or cloth, particularly if you have a fuel-injected vehicle.

Returning to Arizona • You can bring back $400 worth of duty-free goods per family member, plus one quart of liquor per adult. Mexico enjoys favored nation status with the U.S., and certain handicrafts can be imported in excess of the $400 limit. Check with a U.S. Customs office to see what's currently on the list.

Bear in mind that some items can't be imported from any country, including ivory, certain animal skins and sea turtle oil. Customs can advise you what not to buy when you shop across the border.

THE BORDER TOWNS

While none of the border towns are cool in summer, Nogales and Agua Prieta, at nearly 4,000 feet elevation, are a bit more livable. San Luis, below Yuma, is near sea level; expect to sizzle if you plan a summertime visit.

Agua Prieta • This is Mexico's twin to Douglas. The two towns rub shoulders at the border, and stores are less than a block from the boundary. With about 70,000 inhabitants, ten times as many as Douglas, Agua Prieta offers a fair number of shops. They're not as abundant as they are in Nogales or San Luis, however. Downtown here is more of a conventional mix, with curio shops tucked among department stores, *farmacias* and professional offices. Paved highways lead from here into the interior. It's the most direct driving route to Mexico City.

Naco ● A hamlet south of Bisbee, Naco is one of our favorite border towns. If there's such a thing as scruffily cute, this is it. Naco is more like an interior village—uncrowded, with little Mexican shops behind dusty pastel store fronts. You won't find much of a shopping selection here, but there's one good-sized liquor store. The wide (although pot-holed) streets with center dividers give the place a rustic colonial charm.

Nogales ● Opposite Nogales, Arizona, it's the largest of the six border towns, with a population exceeding 200,000. Predictably, it's also the best place to shop. Scores of curio and liquor stores are crowded into **Calle Obregon**, a shopping street that starts just a block from the border. Narrow arcades are stuffed with stalls. Some carry a variety of crafts, curios and general junk, while others specialize in leather goods, fabric, glassware and such. The town also offers several good restaurants.

You'll find inexpensive parking lots on the Arizona side and street parking is plentiful in American Nogales. It can become scarce on weekends, however.

San Luis ● South of Yuma, San Luis is an agricultural community of 50,000 or so. Its weathered old business district offers several shops within two blocks of the border. Selections are fairly good, although it's a distant second to Nogales for shopping variety. You can park free in Friendship Park on the American side. The lot closes at 9 p.m.

Sasabe ● At the bottom of Highway 286 southwest of Tucson, this is the smallest, least crowded and most typically Mexican of all the border towns. A handful of residents occupy its weathered buildings and its matching Arizona twin. Only dirt roads lead south from here, so Sasabe obviously gets very little through traffic. Incidentally, the border is closed between midnight and 8 a.m.

Sonoita ● Opposite Lukeville below Organ Pipe Cactus National Monument, Sonoita is about three miles from the border. A few shops are within walking distance of Lukeville, but there isn't much of a selection. You might like to drive 63 miles south to **Rocky Point** (*Puerto Penasco*), where you can swim, snorkel and fish in the clear waters of the Gulf of California. Remember that you need a Mexican Tourist Card and vehicle permit to go south of Sonoita. The Sonoita-Lukeville border station is closed between midnight and 8 a.m.

Chapter Nineteen

AFTERTHOUGHTS

OUR ARIZONA FAVORITES

We said at the beginning that this book is free of outside bias, for it has no paid listings or advertising. However, it certainly isn't free of ours. So, just for the fun of it, we've compiled "Ten Best" lists of our favorite things in Arizona.

The first selection on each list is our absolute favorite, followed by the next nine in alphabetical order. In this way, we have no losers among the Ten Best, only winners and runners-up.

Arizona's Ten Best towns and cities

1. Tucson ● It has it all: urban conveniences, varied cultural offerings, a world-class university, interesting area attractions, excellent climate (except for peak-summer heat) and surrounding mountains and desert for outdoor enthusiasts.

2. Bisbee ● This old copper mining town has found new life as a tourist and art center. We love the sturdy old downtown and surrounding hills. The mining scars aren't pretty, but they add drama to the setting.

3. Carefree/Cave Creek ● Take your pick of modern (Carefree) or Old West (Cave Creek). They're beyond the Valley of the Sun's spread, in a attractive desert, yet within half an hour of the action.

4. Flagstaff ● Think of it as a mini-Tucson, with colder winters but milder summers. Northern Arizona University and several fine museums give it cultural depth. It's surrounded by natural attractions, and within a short drive of the Grand Canyon.

5. Fountain Hills ● The best of the new planned communities, Fountain Hills offers modern conveniences and beautiful homes in a rugged desert environment.

6. Mesa ● This where we'd live if we lived in the Valley of the Sun. It's on the outer edge of congestion, yet within a short drive of ASU, downtown Phoenix and other lures. We like its oldystle downtown area.

7. Payson ● If we were to settle in the central Arizona mountains, Payson would be our pick. The wooded locale is nice and it's within a reasonable drive of Phoenix.

8. Prescott ● It's an ideal, self-contained little community tucked against forested mountains. Several colleges, art galleries, a handsome old downtown and a friendly Western attitude make this one of Arizona's most desirable cities.

9. Sedona ● We'd retire here if we could afford it, and spend every evening watching the light and shadow show against those fantastic redrock formations.

10. Wickenburg ● If you like to play cowboy, this is the place. A pretty desert setting, an excellent museum, an oldstyle downtown and surrounding dude ranches make this the best little cowtown in Arizona.

Arizona's Ten Best retirement towns

In this list, we tilt more toward places with mild winters and of course, employment isn't a factor.

1. Tucson ● With excellent retirement facilities, affordable housing and the attractions we've already mentioned, the Old Pueblo tops our list again.

2. Apache Junction ● The rugged backdrop of the Superstition Mountains, water-play lures of the nearby Salt River Canyon and affordable housing make this a fine place to retire.

3. Catalina ● The town itself isn't much more than a wide spot on Highway 89. What we're really recommending is the two adjacent retirement villages of **Sun City Vistoso** and **SaddleBrooke.** We like the nearness of Tucson and the adjacent Santa Catalina Mountains.

4. Green Valley ● The surrounding desert is rather bland, but careful planning have created an ideal site for the good life, with ample shopping, reasonable prices and the lures of Tucson not far away.

5. Fountain Hills ● Home prices are on the high side, but otherwise Fountain Hills provides a great retirement environment.

6. Florence ● Mix a historic downtown with some modern housing and a convenient location between Phoenix and Tucson, and you have an excellent retirement community.

7. Prescott ● In addition to its cultural lures, ample shopping and nice setting, Prescott also offers extensive senior programs and good medical facilities. One in four residents is retired.

8. Sun City/Sun City West ● Senior communities were invented here and in next-door Youngtown. Brand-new Sun City West offers some beautifully modern housing.

9. Sedona ● We again select Sedona for its stunning redrock backdrop. With warm summers and rather mild winters, it's a great place to be at leisure—if you can afford the home prices.

10. Yuma ● No, it's not a pretty place. But a good selection of inexpensive homes, mobile home parks, ample shopping facilities and interesting historic lures make Yuma quite attractive. Yes, the town has beastly hot summers. But what the heck; you're retired. Be a Sunbird and fly north.

Arizona's Ten Best places to find a job

Our selections lean more toward practicality than culture and environment. Statistics suggest that these will be the best job market communities in the Nineties. Not surprisingly, most are in the Valley of the Sun.

1. Phoenix ● Without doubt, Phoenix is the job center of Arizona. With an unemployment rate much lower than the state average, and with a broad employment base, this is where we'd start knocking on doors.

2. Buckeye ● This town of 4,000 just west of Phoenix is actively promoting light industry and now has four sizable manufacturing plants. Its labor force has jumped about 40 percent in the past ten years.

3. Chandler ● Fast-growing Chandler offers a mix of space-age firms, high tech, general manufacturing, construction and retailing.

4. Flagstaff ● This dynamic western Arizona city's job count increased more than 30 percent in the past decade. Lumbering, tourism, science, high tech manufacturing and education are the leading sources.

5. Gilbert ● Little Gilbert just keeps growing, and the job market grows along with it. The fastest-growing Arizona city of the Eighties, it saw its employment base increase by 50 percent in that decade.

6. Glendale ● Like its booming neighbors, Glendale has a constantly-expanding job base. In addition to manufacturing, construction, retailing and services, it offers the potential of civil service employment at next-door Luke Air Force Base.

7. Goodyear ● Growing Goodyear has diversified from its aircraft facility to lure such firms as McKesson, Rubbermaid and Intertec Aviation. Its population nearly doubled in the Eighties and job availability increased more than 40 percent.

8. Litchfield Park ● Like neighboring Goodyear, it offers a growing base of light manufacturing and service jobs, with an employment increase of nearly 45 percent in the past decade.

9. Sierra Vista ● This prairie town offers the best job market in southeastern Arizona, which—realistically—is only fair. Although it doesn't have a broad employment base, it's working to attract more light industry and nearby Fort Huachuca employs thousands of civilians.

10. Tucson ● The job market was a bit depressed when the Nineties began, but it should pick up as we move farther into the decade. Like Phoenix, it offers an employment base that is both large and varied, so you should be able to slip into an opening.

Arizona's Ten Best attractions

1. Grand Canyon National Park ● We might even call this incredible gorge *America's* best attraction. The pity is that most people only see it from the rim. To really learn to love the canyon, you should hike down into it or run the wild rapids of the Colorado River.

2. Arizona-Sonora Desert Museum ● If we had time to visit only one museum in Arizona, it would be this one on the outskirts of Tucson. You'll receive a quick education about the flora, fauna and history of the state's great desert reaches—and thus about the state itself.

3. Canyon de Chelly National Monument ● Located in the Navajo Nation, this steep-walled gorge with ancient pueblos tucked into its sheer flanks is often overlooked. Only the Grand Canyon surpasses its grandeur.

4. The Heard Museum ● Devoted exclusively to the study of Native Americans, this outstanding Phoenix museum is the world's best treasury of Indian culture. It tells its story with exhibits, videos and arts and crafts demonstrations.

5. Hoover Dam and Lake Mead National Recreation Area ● When Hoover Dam was completed in 1935, it was the world's highest, holding back the globe's largest man-made lake. It's an awesome thing, worth the drive to the state's far northwest corner.

6. Mission San Xavier del Bac ● The "White Dove of the Desert near Tucson" is one of America's most beautiful early-day missions. It's a near perfect example of Spanish colonial architecture.

7. Monument Valley Tribal Park ● Although smaller than you might have imagined, it contains some of the most dramatic sandstone formations the country. It's on the Arizona-Utah border in the northern Navajo Nation.

8. Oak Creek Canyon ● Awesome redrock shapes, a sparkling stream and thick forests combine to create one of Arizona's most impressive scenes.

9. Organ Pipe Cactus National Monument ● Arizona's largest national monument contains striking examples of the great Sonoran Desert that covers much of southern Arizona and northern Mexico.

10. Wupatki National Monument ● This large park north of Flagstaff preserves scores of pre-Columbian Indian ruins. The largest and most elaborate is Wupatki Pueblo, once a village of several hundred.

USEFUL ARIZONA BOOKS
(in addition to the one you're holding)

As far as we know, all of these books are still in print. If you can't find them at a bookstore, they should be available directly from the publishers. Prices are subject to change, of course.

General travel information

Arizona Travel Planner published by the Arizona Office of Tourism, 1100 W. Washington Ave., Phoenix, AZ 85007. A "quick study" guide to the state, section by section, listing attractions, mileages, campgrounds, chambers of commerce and other essentials. Softcover, 120 pages, **free.**

The Best of Arizona By Don W. Martin and Betty Woo Martin, (c) 1990. Published by Pine Cone Press, P.O. Box 1494, Columbia, CA 95310. Comprehensive, witty and opinionated travel guide, listing Arizona's attractions, restaurants, lodgings, campgrounds, RV parks, annual events and other essentials for visitors. Softcover, 336 pages, **$12.95.**

Grand Canyon National Park by John F. Hoffman, a National Park-ways publication, World-Wide Research and Publishing Co., P.O. Box 3073, Casper, WY 82602. Attractive guide with background, visitor information, maps and attractive color photos. Available at most Grand Canyon National Park museums and gift shops. Softcover, 120 pages, **$5.95.**

Grand Canyon Perspectives by W. Kenneth Hamblin and Joseph R. Murphy, (c) 1969. H & M Distributors, P.O. Box 7085, University Station, Provo, UT 84602. The Grand Canyon as seen from various viewpoints, with detailed sketches of geographic features by illustrator William L. Chesser. Softcover, 48 pages, Available at park museums and gift shops. **$4.25.**

The Grand Canyon: Temple of the World, an Arizona Highways Book, 2039 W. Lewis Ave., Phoenix, AZ 85009. Quotes from various authors who have been moved to pen poetic prose about the canyon, along with the usual Arizona Highways-style beautiful photos. Softcover, 48 pages, **$3.95.**

RVing America's Backroads: Arizona by Kitty Pearson and Jim Vincent, (c) 1989. Published by Trailer Life Books, Agoura, Calif. Full-color, attractively-illustrated guide to Arizona, oriented to the RV set, with suggested driving tours in various areas of the state. Hardcover, 122 pages, **$23.95.**

Scenic Sedona by Lawrence W. Cheek, (c) 1989. An Arizona Highways Book, 2039 W. Lewis Ave., Phoenix, AZ 85009. Prettily-illustrated guide to Sedona, Oak Creek Canyon, Jerome, Mingus Mountain and the Verde Valley. Softcover, 64 pages, **$4.95.**

The Sonoran Desert by Christopher S. Helms, (c) 1980. KC Publications, Inc., Box 14883-A, Las Vegas, NV 89114. Attractive color photos, maps and background on the Sonoran Desert. Softcover, 48 pages, **$4.50.**

Travel Arizona by Joseph Stocker, (c) 1987. An Arizona Highways Book, 2039 W. Lewis Ave., Phoenix, AZ 85009. Sixteen suggested tours of the state, with illustrations and maps; nice color photography. Softcover, 128 pages, **$8.95.**

What Is Arizona Really Like: A Guide to Arizona's Marvels by Reg Manning, (c) 1989. Published by Reganson Cartoon Books, P.O. Box 5242, Phoenix, AZ 85010. Humorously written insider's look at Arizona with cartoon illustrations, by Pulitzer Prize-winning cartoonist for the *Arizona Republic*. Softcover, 120 pages, **$5.95.**

Retirement and relocation

The Phoenix Job Bank, (c) 1990. Published by Bob Adams., Inc., 260 Center St., Holbrook, MA 02343. A complete "how-to" book for job-seekers, with lists of major Phoenix and Tucson employers, job descriptions and techniques for successful job-hunting. Softcover, 288 pages, **$12.95.**

Retirement Living by Sally Ravel and Lee Ann Wolfe, (c) 1990. Published by Conari Press, 713 Euclid Ave., Berkeley, CA 94708. Although it's oriented toward northern California, it contains useful general information in planning for retirement and selecting specific types of retirement communities. Softcover, 256 pages, **$12.95.**

History and general reference

Arizona Place Names, reprint of a 1935 edition by Will C. Barnes, (c) 1988. University of Arizona Press, Tucson. Thorough, comprehensive and scholarly guide to the origin of Arizona's geographic names. Softcover, 504 pages, **$15.95.**

Desert Wildflowers, (c) 1988. An Arizona Highways Book, 2039 W. Lewis Ave., Phoenix, AZ 85009. Gorgeous photos of desert blossoms, with descriptions, zones and times to catch peak blooming periods. Softcover, 112 pages, **$9.95.**

History of Arizona by Robert Woznicki, PH.D. (c) 1987. Messenger Graphics, 110 S. 41st Ave., Phoenix, AZ 85009. A highly-readable treatment of the state's history; not comprehensive, but filled with interesting vignettes and personality sketches. Softcover, 172 pages, **$4.95.**

The Story of Superstition Mountain and the Lost Dutchman Mine by Robert Joseph Allen, (c) 1971. Pocket Books, 1230 Avenue of the Americas, New York, NY 10020. A readable narrative of the Dutchman mine mystery; however it contains some very questionable suppositions about the legendary mine. Softcover, 212 pages, **$3.95.**

Ghost towns and back roads

Travel Arizona: The Back Roads. An Arizona Highways Book, 2039 W. Lewis Ave., Phoenix, AZ 85009. Lots of pretty color photos and route maps. 136 pages, **$9.95.**

Arizona's Best Ghost Towns by Byrd Howell Granger, (c) 1980. Published by Northland Press, P.O. Box N, Flagstaff, AZ 86002. A helpful guide with maps and nice sketches. Softcover, 142 pages; **$12.95.**

Dining

100 Best Restaurants in Arizona by John and Joan Bogert, issued annually. Published by Arizona Desert Minerals Company, Inc., P.O. Box 10462, Phoenix, AZ 85064-0462. Reviews of restaurants throughout the state; focused mostly in Phoenix and Tucson. Softcover, 208 pages, **$3.95.**

Hiking and camping

A Hiker's Guide to Arizona by Steward Aitchison and Bruce Grubbs, (c) 1987. Falcon Press, P.O. Box 279, Billings, MT 59103. A well-written guide with maps and black and white photos. Softcover, 160 pages, **$9.95.**

Outdoors in Arizona: A Guide to Camping by Bob Hirsch, (c) 1986. An Arizona Highways Book, 2039 W. Lewis Ave., Phoenix, AZ 85009. A good mix of campsite listings, color photos and history and vignettes about the state's out-of-doors. Softcover, 128 pages, **$12.95.**

Outdoors in Arizona: A Guide to Hiking and Backpacking by John Annerino, (c) 1987. An Arizona Highways Book, 2039 W. Lewis Ave., Phoenix, AZ 85009. Suggested hikes from desert to mountain to prairie, with maps and photos. Softcover, 136 pages, **$12.95.**

Indians: today and yesterday

A Clash of Cultures: Fort Bowie and the Chiricahua Apaches by Robert M. Utley, (c) 1977. For sale by the Superintendent of Documents, U.S. Government Printing Office, Washington, DC 20402. Also available at national monuments and historic sites, particularly in southeastern Arizona. Softcover, 88 pages, **$2.95.**

American Indians of the Southwest by Bertha P. Dutton, (c) 1984. University of New Mexico Press. A good general guide to present and past Southwestern Indians. Softcover, 286 pages, **$7.95.**

The Complete Family Guide to Navajo-Hopi Land by Bonnie Brown and Carol D. Bracken, (c) 1986. Published by Bonnie Brown and Carol Bracken, P.O. Box 2914, Page, AZ 86040. It's a bit unprofessionally done, but helpful, with lists of attractions, places to dine and sleep; several children's pages to amuse the youngsters. Softcover, 112 pages, **$7.95.**

Geronimo: A Man, His Time, His Place by Angie Debo, (c) 1976. University of Oklahoma Press, Norman, OK 73019. An award-winning biography of the famous Apache warrior; probably the most comprehensive Geronimo study ever written. Softcover, 480 pages, **$10.95.**

Hohokam Indians of the Tucson Basin by Linda M. Gregonis and Karl J. Reinhard, (c) 1979. University of Arizona Press, Tucson. Scholarly, readable view of Tucson's prehistoric peoples. Softcover, 48 pages, **$1.95**

Southwestern Indian Tribes by Tom Bahti, (c) 1989. KC Publications, Inc., Box 14883-A, Las Vegas, NV 89114. Attractive easy-reference guide to Arizona and New Mexico tribes with maps and color and black and white illustrations; nice detail photos of artifacts. Softcover, 72 pages, **$4.50.**

Visitor's Guide to Arizona's Indian Reservations by Boye De Mente, (c) 1988. Phoenix Books/Publishers, P.O. Box 32008, Phoenix, AZ 85064. A thorough, well-written guide with lots of detail and maps. Softcover, 160 pages, **$6.**

HOW TO TALK LIKE AN ARIZONAN

Well, of course Arizonans speak English, but there's a sprinkling of Spanish and Indian words in there. And many Arizona place names have Spanish and Indian roots. This pronunciation guide, prepared with the aid of Brian C. Catts of the University of Arizona's Office of Public Service, will help you talk like a native.

Ajo *(AH-hoe)* — Town in southern Arizona; means "garlic" in Spanish.

Anasazi *(Ana-SAH-zee)* — Early Arizona Indian tribe; the name means "the ancient ones."

Apache *(Ah-PAH-chee)* — Central and southeastern Arizona tribe.

Arcosanti *(Ar-ko-SAN-tee)* — Futuristic habitat north of Phoenix, built by Italian visionary-architect Paolo Soleri.

Athabaskan *(A-tha-BAS-kan)* — Canadian Indian tribe; ancestors of the Navajo and Apache.

Bowie *(BOO-ee)* — Fort in southeastern Arizona, now a national historic site; also a tiny town on Interstate 10.

Canyon de Chelly *(du SHAY)* — Arizona national monument.

Canyon del Muerto *(MWAIR-toh)* — "Canyon of Death," a ravine adjacent to Canyon de Chelly.

Carne *(CAR-nay)* — Meat.

Cerveza fria, por favor *(Sehr-VE-sa FREE-ah, por fah-VOR)* — "Bring me a cold one, please."

Chemehuevi *(Tchem-e-H'WAY-vee)* — Southern Colorado River tribe of Yuman origin; located mostly in southeastern California. Meaning is unknown.

Chinle *(Chin-LEE)* Navajo town, the gateway to Canyon de Chelly National Monument.

Chiricahua *(Cheer-i-COW-wa)* — Southeastern Arizona Apache tribe made famous by Cochise and Geronimo's rebellions; also the name of a mountain range and national monument.

Cholla *(CHOY-ya)* — Large family of Arizona cactus.

Coconino *(Co-co-NEE-no)* — Arizona place name, given to a national forest, county and plateau south of the Grand Canyon.

Colorado *(Coh-lo-RAH-doh)* — Red; obviously, a very common Arizona geographic name.

El Tovar *(El To-VAR)* — Historic hotel at South Rim of Grand Canyon National Park.

Gila *(HEE-la)* — A river in southern Arizona.

Guadalupe Hidalgo *(Wa-da-LU-pay Hee-DAL-go)* The treaty ending the Mexican War, signed in 1848.

Havasupai *(Hah-vah-SOO-pie)* — "Blue-green water people" who occupy beautiful Havasu Canyon, tributary of the Grand Canyon; also called Supai.

Hohokam *(Hoe-hoe-KAHM)* — Prehistoric Indian tribe occupying deserts of Southern Arizona about AD 200 to 500; means "those who have gone."

Huachuca *(Hwa-CHOO-ka)* — Army fort in southern Arizona with an historic museum; also the name of a mountain range.

Hopi *(HOE-pee)* — Indian tribe, probably descended from the Anasazi.

Hotevilla *(HOAT-vih-la)* — Hopi village on Third Mesa. The name means "skinned back" or cleared off.

Hualapai *(HWAL-a-pie or WAH-lah-pie)* — Western Arizona Indian tribe; the name means "pine tree people."

Huevos Rancheros *(WHEY-vose ran-CHER-ohs)* — Popular Spanish-style breakfast with eggs and picante sauce.

Javalina *(Ha-va-LEE-na)* — Wild boar.

Kykotsmovi *(Kee-KOTS-mo-vee)* — Hopi tribal administrative center, on Third Mesa below Oraibi, also called New Oraibi. It means "the place of the mound of ruins."

Maricopa *(Ma-ri-KOH-pah)* — A name given to the Pipa tribe, which shares a reservation with the Pima.

Mescalero *(Mess-kah-LAIR-O)* — Eastern Arizona and Western New Mexico Apache tribe. The name is Spanish, referring to mescal cactus, a traditional food source.

Moenkopi *(Mu-en-KO-pee)* — Hopi village on Third Mesa; means "place of running water."

Mogollon *(MUGGY-yon)* — Ancient Indian tribe occupying eastern Arizona about AD 200 to 500; also Mogollon Rim, the abrupt southern edge of the Colorado Plateau.

Mohave *(Mo-HA-vay)* — Arizona place name, referring to Indian tribe and a county along the western border.

Mojave — Same pronunciation as above, with Spanish spelling, commonly used in California.

Navajo *(NAH-VAH-hoe)* — America's largest Indian tribe, descended from the Athabascan band of Canada.

Nogales *(No-GAH-less)* Twin Arizona-Mexico border towns; the word is Spanish for "walnuts."

Ocotillo *(O-co-TEE-yo)* — Spiny-limbed desert bush with red spear-like blossoms.

Oraibi *(Oh-RYE-bee)* — Hopi settlement on Third Mesa; means "place of the Orai stone."

Paloverde *(PAW-lo-VAIR-day)* — Desert tree distinctive for the green bark of its limbs.

Papago *(PAH-pa-go)* — Spanish word for "bean eaters," referring to a Southern Arizona Indian tribe, which has since readopted its traditional name of "Tohono O'odham."

Pima *(PEE-mah)* — Central and southern Arizona tribe. The name was a Spanish mistake. When questioned by early explorers, they responded *"Pinyi-match,"* which means "I don't understand." The Spanish thought they were identifying themselves.

Prescott *(PRESS-kit)* — Town in central Arizona.

Quechan *(KEE-chan or KAY-chan)* — Indian tribe near Yuma area; also known as Yuma Indians.

Saguaro *(Sa-WHA-ro)* — Large cactus; its blossom is Arizona's state flower.

San Xavier *(Sahn Ha-vee-YAY)* — Spanish mission south of Tucson; some locals pronounce it *Ha-VEER*.

Sichomovi *(si-CHO-MO-vee* — Hopi settlement on First Mesa; means "a hill where the wild currants grow."

Sinagua *(Si-NAU-wa)* — Ancient north central Arizona tribe; lived in the area about 900-1000 A.D. It comes from the Spanish words *sin agua*— "without water."

Shungopovi *(Shung-O-PO-vee)* — Hopi settlement on Second Mesa; means "a place by the spring where tall reeds grow."

Tempe *(Tem-PEE)* — City east of Phoenix.

Tohono O'odham *(To-HO-no ah-toon)* — Traditional tribal name of the Papago Indians. It means "people of the desert who have emerged from the earth."

Tubac *(TU-bahk)* — Arizona's first settlement; below Tucson.

Tumacacori *(Too-mawk-ka-COR-ee)* — Spanish mission below Tucson; now a national monument.

Tusayan *(TU-sigh-yan or TUSSY-yan)* — Sinagua Indian ruin near Desert View in Grand Canyon National Park; also a community just outside the park's south entrance station.

Ute *(Yoot)* — Large Great Basin Indian tribe; few members are in Arizona. The name simply means "the tribe" in the Shoshoni and Comanche language.

Verde *(VAIR-day)* — Spanish for "green."

Wahweap *(WAH-weep)* — Ute Indian for "bitter water"; the name of a large marina at Glen Canyon National Recreation Area.

Wupatki *(Wu-PAT-key)* — National monument northeast of Flagstaff. The word is Hopi for "tall house."

Yaqui *(Ya-KEE)* — Small Indian tribe southwest of Tucson, near Tohono O'odham Reservation. Origin of name unknown; it might simply mean "the people," a self-reference commonly used by many early tribes. Yaqui are more numerous in northern Mexico and may be an off-shoot of early Apache tribes.

Yavapai *(YA-va-pie)* — Central Arizona tribe. Origin of the name is not sure; might mean "crooked mouth people" or "people of the sun."

Yuma *(YOO-mah)* — Large tribal group near the city of Yuma; the name is derived from *lum,* which means tribe. Original name is Quechan.

INDEX

Page numbers of main community listings are indicated in **bold face** type.